JOURNALS
DOROTHY WOR

D0176029

DOROTHY WORDSWORTH

Born at Cockermouth, Cumberland, 25 December 1771
Died at Rydal Mount, Westmorland, 25 January 1855

JOURNALS OF
DOROTHY WORDSWORTH

The Alfoxden Journal 1798
The Grasmere Journals 1800–1803

WITH AN INTRODUCTION BY HELEN DARBISHIRE

SECOND EDITION BY
MARY MOORMAN

Oxford New York
OXFORD UNIVERSITY PRESS

Oxford University Press, Walton Street, Oxford OX2 6DP

Oxford New York Toronto
Delhi Bombay Calcutta Madras Karachi
Petaling Jaya Singapore Hong Kong Tokyo
Nairobi Dar es Salaam Cape Town
Melbourne Auckland

and associated companies in
Berlin Ibadan

Oxford is a trade mark of Oxford University Press

The Alfoxden Journal and The Grasmere Journals first published in The
World's Classics 1958
This second edition, with new material by Mary Moorman, first published as an
Oxford University Press paperback 1971
Reprinted 1973 (with corrections), 1974, 1976, 1978, 1980, 1981, 1983, 1985, 1987, 1988

British Library Cataloguing in Publication Data
Data available

Library of Congress Cataloging in Publication Data
Wordsworth, Dorothy, 1771–1855.
Journals of Dorothy Wordsworth.
(Oxford paperbacks)
Includes index.
1. Wordsworth, Dorothy, 1771–1855—Diaries.
2. Authors, English—19th century—Diaries. I. Moorman,
Mary Trevelyan, 1905– . II. Title.
PR5849.A8 1987 828'.703 [B] 87–14133
ISBN 0–19–281103–7 (pbk.)

Printed in Great Britain by
Richard Clay Ltd.
Bungay, Suffolk

CONTENTS

PREFACE TO THE 1971 EDITION

IN preparing the Journals of Dorothy Wordsworth for this new edition, which is to replace that in The World's Classics (1958), edited by Helen Darbishire, a number of corrections have been made in the annotation, which Miss Darbishire based on the work of Knight, de Selincourt, and on Gordon Graham Wordsworth's (G. G. W.) manuscript notes at Grasmere. As space in this edition is no longer so restricted, many new notes have been added, both topographical and biographical, which seemed desirable for the better understanding of the journals. G. G. W.'s notes on places and characters have been kept in their original form. More of the shorter poems of Wordsworth referred to in the journals have been added to Appendix I, especially those, like 'I have thoughts that are fed by the sun', which are not widely known. Two poems by Dorothy Wordsworth are also included, as Appendix II.

The text of the Grasmere Journals, which Miss Darbishire founded on four notebooks preserved in the Wordsworth Library at Grasmere, has been carefully revised from the MSS. The punctuation now conforms much more closely to D. W.'s than has been the case in previous editions. The same applies to capital letters, and to the use of italics for the titles of books and poems: Dorothy did not underline these words, and consequently I have not italicized them.

Her method of dating the journal entries has also been followed more closely. She usually started with the day of the week, followed by the date, with or without the name of the month. By giving the month and year in the headline on each page, it has been possible to retain her dating unchanged. Where she dates wrongly, as she not infrequently does, the actual date has been given in a footnote.

Certain words and phrases, hitherto considered illegible, have been deciphered or at least guessed at, and a few more erased sentences recovered.[1] Some of these erasures were made by Dorothy herself, when she had inadvertently recorded an incident or description on the wrong day. She did not write up her journal every day, but usually every third or fourth— sometimes with longer gaps—so that slips of memory were easily made. In these cases the same sentence is sometimes found again a day or two later, with slight variations. I have not recorded all of these repetitions in the notes, but if there are any interesting variants in the erased sentences I have done so.

The more important of the recovered sentences have now been indicated by a footnote. Besides the erasures, two pages have been roughly torn out—one containing entries for 5–9 November 1801 and the other for 26–28 June 1802. When Christopher Wordsworth quoted a few extracts from the Grasmere Journals in his *Memoirs* of Wordsworth in 1851, the first of these pages was certainly there, for he transcribed two sentences from it.[2] William Knight, who gave extracts from the Journals in his *Life* of Wordsworth (1889) and published a fuller but still very incomplete edition of them in 1897, omitted purposely what he calls 'trivial' details, which in fact included almost all references to the Wordsworths' health.

The most serious disaster that befell the journals was the loss, at some unknown date, of the MS. of the Alfoxden Journal. Knight transcribed and published portions of it with the other Journals in 1897, and the text printed here is necessarily from that transcription. At some time between 1897 and de Selincourt's edition of 1941, the Journal disappeared. As far as is known, the only MS. now remaining of any part of it is a copy in the Alfoxden Notebook, in Wordsworth's hand, of the opening sentences of the first entry—20 January 1798. Probably the poet copied out the fragment as being useful to the verse he was writing at the time.

I am grateful to two people for their generous assistance in examining the MSS.—Miss Nesta Clutterbuck, formerly

---

[1] The work of recovering erasures was begun by Miss Darbishire in the World's Classics edition.

[2] *Memoirs of William Wordsworth*, by Christopher Wordsworth, D.D., vol. 1, p. 177.

Librarian at the Wordsworth Library, and Mr. Paul F. Betz of Georgetown University, Washington, D.C.—and also to Miss Catharine Carver of the Oxford University Press for her great interest and assistance in the whole project.

MARY MOORMAN

INTRODUCTION

DOROTHY WORDSWORTH comes to us not only as the friend and treasured companion of two great poets—'Wordsworth's exquisite sister' Coleridge called her, himself touched by her subtle influence—she comes as herself, a rare being who has revealed herself in a living world.

Of her life there is little to tell, but a few facts are significant. Born in 1771, a year and a half after William, in Cockermouth, within hail of the mountains, she spent her later childhood, after her parents' early death, with relatives—first with her kindly 'Aunt' Threlkeld at Halifax, then with her unsympathetic grandparents at Penrith, and finally with her friendly Uncle and Aunt Cookson in Norfolk. The physical separation from her three brothers was a sore trial. The loss of their parents kept them closely united in affection, especially William, Dorothy, and John the Sailor; and it is significant that their Penrith neighbours, the Hutchinsons, likewise left orphans in the same period, were in a special way drawn to the Wordsworths: Mary, nearly William's age, became his wife, Sara and Joanna as well as Mary were Dorothy's close friends, and the brothers, especially Tom, familiar companions of them all.

William and Dorothy had long cherished a plan to live together and in 1795, by the help of a legacy from William's friend Raisley Calvert, they were installed in a friend's house at Racedown in Dorset. Two years later, in order to be in reach of Coleridge at Nether Stowey, they moved to Alfoxden near Holford on the Quantock hills. The three friends met almost daily, rambling on the hills, exchanging their impressions and their thoughts, 'three persons and one soul'. The two poets were plunged in far-reaching speculations about the nature of poetry; Dorothy, entranced but not partaking in the argument, could and did provide them with the living material of poetry. She could express her sensitive delight in earth and sea and sky from moment to moment as they walked and talked, no less than she could record it afterwards in her diary. It was an important moment in her life when she took up a notebook and began to write her Alfoxden Journal.

> *Alfoxden.* 20th January 1798. The green paths down the hill-sides are channels for streams. The young wheat is streaked by silver lines of water running between the ridges, the sheep are gathered together on the slopes. After the wet dark days, the country seems more populous.

Wordsworth himself copied these sentences into a notebook of his own, a notebook which he began to fill at Alfoxden with drafts of the poems he was composing. He must have thought them worth remembering, and we know from her own record that she continued to write her journal at Grasmere '*to please William*'.

It was not till December 1799, after the *annus mirabilis* at Alfoxden which bore fruit in the *Lyrical Ballads*, and after their sojourn in Germany which saw the beginnings of *The Prelude* as we know it, that Dorothy had the happiness of settling with William in a house of their own at Grasmere.

Dove Cottage holds the heart of her experience, and her Grasmere Journals record it day by day. They are like a clear mirror in which are reflected whatever there is in her that makes her beautiful to us, and memorable. De Quincey said, 'she was the very wildest (in the sense of the most natural) person that I have ever known; and also the truest, most inevitable, and at the same time the quickest and readiest in her sympathy with either joy or sorrow, with laughter or with tears, with the realities of life or the larger realities of the poets'. There is, alas! no portrait of Dorothy except for a sad one taken in her old age. But De Quincey tells us of his impression of her in youth; he writes of her 'Gipsy Tan', from constant exposure to sun and wind—and of her eyes, 'not soft like Mrs W's, nor bold: but they were wild and startling'. We knew this already from her brother's unforgettable lines commemorating their visit together to Tintern Abbey; he reads

> My former pleasures *in the shooting lights*
> Of thy wild eyes.

Thelwall, the notorious radical, who paid them a friendly visit at Alfoxden, noticed the same feature in Dorothy in verses less inspired:

> Alfoxden's musing tenant [he writes] and *the maid*
> *Of ardent eye* who with fraternal love
> Sweetens his solitude

When we meet Dorothy for the first time we feel her as more alive than anyone we have met before, most of all in her eyes and in her quick movements. She said of herself: 'It is natural to me to do everything as quick as I can, and at the same time.' This quickness and ardour which belonged to her physical being were naturally a part of her inner self. Coleridge's first recorded impression of her tells how he valued her mind, her sensibility, and her character—all vital and unique. His words carry the quickening power that her presence could always communicate.

Wordsworth and his exquisite sister are with me [this was in June 1797]. She is a woman indeed: in mind I mean, and heart; for her person is such that if you expected to see a pretty woman, you would think her ordinary; if you expected to see an ordinary woman you would think her pretty! But her manners are simple, ardent, impressive. In every motion her most innocent soul beams out so brightly, that who saw would say 'Guilt was a thing impossible in her'. Her information various. Her eye watchful in minutest observation of nature; and her taste a perfect electrometer. It bends, protrudes, and draws in, at subtlest beauties and most recondite faults.

To meet Dorothy Wordsworth we have only to open her journal and enter her world. It is the world which is the world of all of us, the world of man and nature, *her part of it, as she saw it.* Coleridge speaks of 'her eye watchful in minutest observation of nature'. So it was; and he owed to it, along with much else, a lovely image in *Christabel*:

> The one red leaf, the last of its clan,
> That dances as often as dance it can,
> Hanging so light, and hanging so high,
> On the topmost twig that looks up at the sky.

Dorothy had first noted this in her journal:

7th [March 1798]. One only leaf upon the top of a tree—the sole remaining leaf—danced round and round like a rag blown by the wind.

xiv INTRODUCTION

Her ear was as sensitive as her eye. At Alfoxden they often walked in the woods, and the sea, not more than two miles away, was a presence never long forgotten.

22nd [February 1798]. The sea very black, and making a loud noise as we came through the wood, loud as if disturbed, and the wind was silent.

The 'background' noise at Grasmere was not the sea but the pervading sound of becks and falls. Dorothy is keenly aware of this enlivenment of the air in mountain country. On an evening after rain she speaks of 'the hills, the stars and the white waters with their ever-varying, yet ceaseless sound'. And on another day she tells how 'William lay listening to the waterfalls and the Birds: there was no one waterfall above another—it was a sound of waters in the air—the voice of the air'. In this great 'world of eye and ear' it was not only minute observation that Dorothy gave to Nature, she gave a complete and loving surrender to what Wordsworth called the 'moods of time and season'. As we follow her from day to day we are never allowed to forget the season of the year, the time of day—and the weather!

The weather, we may notice, is kindly treated, like a familiar neighbour:

30th [May 1800]. It rained very mildly and sweetly.
[4th December 1800]. Langdale covered with snow. . . . Cold and slippery but exceedingly pleasant.
21st [March 1798]. A quiet shower of snow was in the air.

The tranquil daily record flowers ever and again into phrases like these, which seem to slip from her pen as easily as a raindrop slides from a leaf:

2nd October [1800]. A showery evening. The moonlight lay upon the hills like snow.

and on 31st October (the next full moon)

The moon shone like herrings in the water.

16th [March 1802]. The moon was a good height above the mountains. She seemed far and distant in the sky there were two stars beside her, that twinkled in and out, and seemed almost like butterflies in motion and lightness.

Wordsworth, we know, drew sustenance for his poetry from Dorothy's journal. He would make her read out a passage which could revive his memory, as he did with the record of the daffodils by Ullswater. His poem, 'I wandered lonely as a cloud', owes much to Dorothy's prose description:

> ... I never saw daffodils so beautiful they grew among the mossy stones about and about them, some rested their heads upon these stones as on a pillow for weariness and the rest tossed and reeled and danced and seemed as if they verily laughed with the wind that blew upon them over the lake, they looked so gay ever glancing ever changing. This wind blew directly over the lake to them. There was here and there a little knot and a few stragglers a few yards higher up but they were so few as not to disturb the simplicity and unity and life of that one busy highway.

Dorothy was not only the source of poetry in others, she was a creator in her own right. She has noted in her journal one grave evening by the side of Rydal:

> ... when I saw this lowly Building in the waters among the Dark and lofty hills, with that bright soft light upon it, it made me more than half a poet.

She tried her hand at verse, encouraged by her brother, urged by her friends, but she could not accomplish it to her satisfaction. Yet her own words hit the truth: she *was* more than half a poet: she was a poet in prose. She had not only the 'eye watchful in minutest observation of nature' which rejoiced Coleridge, not only the unusual depth of sensibility that struck De Quincey—she had the poetic imagination. She saw things alive and she saw them *whole*, with the unity which belongs to things seen by painter or poet. In that description of the daffodils by the lake the last words drive this home: '*the simplicity and unity and life* of that one busy highway'. But the unity and life are implicit in every touch of the picture. So it is when she describes a tree: it is alive and whole as a human being is alive—a being in itself:

Tuesday 24th [November 1801]. We were stopped at once, at the distance perhaps of 50 yards from our favourite Birch tree. It was yielding to the gusty wind with all its tender twigs, the sun shone upon it and it glanced in the wind like a flying sunshiny shower. It was a tree in shape with stem and branches but it was like a Spirit of water. . . . The other Birch trees that were near it looked bright and chearful, but it was a creature by its own self among them.

Or of a hill or mountain:

Helm Crag rose very bold and craggy, *a being by itself*, and behind it was the large Ridge of mountain smooth as marble and snow white.

And so it is with every part of the beloved landscape, which is so much more than landscape to her.

Saturday 23rd [*October 1802*]. It is a breathless grey day that leaves the golden woods of autumn quiet in their own tranquillity, stately and beautiful in their decaying, the lake is a perfect mirror.

It is the same with human beings, whether neighbours whom she knows familiarly like old Fleming, the inn-keeper:

22nd [*December 1801*]. We overtook old Fleming at Rydale, leading his little Dutchman-like grandchild along the slippery road. The same pace seemed to be natural to them both, the old man and the little child, and they went hand in hand, the grandfather cautious, yet looking proud of his charge;

or a passing stranger like the little lass travelling with the highlander and his carts:

Sunday 14th February 1802. The carman was cheering his horses and talking to a little lass about 10 years of age who seemed to make him her companion. She ran to the wall and took up a large stone to support the wheel of one of his carts and ran on before with it in her arms to be ready for him. She was a beautiful creature and there was something uncommonly impressive in the lightness and joyousness of her manner. Her business seemed to be all pleasure—pleasure in her own motions—and the man looked at her as if he too was pleased and spoke to her in the same tone in which he spoke to his horses. There was a wildness in her whole figure, not the wildness of a Mountain lass but a *Road* lass, a traveller from her Birth. . . .

In all these passages there is something that Wordsworth and Coleridge called imagination, that power which, as Lamb said, 'draws all things to one: which makes things animate or inanimate, beings with their attributes, subjects with their accessories take one colour and serve to one effect'.

There is something else that imagination does, the simplest thing, the central thing. It pierces through the familiar surface to something nearer to life itself than what we ordinarily see. The effect is visionary. Wordsworth called imagination 'the vision and the faculty divine'. Here is Dorothy in the Quantock hills one early morning that began in fog, then cleared:

1st March [*1798*]. . . . The shapes of the mist, slowly moving along, exquisitely beautiful; passing over the sheep they almost seemed to have more of life than those quiet creatures. The unseen birds singing in the mist.

There is magic here. The moving, changing mists that seem more alive than the quiet sheep—the unseen birds singing in the mist, make us forget to wonder at the perfect prose, perfect in its choice of words, in its repetitions and cadences. 'Dorothy Wordsworth', said Ernest de Selincourt, 'is probably the most remarkable and the most distinguished of English writers who never wrote a line for the general public.' Her prose is as lively and natural, as inevitable in its movement as a mountain stream, its language as transparently clear. She never thought of herself as a writer. 'I should detest', she said, 'the idea of setting myself up as an author.' She never strains after an effect. The very *naïveté* of her expressions and the way one follows another are a delight. Resting on an expedition up the valley, 'Wm and C[oleridge] repeated and read verses. I drank a little Brandy and water, and was in Heaven.' She wrote as she lived, in the way that was natural to her. That is why we listen to what she tells us as we might listen to a thrush singing.

But like all good writers she had her own initiation. She loved listening to the natural country speech of her neighbours with its salty freshness and drive, its lilt and flavour; and, after all, she was well used to hear her brother talk, and she was steeped in his poetry, as well as in that of the great poets whom he loved,—most of all Shakespeare, Spenser, and Milton. She had received all unconsciously an exceptional education in the art of good English.

To many readers the journals will have their liveliest interest and their lasting value not as a work of imagination or an example of exquisite prose but as a record of part of the life of a great poet, and as in the simplest way a human document. William and Dorothy, and for a time their sailor brother John, are before us day by day and hour by hour in their frugal cottage life. Coleridge is a frequent visitor, and when not present always intimately with them through letters passing to and from Keswick; Mary and Sara Hutchinson come for long periods. Wordsworth is seen in his daily life: he works in the garden, he sticks peas, he fishes in the lake, he sleeps badly, sometimes he sleeps well, he tires himself out with composing, worries unreasonably over a bad patch, he 'kindles' and composes rapidly, he 'wastes his mind in the magazines' (seldom), he walks day and night, generally with Dorothy (he was a confirmed night walker). We have the faithful record of a poet at home.

On 27th March 1802, 'At breakfast Wm wrote part of an ode [*Ode: Intimations of Immortality*]. Mr Olliff sent the dung and Wm went to work in the garden.'

And this is how a lyric was born in that same fruitful spring:

Sunday Morning [*14th March*]. William had slept badly—he got up at 9 o'clock, but before he rose he had finished the Beggar Boys—and while we were at Breakfast that is (for I had breakfasted) he, with his Basin of Broth before him untouched and a little plate of Bread and butter he wrote the Poem to a Butterfly! He ate not a morsel, nor put on his stockings but sate with his shirt neck unbuttoned, and his waistcoat open while he did it. The thought first came upon him as we were talking about the pleasure we both always feel at the sight of a Butterfly. I told him that I used to chase them a little but that I was afraid of brushing the dust off their wings, and did not catch them.

Dorothy was with him in his poetry as she was in his life. She reveals herself in her journals with complete simplicity, a woman of sensibility easily moved to tears, and equally to sheer delight, keenly alive to the human needs of friends and neighbours, devoted to her brother as the centre and core of her life. The relation between these two was as intimate, perhaps, as the relation between brother and sister can be. He was a sensitive, reserved boy, and Dorothy early took the place, as far as might be, of the mother lost to them in childhood. She understood him as no one else did. In his worst time of stress she 'preserved him still a poet', as he said. She knew his vital needs. Though her supreme happiness was in ministering to him in their shared solitude, and though to give this up was inevitably a pain and a poignant sadness, yet she knew that he needed marriage to fulfil himself and she rejoiced in his taking to wife their long known and well-loved friend Mary Hutchinson, his first love, whom she accepted simply as her sister. On their return to Grasmere after the wedding the journal records: 'the first walk that I had taken with my Sister.'

William and Dorothy, both unusual people, unusually endowed, had in a degree that goes beyond our ordinary ken the capacity for passionate affection towards their intimates. The special relation between these two, with its special intensity enhanced by circumstance, was rooted only more firmly in the new ground of his happy marriage. Dorothy was always happy with children and she cherished William's children as her own. With Mary she lived in unbroken harmony through all the days of her prime. She never had robust health, as the journal, which reveals so much, cannot conceal. In her fifty-seventh year she was struck down by an illness which gradually invaded her mind as well as her body.[1] She died in 1855 after a prolonged period of life-in-death. Once or twice in these shrouded years

[1] In April 1829, D. W.'s illness, which has never been sufficiently defined, began with a violent attack of gall-stones while staying with her nephew John W. in his Leicestershire curacy. She partially recovered, but was obliged thenceforward to lead a carefully sheltered life, and even so recurrent attacks often brought her near to death. In June 1835 she was very ill, and it was after this attack that her mind was found to be affected. She remembered the distant past, but had little notion of what was going on around her. She had also lost the use of her legs and could not walk. She was fretful and at times violent, though with many gleams of sense and even wit; her memory of her brother's poetry was quite unimpaired and she would often recite it. She was in fact a victim of arteriosclerosis, which eventually affects the brain. This condition may easily be produced if gall-stones are not cleared up by medical or surgical means, which in those days was not possible. The notion put about recently, that D. W.'s mind was affected by emotional distress, is not tenable. Her illness had purely physical causes, and if she had lived in our own age could have been treated so that the mental condition would not have arisen. (M. M.)

the veil is lifted—as in the following letter to a well-loved cousin:

Rydal Mount, Sunday, October 8th, 1837

My dear Cousin Edward,

A madman might as well attempt to relate the history of his doings and those of his fellows in confinement, as to tell you one hundredth part of what I have felt, suffered and done. Thro' God's mercy I am now calm and easy, and I trust my dear Brother's eyes are in a fair way of perfect recovery. . . . I have not seen dear Charles Lamb's book [she means Talfourd's *Life and Letters of Charles Lamb*]. His Sister still survives, a solitary twig patiently enduring the storm of life. In losing her Brother she lost her all—all but the remembrance of him, which chears her the day through.

We can be grateful for this glimpse of the true, loving Dorothy, faithful as she always was in confronting her lot, alive and outgoing in her sympathy for others. But the Dorothy who lives for posterity is the Dorothy of the early journals. For if what her brother said of genius is true, then Dorothy Wordsworth had genius: 'Of genius in the fine Arts the only infallible sign is the widening the sphere of human sensibility for the delight, honour and benefit of human nature.'

HELEN DARBISHIRE

Grasmere, January 1958

ABBREVIATIONS, ETC.,
USED IN TEXT AND NOTES

D. W.	Dorothy Wordsworth
W., Wm, W. W.	William Wordsworth
R. W.	Richard Wordsworth, brother of W. W.
C. W.	Christopher Wordsworth, brother of W. W.
G. G. W.	Gordon Graham Wordsworth, grandson of W. W.
C., S. T. C.	Samuel Taylor Coleridge
M. H.	Mary Hutchinson, later W. W.'s wife
S. H.	Sara Hutchinson, sister of M. H.
E. de S.	Ernest de Selincourt
W. K.	William Knight
H. D.	Helen Darbishire

P.W.	*The Poetical Works of William Wordsworth*, vols. I–V, edited by E. de Selincourt and H. Darbishire, 1940–9
E.Y.	*The Letters of William and Dorothy Wordsworth: The Early Years*, edited by E. de Selincourt, revised by C. L. Shaver, 1967
Griggs	*Collected Letters of Samuel Taylor Coleridge*, edited by E. L. Griggs, vols. I and II, 1956
CNB	*Notebooks of Samuel Taylor Coleridge*, edited by Kathleen Coburn, vol. I, 1957
[?]	= word or words illegible in MS.

Words included in square brackets are editorial conjectures.

THE
ALFOXDEN JOURNAL
1798

ALFOXDEN, *20th January 1798*.[1] The green paths down the hillsides are channels for streams. The young wheat is streaked by silver lines of water running between the ridges, the sheep are gathered together on the slopes. After the wet dark days, the country seems more populous. It peoples itself in the sunbeams. The garden, mimic of spring, is gay with flowers. The purple-starred hepatica spreads itself in the sun, and the clustering snow-drops put forth their white heads, at first upright, ribbed with green, and like a rosebud;[2] when completely opened, hanging their heads downwards, but slowly lengthening their slender stems. The slanting woods of an unvarying brown, showing the light through the thin net-work of their upper boughs. Upon the highest ridge of that round hill covered with planted oaks, the shafts of the trees show in the light like the columns of a ruin.

21st. Walked on the hill-tops—a warm day. Sate under the firs in the park. The tops of the beeches of a brown-red, or crimson. Those oaks, fanned by the sea breeze, thick with feathery sea-green moss,[3] as a grove not stripped of its leaves. Moss cups more proper than acorns for fairy goblets.

22nd. Walked through the wood to Holford. The ivy twisting round the oaks like bristled serpents. The day cold—a warm shelter in the hollies, capriciously bearing berries. Query: Are the male and female flowers on separate trees?

[1] W. W. copied the first four sentences of this entry (20 January), the only portion of the Alfoxden Journal of which a MS. copy exists, into a notebook (now called the Alfoxden Notebook), perhaps because he wanted it for the purposes of his poetry. The lines 'these populous slopes etc.', printed in *P.W.*, vol. v, p. 341, echo some of its phrases.

[2] In all previous editions, including that in The World's Classics (1958), the semi-colon supplied here after 'rosebud' has been omitted, thus destroying the sense of D.W.'s comparison.

[3] Cf. 'The Thorn', stanza II, p. 167.

23rd. Bright sunshine, went out at 3 o'clock. The sea perfectly calm blue, streaked with deeper colour by the clouds, and
tongues or points of sand; on our return of a gloomy red. The
sun gone down. The crescent moon, Jupiter, and Venus. The
sound of the sea distinctly heard on the tops of the hills, which
we could never hear in summer. We attribute this partly to
the bareness of the trees, but chiefly to the absence of the
singing of birds, the hum of insects, that noiseless noise which
lives in the summer air. The villages marked out by beautiful
beds of smoke. The turf fading into the mountain road. The
scarlet flowers of the moss.

24th. Walked between half-past three and half-past five.
The evening cold and clear. The sea of a sober grey, streaked
by the deeper grey clouds. The half dead sound of the near
sheep-bell, in the hollow of the sloping coombe, exquisitely
soothing.

25th. Went to Poole's[1] after tea. The sky spread over with
one continuous cloud,[2] whitened by the light of the moon,
which, though her dim shape was seen, did not throw forth so
strong a light as to chequer the earth with shadows. At once the
clouds seemed to cleave asunder, and left her in the centre of a
black-blue vault.[3] She sailed along, followed by multitudes of
stars, small, and bright, and sharp. Their brightness seemed
concentrated, (half-moon).

26th. Walked upon the hill-tops; followed the sheep tracks
till we overlooked the larger coombe. Sat in the sunshine. The
distant sheep-bells, the sound of the stream; the woodman
winding along the half-marked road with his laden pony; locks
of wool still spangled with the dewdrops; the blue-grey sea,
shaded with immense masses of cloud, not streaked; the sheep
glittering in the sunshine. Returned through the wood. The
trees skirting the wood, being exposed more directly to the
action of the sea breeze, stripped of the net-work of their upper
boughs, which are stiff and erect, like black skeletons; the

[1] Thomas Poole (1765–1837) of Nether Stowey, Coleridge's friend. It was he
who secured Alfoxden House for the Wordsworths.

[2] The phraseology of this entry should be compared with *Christabel*, l. 16, 'The
thin grey cloud is spread on high', etc. It is the first of several entries in the Journal
which seem particularly to have pleased Coleridge. *Christabel* was written in the
following April (1798).

[3] Cf. W. W.'s 'A Night-Piece', p. 174.

ground strewed with the red berries of the holly. Set forward before two o'clock. Returned a little after four.

27th. Walked from seven o'clock till half-past eight. Upon the whole an uninteresting evening. Only once while we were in the wood the moon burst through the invisible veil which enveloped her, the shadows of the oaks blackened, and their lines became more strongly marked. The withered leaves were coloured with a deeper yellow, a brighter gloss spotted the hollies; again her form became dimmer; the sky flat, unmarked by distances, a white thin cloud. The manufacturer's dog makes a strange, uncouth howl, which it continues many minutes after there is no noise near it but that of the brook. It howls at the murmur of the village stream.

28th. Walked only to the mill.

29th. A very stormy day. William walked to the top of the hill to see the sea. Nothing distinguishable but a heavy blackness. An immense bough riven from one of the fir trees.

30th. William called me into the garden to observe a singular appearance about the moon. A perfect rainbow, within the bow one star, only of colours more vivid. The semi-circle soon became a complete circle, and in the course of three or four minutes the whole faded away. Walked to the blacksmith's and the baker's; an uninteresting evening.

31st. Set forward to Stowey at half-past five. A violent storm in the wood; sheltered under the hollies. When we left home the moon immensely large, the sky scattered over with clouds. These soon closed in, contracting the dimensions of the moon without concealing her.[1] The sound of the pattering shower, and the gusts of wind, very grand. Left the wood when nothing remained of the storm but the driving wind, and a few scattering drops of rain. Presently all clear, Venus first showing herself between the struggling clouds; afterwards Jupiter appeared. The hawthorn hedges, black and pointed, glittering with millions of diamond drops; the hollies shining with broader patches of light. The road to the village of Holford glittered like another stream. On our return, the wind high—a violent

[1] Cf. *Christabel*, l. 18:

> The moon is behind, and at the full;
> And yet she looks both small and dull.

storm of hail and rain at the Castle of Comfort.[1] All the Heavens seemed in one perpetual motion when the rain ceased; the moon appearing, now half veiled, and now retired behind heavy clouds, the stars still moving, the roads very dirty.

1st February. About two hours before dinner, set forward towards Mr Bartholemew's.[2] The wind blew so keen in our faces that we felt ourselves inclined to seek the covert of the wood. There we had a warm shelter, gathered a burthen of large rotten boughs blown down by the wind of the preceding night. The sun shone clear, but all at once a heavy blackness hung over the sea. The trees almost *roared*, and the ground seemed in motion with the multitudes of dancing leaves, which made a rustling sound, distinct from that of the trees. Still the asses pastured in quietness under the hollies, undisturbed by these forerunners of the storm. The wind beat furiously against us as we returned. Full moon. She rose in uncommon majesty over the sea, slowly ascending through the clouds. Sat with the window open an hour in the moonlight.

2nd. Walked through the wood, and on to the Downs before dinner; a warm pleasant air. The sun shone, but was often obscured by straggling clouds. The redbreasts made a ceaseless song in the woods. The wind rose very high in the evening. The room smoked so that we were obliged to quit it. Young lambs in a green pasture in the Coombe,[3] thick legs, large heads, black staring eyes.

3rd. A mild morning, the windows open at breakfast, the redbreasts singing in the garden. Walked with Coleridge over the hills.[4] The sea at first obscured by vapour; that vapour afterwards slid in one mighty mass along the sea-shore; the islands and one point of land clear beyond it. The distant country (which was purple in the clear dull air), overhung by straggling clouds that sailed over it, appeared like the

[1] A public house at Dodington, halfway between Holford and Nether Stowey.

[2] John Bartholomew, who lived at Putsham (then known as Potsham) on the road to Minehead, rented Alfoxden and sub-let it to the Wordsworths.

[3] i.e. Hodder's Combe, the nearest of the Quantock Combes to Alfoxden, being immediately over the ridge of the hill above the house.

[4] Unless Knight's transcript is in error, D. W. must have misdated the entries for 3, 4, and 5 February. Coleridge had paid a long visit to Shrewsbury, staying with the Wedgwoods at Cote House, Bristol, for a week on the way back, and only returned to Nether Stowey on 9 February, so he could not have walked with D. W. on these three days. See his letter of 8 February (really 9th) in Griggs, vol. i, p. 383.

darker clouds, which are often seen at a great distance apparently motionless, while the nearer ones pass quickly over them, driven by the lower winds. I never saw such a union of earth, sky, and sea. The clouds beneath our feet spread themselves to the water, and the clouds of the sky almost joined them. Gathered sticks in the wood; a perfect stillness. The redbreasts sang upon the leafless boughs. Of a great number of sheep in the field, only one standing. Returned to dinner at five o'clock. The moonlight still and warm as a summer's night at nine o'clock.

4th. Walked a great part of the way to Stowey with Coleridge.[1] The morning warm and sunny. The young lasses seen on the hill-tops, in the villages and roads, in their summer holiday clothes—pink petticoats and blue. Mothers with their children in arms, and the little ones that could just walk, tottering by their side. Midges or small flies spinning in the sunshine; the songs of the lark and redbreast; daisies upon the turf; the hazels in blossom; honeysuckles budding. I saw one solitary strawberry flower under a hedge. The furze gay with blossom. The moss rubbed from the pailings by the sheep, that leave locks of wool, and the red marks with which they are spotted, upon the wood.[2]

5th. Walked to Stowey with Coleridge, returned by Woodlands;[3] a very warm day. In the continued singing of birds distinguished the notes of a blackbird or thrush. The sea overshadowed by a thick dark mist, the land in sunshine. The sheltered oaks and beeches still retaining their own leaves. Observed some trees putting out red shoots. Query: What trees are they?

6th. Walked to Stowey over the hills, returned to tea, a cold and clear evening, the roads in some parts frozen hard. The sea hid by mist all the day.

7th. Turned towards Potsham, but finding the way dirty, changed our course. Cottage gardens the object of our walk. Went up the smaller Coombe to Woodlands, to the blacksmith's, the baker's, and through the village of Holford. Still

---

[1] See n. 4, p. 4, on the date of this walk and that on the next day.

[2] This observation is found also in *The Excursion*, i. 742–5. In its first form, *The Ruined Cottage*, the poem was being written at this very time.

[3] A hamlet just beyond Holford from Alfoxden; the house there was later inhabited by John Kenyon, who first introduced Browning to Elizabeth Barrett and to whom Browning dedicated *Dramatic Romances* and Elizabeth her *Aurora Leigh.*

misty over the sea. The air very delightful. We saw nothing very new, or interesting.

8th. Went up the Park, and over the tops of the hills, till we came to a new and very delicious pathway, which conducted us to the Coombe. Sat a considerable time upon the heath. Its surface restless and glittering with the motion of the scattered piles of withered grass, and the waving of the spiders' threads.[1] On our return the mist still hanging over the sea, but the opposite coast clear, and the rocky cliffs distinguishable. In the deep Coombe, as we stood upon the sunless hill, we saw miles of grass, light and glittering, and the insects passing.

9th. William gathered sticks. . . .

10th. Walked to Woodlands, and to the waterfall. The adder's-tongue and the ferns green in the low damp dell. These plants now in perpetual motion from the current of the air; in summer only moved by the drippings of the rocks. A cloudy day.

11th. Walked with Coleridge near to Stowey. The day pleasant, but cloudy.

12th. Walked alone to Stowey. Returned in the evening with Coleridge. A mild, pleasant, cloudy day.

13th. Walked with Coleridge through the wood. A mild and pleasant morning, the near prospect clear. The ridges of the hills fringed with wood, showing the sea through them like the white sky, and still beyond the dim horizon of the distant hills, hanging as it were in one undetermined line between sea and sky.

14th. Gathered sticks with William in the wood, he being unwell and not able to go further. The young birch trees of a bright red, through which gleams a shade of purple. Sat down in a thick part of the wood. The near trees still, even to their topmost boughs, but a perpetual motion in those that skirt the wood. The breeze rose gently; its path distinctly marked, till it came to the very spot where we were.

15th. Gathered sticks in the further wood. The dell green with moss and brambles, and the tall and slender pillars of the unbranching oaks. I crossed the water with letters; returned to Wm and Basil.[2] A shower met us in the wood, and a ruffling breeze.

---

[1] Cf. *The Ancient Mariner*, l. 184, 'restless gossameres'.

[2] The little son of W. W.'s friend Basil Montagu. He lived with the Wordsworths from 1795 until July 1798.

16th. Went for eggs into the Coombe, and to the baker's; a hail shower; brought home large burthens of sticks, a starlight evening, the sky closed in, and the ground white with snow before we went to bed.

17th. A deep snow upon the ground. Wm and Coleridge walked to Mr Bartholemew's, and to Stowey. Wm returned, and we walked through the wood into the Coombe to fetch some eggs. The sun shone bright and clear. A deep stillness in the thickest part of the wood, undisturbed except by the occasional dropping of the snow from the holly boughs; no other sound but that of the water, and the slender notes of a redbreast, which sang at intervals on the outskirts of the southern side of the wood. There the bright green moss was bare at the roots of the trees, and the little birds were upon it. The whole appearance of the wood was enchanting; and each tree, taken singly, was beautiful. The branches of the hollies pendent with their white burden, but still showing their bright red berries, and their glossy green leaves. The bare branches of the oaks thickened by the snow.

18th. Walked after dinner beyond Woodlands. A sharp and very cold evening; first observed the crescent moon, a silvery line, a thready bow, attended by Jupiter and Venus in their palest hues.

19th. I walked to Stowey before dinner; Wm unable to go all the way. Returned alone; a fine sunny, clear, frosty day. The sea still, and blue, and broad, and smooth.

20th. Walked after dinner towards Woodlands.

21st. Coleridge came in the morning, which prevented our walking. Wm went through the wood with him towards Stowey; a very stormy night.

22nd. Coleridge came in the morning to dinner. Wm and I walked after dinner to Woodlands; the moon and two planets; sharp and frosty. Met a razor-grinder with a soldier's jacket on, a knapsack upon his back, and a boy to drag his wheel. The sea very black, and making a loud noise as we came through the wood, loud as if disturbed, and the wind was silent.

23rd. William walked with Coleridge in the morning. I did not go out.

24th. Went to the hill-top. Sat a considerable time overlooking the country towards the sea. The air blew pleasantly round us. The landscape mildly interesting. The Welsh hills capped by a huge range of tumultuous white clouds. The sea, spotted with white, of a bluish grey in general, and streaked with darker lines. The near shores clear; scattered farm houses, half-concealed by green mossy orchards, fresh straw lying at the doors; hay-stacks in the fields. Brown fallows, the springing wheat, like a shade of green over the brown earth, and the choice meadow plots, full of sheep and lambs, of a soft and vivid green; a few wreaths of blue smoke, spreading along the ground; the oaks and beeches in the hedges retaining their yellow leaves; the distant prospect on the land side, islanded with sunshine; the sea, like a basin full to the margin; the dark fresh-ploughed fields; the turnips of a lively rough green. Returned through the wood.

25th. I lay down in the morning, though the whole day was very pleasant, and the evening fine. We did not walk.

26th. Coleridge came in the morning, and Mr and Mrs Crewkshank;[1] walked with Coleridge nearly to Stowey after dinner. A very clear afternoon. We lay sidelong upon the turf, and gazed on the landscape till it melted into more than natural loveliness. The sea very uniform, of a pale greyish blue, only one distant bay, bright and blue as a sky; had there been a vessel sailing up it, a perfect image of delight. Walked to the top of a high hill to see a fortification. Again sat down to feed upon the prospect; a magnificent scene, *curiously* spread out for even minute inspection, though so extensive that the mind is afraid to calculate its bounds. A winter prospect shows every cottage, every farm, and the forms of distant trees, such as in summer have no distinguishing mark. On our return, Jupiter and Venus before us. While the twilight still overpowered the light of the moon, we were reminded that she was shining bright above our heads, by our faint shadows going before us. We had seen her on the tops of the hills, melting into the blue sky. Poole called while we were absent.

27th. I walked to Stowey in the evening. Wm and Basil went with me through the wood. The prospect bright, yet *mildly* beautiful. The sea big and white, swelled to the very shores, but round and high in the middle. Coleridge returned with me, as far as the wood. A very bright moonlight night. Venus almost

[1] John Cruikshank was agent at Stowey of Lord Egmont.

like another moon. Lost to us at Alfoxden long before she goes down the large white sea.

．　　．　　．　　．　　．¹

1st March. We rose early. A thick fog obscured the distant prospect entirely, but the shapes of the nearer trees and the dome of the wood dimly seen and dilated. It cleared away between ten and eleven. The shapes of the mist, slowly moving along, exquisitely beautiful; passing over the sheep they almost seemed to have more of life than those quiet creatures. The unseen birds singing in the mist.

2nd. Went a part of the way home with Coleridge in the morning. Gathered fir-apples afterwards under the trees.

3rd. I went to the shoemaker's. William lay under the trees till my return. Afterwards went to the secluded farm house in search of eggs, and returned over the hill. A very mild, cloudy evening. The rose trees in the hedges and the elder budding.

4th. Walked to Woodlands after dinner, a pleasant evening.

5th. Gathered fir-apples. A thick fog came on. Walked to the baker's and the shoemaker's, and through the fields towards Woodlands. On our return, found Tom Poole in the parlour. He drank tea with us.

6th. A pleasant morning, the sea white and bright, and full to the brim. I walked to see Coleridge in the evening. William went with me to the wood. Coleridge very ill. It was a mild, pleasant afternoon, but the evening became very foggy; when I was near Woodlands, the fog overhead became thin, and I saw the shapes of the Central Stars. Again it closed, and the whole sky was the same.

7th. William and I drank tea at Coleridge's. A cloudy sky. Observed nothing particularly interesting—the distant prospect obscured. One only leaf upon the top of a tree—the sole remaining leaf—danced round and round like a rag blown by the wind.²

8th. Walked in the Park in the morning. I sate under the fir trees. Coleridge came after dinner, so we did not walk again. A foggy morning, but a clear sunny day.

9th. A clear sunny morning, went to meet Mr and Mrs Coleridge. The day very warm.

¹ Probably Knight's deletion.
² Cf. *Christabel*, l. 49: 'The one red leaf, the last of its clan', etc.

10th. Coleridge, Wm, and I walked in the evening to the top of the hill. We all passed the morning in sauntering about the park and gardens, the children playing about, the old man at the top of the hill gathering furze; interesting groups of human creatures, the young frisking and dancing in the sun, the elder quietly drinking in the life and soul of the sun and air.

11th. A cold day. The children went down towards the sea. William and I walked to the top of the hills above Holford. Met the blacksmith. Pleasant to see the labourer on Sunday jump with the friskiness of a cow upon a sunny day.

12th. Tom Poole returned with Coleridge to dinner, a brisk, cold, sunny day; did not walk.

13th. Poole dined with us. William and I strolled into the wood. Coleridge called us into the house.

. . . . . [1]

15th. I have neglected to set down the occurrences of this week, so I do not recollect how we disposed of ourselves to-day.

16th. William, and Coleridge, and I walked in the Park a short time. I wrote to ——.[2] William very ill, better in the evening; and we called round by Potsham.

17th. I do not remember this day.

18th. The Coleridges left us. A cold, windy morning. Walked with them half way. On our return, sheltered under the hollies, during a hail-shower. The withered leaves danced with the hailstones. William wrote a description of the storm.[3]

19th. Wm and Basil and I walked to the hill-tops, a very cold bleak day. We were met on our return by a severe hailstorm. William wrote some lines describing a stunted thorn.[4]

20th. Coleridge dined with us. We went more than half way home with him in the evening. A very cold evening, but clear. The spring seemingly very little advanced. No green trees, only the hedges are budding, and looking very lovely.

[1] Probably Knight's deletion.

[2] Possibly Charles Lloyd, whose poems had been published with Lamb's and Coleridge's in 1797. At this time he was trying to involve D. W. in his attempts to create ill-feeling between C. and Lamb. See Griggs, vol. 1, p. 403 n., and E. K. Chambers, *A Sheaf of Studies*, p. 68.

[3] See 'A whirl-blast from behind the hill', p. 175.

[4] See 'The Thorn', p. 167.

> Not higher than a two years' child
> It stands, erect, this aged Thorn.

21st. We drank tea at Coleridge's. A quiet shower of snow was in the air during more than half our walk. At our return the sky partially shaded with clouds. The horned moon was set. Startled two night birds from the great elm tree.

22nd. I spent the morning in starching and hanging out linen; walked *through* the wood in the evening, very cold.

23rd. Coleridge dined with us. He brought his ballad finished.[1] We walked with him to the Miner's house. A beautiful evening, very starry, the horned moon.

24th. Coleridge, the Chesters,[2] and Ellen Cruikshank called. We walked with them through the wood. Went in the evening into the Coombe to get eggs; returned through the wood, and walked in the park. A duller night than last night: a sort of white shade over the blue sky. The stars dim. The spring continues to advance very slowly,[3] no green trees, the hedges leafless; nothing green but the brambles that still retain their old leaves, the evergreens, and the palms, which indeed are not absolutely green. Some brambles I observed to-day budding afresh, and those have shed their old leaves. The crooked arm of the old oak tree points upwards to the moon.

25th. Walked to Coleridge's after tea. Arrived at home at one o'clock. The night cloudy but not dark.[4]

26th. Went to meet Wedgwood[5] at Coleridge's after dinner. Reached home at half-past twelve, a fine moonlight night; half moon.

27th. Dined at Poole's. Arrived at home a little after twelve, a partially cloudy, but light night, very cold.

28th. Hung out the linen.

29th. Coleridge dined with us.

30th. Walked I know not where.

31st. Walked.

[1] Presumably *The Ancient Mariner*, although C. had told Joseph Cottle in February that it was 'finished'. The expression 'the horned moon' twice in quick succession in this and the entry for 21 March, seems to indicate the influence of the poem. Cf. ll. 210–11,

> The hornéd Moon, with one bright Star
> Within the nether tips.

[2] John Chester, of Nether Stowey, accompanied C. and the Wordsworths to Germany in September.

[3] Coleridge, *Christabel*.   [4] Cf. *Christabel*, l. 15.

[5] Thomas Wedgwood (1771–1805), who with his brother Josiah became at this time Coleridge's benefactor. Thomas was an early experimenter in the behaviour of light, and also a student of educational theories.

1st April. Walked by moonlight.

2nd. A very high wind. Coleridge came to avoid the smoke; stayed all night. We walked in the wood, and sat under the trees. The half of the wood perfectly still, while the wind was making a loud noise behind us. The still trees only gently bowed their heads, as if listening to the wind. The hollies in the thick wood unshaken by the blast; only, when it came with a greater force, shaken by the rain drops falling from the bare oaks above.

3rd. Walked to Crookham,[1] with Coleridge and Wm, to make the appeal. Left Wm there, and parted with Coleridge at the top of the hill. A very stormy afternoon. . . .[2]

4th. Walked to the sea-side in the afternoon. A great commotion in the air, but the sea neither grand nor beautiful. A violent shower in returning. Sheltered under some fir trees at Potsham.

5th. Coleridge came to dinner. William and I walked in the wood in the morning. I fetched eggs from the Coombe.

6th. Went a part of the way home with Coleridge. A pleasant warm morning, but a showery day. Walked a short distance up the lesser Coombe, with an intention of going to the source of the brook,[3] but the evening closing in, cold prevented us. The Spring still advancing very slowly. The horse-chestnuts budding, and the hedgerows beginning to look green, but nothing fully expanded.

7th. Walked before dinner up the Coombe, to the source of the brook, and came home by the tops of the hills; a showery morning, at the hilltops; the view opened upon us very grand.

8th. Easter Sunday. Walked in the morning in the wood, and half way to Stowey; found the air at first oppressively warm, afterwards very pleasant.

9th. Walked to Stowey, a fine air in going, but very hot in returning. The sloe in blossom, the hawthorns green, the larches in the park changed from black to green in two or three days. Met Coleridge in returning.

---

[1] i.e. Crowcombe, on the western side of the Quantocks. 'The appeal' was an appeal against house-tax. See *E. Y.*, p. 220.

[2] Probably Knight's omission.

[3] Coleridge was planning a long poem to be called *The Brook*. See his *Biographia Literaria*, ch. x.

10th. I was hanging out linen in the evening. We walked to Holford. I turned off to the baker's, and walked beyond Woodlands, expecting to meet William, met him on the hill; a close warm evening . . .[1] in bloom.

11th. In the wood in the morning, walked to the top of the hill, then I went down into the wood. A pleasant evening, a fine air, the grass in the park becoming green, many trees green in the dell.

12th. Walked in the morning in the wood. In the evening up the Coombe, fine walk. The Spring advances rapidly, multitudes of primroses, dog-violets, periwinkles, stitchwort.

13th. Walked in the wood in the morning. In the evening went to Stowey. I staid with Mrs[2] Coleridge. Wm went to Poole's. Supped with Mrs[2] Coleridge.

14th. Walked in the wood in the morning. The evening very stormy, so we staid within doors. Mary Wollstonecraft's life,[3] etc., came.

15th. Set forward after breakfast to Crookham, and returned to dinner at three o'clock. A fine cloudy morning. Walked about the squire's grounds. Quaint waterfalls about, about which Nature was very successfully striving to make beautiful what art had deformed—ruins, hermitages, etc. etc. In spite of all these things, the dell romantic and beautiful, though everywhere planted with unnaturalised trees. Happily we cannot shape the huge hills, or carve out the valleys according to our fancy.

16th. New moon. William walked in the wood in the morning. I neglected to follow him. We walked in the park in the evening. . . .

17th. Walked in the wood in the morning. In the evening upon the hill. Cowslips plentiful.

18th. Walked in the wood, a fine sunny morning, met Coleridge returned from his brother's. He dined with us. We drank tea, and then walked with him nearly to Stowey. . . .

19th. . . .

[1] Probably a word illegible to Knight.

[2] Printed in all editions hitherto as 'Mr', but clearly a misreading for 'Mrs'. C. was away in Devonshire visiting his brother George at Ottery. See under 18 April below.

[3] William Godwin's memoir of his wife, Mary Wollstonecraft, had just been published.

20th. Walked in the evening up the hill dividing the Coombes. Came home the Crookham way, by the thorn, and the 'little muddy pond'. Nine o'clock at our return. William all the morning engaged in wearisome composition. The moon crescent. Peter Bell begun.[1]

21st, 22nd, 23rd. . . .

24th. Walked a considerable time in the wood. Sat under the trees, in the evening walked on the top of the hill, found Coleridge on our return and walked with him towards Stowey.

25th. Coleridge drank tea, walked with him to Stowey.

26th. William went to have his picture taken.[2] I walked with him. Dined at home. Coleridge and he drank tea.

27th. Coleridge breakfasted and drank tea, strolled in the wood in the morning, went with him in the evening through the wood, afterwards walked on the hills: the moon, a many-coloured sea and sky.

Saturday, 28th. A very fine morning, warm weather all the week.

Sunday, 6th May. Expected the painter, and Coleridge. A rainy morning—very pleasant in the evening. Met Coleridge as we were walking out. Went with him to Stowey; heard the nightingale; saw a glow-worm.

7th. Walked in the wood in the morning. In the evening, to Stowey with Coleridge who called.

8th. Coleridge dined, went in the afternoon to tea at Stowey. A pleasant walk home.

9th. . . . Wrote to Coleridge.

Wednesday, 16th. Coleridge, William, and myself set forward to the Chedder rocks; slept at Bridgewater.

Thursday, 22nd.[3] Walked to Chedder. Slept at Cross.

---

[1] On this day also Coleridge wrote 'Fears in Solitude'. 'The little muddy pond' is from *The Thorn*, verse 3. See below, p. 168.

[2] This was the earliest known portrait of W. W. It was done by W. Shuter, for Joseph Cottle of Bristol, publisher of *Lyrical Ballads*. The original is in the Wordsworth Collection at Cornell University.

[3] 22 May 1798 was in fact a Tuesday. It is probable that this second expedition to Cheddar began on Thursday, 24 May. Wordsworth went on alone to Bristol to see Cottle.

THE
GRASMERE JOURNALS
1800–1803

I. *14 May to 22 December 1800*

May 14 1800 [*Wednesday*]. Wm and John set off into Yorkshire[1] after dinner at ½ past 2 o'clock, cold pork in their pockets.
I left them at the turning of the Low-wood bay under the trees.
My heart was so full that I could hardly speak to W. when I
gave him a farewell kiss. I sate a long time upon a stone at the
margin of the lake, and after a flood of tears my heart was
easier. The lake looked to me I knew not why dull and melancholy, and the weltering on the shores seemed a heavy sound. I
walked as long as I could amongst the stones of the shore. The
wood rich in flowers. A beautiful yellow, palish yellow flower,
that looked thick round and double, and smelt very sweet—I
supposed it was a ranunculus[2]—Crowfoot, the grassy-leaved
Rabbit-toothed white flower,[3] strawberries, geranium—scentless violet, anemones two kinds, orchises, primroses. The heckberry[4] very beautiful, the crab coming out as a low shrub. Met
a blind man, driving a very large beautiful Bull and a cow—he
walked with two sticks. Came home by Clappersgate.[5] The
valley very green, many sweet views up to Rydale head when
I could juggle away the fine houses, but they disturbed me
even more than when I have been happier. One beautiful view
of the Bridge,[6] without Sir Michael's.[7] Sate down very often,
though it was cold. I resolved to write a journal of the time till
W. and J. return, and I set about keeping my resolve because I
will not quarrel with myself, and because I shall give Wm

[1] i.e. to Gallow Hill, Brompton, near Scarborough, to visit M. H.
[2] Globe-flower (*Trollius Europeus*). For the local name see under 3 June.
[3] Stitchwort (*Stellaria holostea*).
[4] Local name for the bird-cherry (*Prunus padus*).
[5] See p. 17, n. 2.   [6] Pelter Bridge, Rydal.
[7] Rydal Hall, the seat of Sir Michael le Fleming.

Pleasure by it when he comes home again. At Rydale a woman of the village, stout and well dressed, begged a halfpenny—she had never she said done it before, but these hard times— — Arrived at home with a bad head-ach, set some slips of privett. The evening cold, had a fire—my face now flame-coloured. It is nine o'clock. I shall soon go to bed. A young woman begged at the door—she had come from Manchester on Sunday morn: with two shillings and a slip of paper which she supposed a Bank note—it was a cheat. She had buried her husband and three children within a year and a half—all in one grave— burying very dear—paupers all put in one place—20 shillings paid for as much ground as will bury a man—a stone to be put over it or the right will be lost—11/6 each time the ground is opened. Oh! that I had a letter from William!

May 15 Thursday. A coldish dull morning—hoed the first row of peas, weeded etc. etc., sat hard to mending till evening. The rain which had threatened all day came on just when I was going to walk.

Friday morning [16th]. Warm and mild, after a fine night of rain. Transplanted raddishes after breakfast, walked to Mr Gell's[1] with the Books, gathered mosses and plants. The woods extremely beautiful with all autumnal variety and softness. I carried a basket for mosses, and gathered some wild plants. Oh! that we had a book of botany.[2] All flowers now are gay and deliciously sweet. The primrose still pre-eminent among the later flowers of the spring. Foxgloves very tall, with their heads budding. I went forward round the lake at the foot of Loughrigg fell. I was much amused with the business of a pair of stone chats.[3] Their restless voices as they skimmed along the water following each other their shadows under them, and their returning back to the stones on the shore, chirping with the same unwearied voice. Could not cross the water so I went round by the stepping-stones. The morning clear but

[1] Mr. Gell lived in a cottage on the site of the house now called Silver How. (G. G. W.) He was Sir William Gell (1777–1836, knighted 1803), the archaeologist and topographer. The identification was made by C. W. in his *Memoirs of W. W.* (1851).

[2] In March 1801 the Wordsworths acquired Withering's *An Arrangement of British Plants according to the latest Improvements of the Linnean System* (1796), in 4 vols. The book, containing some marginal notes by both D. W. and W. W., is now in the Wordsworth Library.

[3] D. W. probably means, from her description, sand-pipers.

cloudy, that is the hills were not overhung by mists. After dinner Aggy[1] weeded onions and carrots. I helped for a little—wrote to Mary Hutchinson—washed my head—worked. After tea went to Ambleside—a pleasant cool but not cold evening. Rydale was very beautiful with spear-shaped streaks of polished steel. No letters!—only one newspaper. I returned by Clappersgate.[2] Grasmere was very solemn in the last glimpse of twilight it calls home the heart to quietness. I had been very melancholy in my walk back. I had many of my saddest thoughts and I could not keep the tears within me. But when I came to Grasmere I felt that it did me good. I finished my letter to M. H. Ate hasty pudding, and went to bed. As I was going out in the morning I met a half crazy old man. He shewed me a pincushion and begged a pin, afterwards a halfpenny. He began in a kind of indistinct voice in this manner: 'Matthew Jobson's lost a cow. Tom Nichol has two good horses strayed. Jim Jones's cow's brokken her horn, etc. etc.' He went into Aggy's and persuaded her to give him some whey and let him boil some porridge. She declares he ate two quarts.

Saturday [*17th*]. Incessant rain from morning till night. T. Ashburner[3] brought us coals. Worked hard and read Midsummer Night's Dream, Ballads—sauntered a little in the garden. The Skobby[4] sate quietly in its nest rocked by the winds and beaten by the rain.

Sunday 19th.[5] Went to church, slight showers, a cold air. The mountains from this window look much greener and I think the valley is more green than ever. The corn begins to shew itself. The ashes are still bare. Went part of the way home with Miss Simpson.[6] A little girl from Coniston came to beg. She had lain out all night—her step-mother had turned her out of doors. Her father could not stay at home 'She flights so'.

---

[1] The Fisher family, John with his wife Agnes (Aggy) and his sister Mary, the 'old Molly' who acted as servant to Dorothy and William, lived at Sykeside, the cottage across the road from Dove Cottage to the south-west.

[2] Not the village so named, but the road under Loughrigg Fell along the banks of the Rothay.

[3] Thomas Ashburner lived in the cottage now rebuilt opposite Dove Cottage. He supplied the Wordsworths with coal from Keswick.

[4] Local name for chaffinch.　　　　　　　　　[5] Actually the 18th.

[6] Daughter of the Revd. Joseph Simpson, vicar of Wythburn by Thirlmere, who lived at High Broadrain on the Keswick road. See *The Excursion*, VII. 31–291.

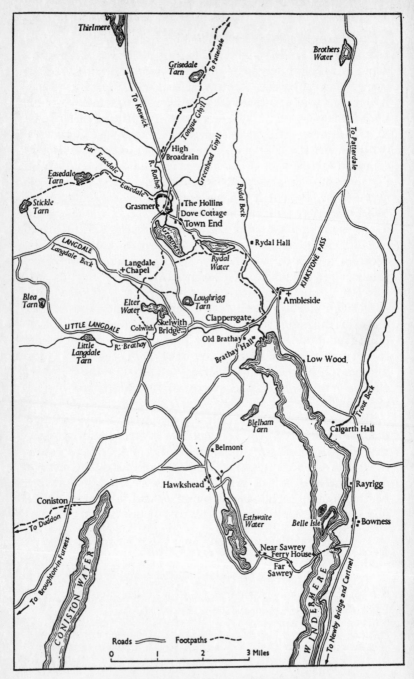

THE SOUTHERN LAKE DISTRICT

Walked to Ambleside in the evening round the lake. The prospect exceedingly beautiful from Loughrigg fell. It was so green,
that no eye could be weary of reposing upon it. The most
beautiful situation for a house in the field next to Mr Benson's.[1]
It threatened rain all the evening but was mild and pleasant.
I was overtaken by 2 Cumberland people on the other side of
Rydale who complimented me upon my walking. They were
going to sell cloth, and odd things which they make themselves in Hawkshead and the neighbourhood. The post was
not arrived so I walked thro' the town, past Mrs Taylor's, and
met him. Letters from Coleridge and Cottle.[2] John Fisher over-
took me on the other side of Rydale. He talked much about the
alteration in the times, and observed that in a short time there
would be only two ranks of people, the very rich and the very
poor, for those who have small estates says he are forced to sell,
and all the land goes into one hand. Did not reach home till
10 o'clock.

Monday [19th]. Sauntered a good deal in the garden, bound
carpets, mended old clothes. Read Timon of Athens. Dried
linen. Molly weeded the turnips, John stuck the peas. We had
not much sunshine or wind but no rain till about 7 o'clock when
we had a slight shower just after I had set out upon my walk.
I did not return but walked up into the Black Quarter.[3] I
sauntered a long time among the rocks above the church. The
most delightful situation possible for a cottage commanding
two distinct views of the vale and of the lake, is among those
rocks. I strolled on, gathered mosses, etc. The quietness and
still seclusion of the valley affected me even to producing the
deepest melancholy. I forced myself from it. The wind rose
before I went to bed. No rain—Dodwell and Wilkinson called
in my absence.

Tuesday Morning [20th]. A fine mild rain. After Breakfast the
sky cleared and before the clouds passed from the hills I went to
Ambleside. It was a sweet morning. Everything green and over-
flowing with life, and the streams making a perpetual song with
the thrushes and all little birds, not forgetting the Stone chats.

[1] The Bensons lived at Tail End (now Dale End) on the western side of the lake.
[2] Joseph Cottle of Bristol, who had published *Lyrical Ballads* for Wordsworth and
Coleridge in 1798.
[3] The name given by the W.s to Easedale, during their first year's residence at
Grasmere. It does not appear in the journal after November 1800. (G. G. W.)

The post was not come in. I walked as far as Windermére,[1] and met him there. No letters! no papers. Came home by Clappersgate. I was sadly tired, ate a hasty dinner and had a bad headach. Went to bed and slept at least 2 hours. Rain came on in the Evening—Molly washing.

Wednesday [*21st*]. Went often to spread the linen which was bleaching—a rainy day and very wet night.

Thursday [*22nd*]. A very fine day with showers—dried the linen and starched. Drank tea at Mr Simpson's.[2] Brought down Batchelor's Buttons (Rock Ranunculus) and other plants —went part of the way back. A showery, mild evening—all the peas up.

Friday 23rd. Ironing till tea time. So heavy a rain that I could not go for letters—put by the linen, mended stockings etc.

Saturday May 24th. Walked in the morning to Ambleside. I found a letter from Wm and from Mary Hutchinson and Douglass.[3] Returned on the other side of the lakes—wrote to William after dinner, nailed up the beds, worked in the garden, sate in the evening under the trees. I went to bed soon with a bad head-ache. A fine day.

Sunday [*25th*]. A very fine warm day, had no fire. Read Macbeth in the morning, sate under the trees after dinner. Miss Simpson came just as I was going out and she sate with me. I wrote to my Brother Christopher, and sent John Fisher to Ambleside after tea. Miss Simpson and I walked to the foot of the lake—her Brother met us. I went with them nearly home and on my return found a letter from Coleridge and from Charles Lloyd,[4] and three papers.

Monday May 26. A very fine morning, worked in the garden till after 10 when old Mr Simpson came and talked to me till after 12. Molly weeding. Wrote letters to J. H.,[5] Coleridge, C. Ll., and W. I walked towards Rydale and turned aside at my favorite field. The air and the lake were still—one cottage

---

[1] i.e. the head of the lake, not the modern town.

[2] The Revd. Joseph Simpson. See under 18 May.

[3] Charles Douglas of Jamaica, a Cambridge friend of W.'s, now a barrister. In 1796 W. while at Racedown had lent him £200. See *E.Y.*, p. 182.

[4] Charles Lloyd (1775–1839), son of the Birmingham banker, had lived with C. at Nether Stowey in 1798. In 1800 he settled with his family at Old Brathay, near Clappersgate village.

[5] Joanna Hutchinson, youngest sister of M. H.

light in the vale, had so much of day left that I could distinguish objects, the woods; trees and houses. Two or three different kinds of Birds sang at intervals on the opposite shore. I sate till I could hardly drag myself away I grew so sad. 'When pleasant thoughts,' etc. . . .[1]

Tuesday 27th. I walked to Ambleside with letters—met the post before I reached Mr Partridge's,[2] one paper, only a letter for Coleridge—I expected a letter from Wm. It was a sweet morning, the ashes in the valley nearly in full leaf but still to be distinguished, quite bare on the higher grounds. I was warm in returning, and becoming cold with sitting in the house—I had a bad head-ach—went to bed after dinner, and lay till after 5— not well after tea. I worked in the garden, but did not walk further. A delightful evening before the Sun set but afterwards it grew colder. Mended stockings etc.

Wednesday [*28th*]. In the morning walked up to the rocks above Jenny Dockeray's[3] sate a long time upon the grass the prospect divinely beautiful. If I had three hundred pounds and could afford to have a bad interest for my money I would buy that estate, and we would build a cottage there to end our days in. I went into her garden and got white and yellow lilies, periwinkle, etc., which I planted. Sate under the trees with my work. No fire in the morning. Worked till between 7 and 8, and then watered the garden, and was about to go up to Mr Simpson's, when Miss S. and her visitors passed the door. I went home with them, a beautiful evening the crescent moon hanging above Helm crag.

Thursday [*29th*]. In the morning worked in the garden a little, read King John. Miss Simpson, and Miss Falcon and Mr S. came very early. Went to Mr Gell's boat before tea. We fished upon the lake and amongst us caught 13 Bass. Miss Simpson brought gooseberries *and cream*. Left the water at near nine o'clock, very cold. Went part of the way home with the party.

[1] 'Lines written in Early Spring':
> In that sweet mood when pleasant thoughts
> Bring sad thoughts to the mind.

[2] Edward Partridge, a manufacturer of linseys at Ambleside.

[3] Jenny Dockray lived either in Underhow or Dockray, two ancient farmhouses south of Butterlip How and east and west of the Easedale road, both formerly occupied by the Dockray family. (G. G. W.)

Friday [*30th*]. In the morning went to Ambleside, forgetting that the post does not come till the evening. How was I grieved when I was so informed. I walked back resolving to go again in the evening. It rained very mildly and sweetly in the morning as I came home, but came on a wet afternoon and evening—but chilly. I caught Mr Olliff's[1] Lad as he was going for letters, he brought me one from Wm and 2 papers. I planted London pride upon the wall and many things on the Borders. John sodded the wall. As I came past Rydale in the morning I saw a Heron swimming with only its neck out of water—it beat and struggled amongst the water when it flew away and was long in getting loose.

Saturday [*31st*]. A sweet mild rainy morning. Grundy the carpet man called. I paid him 1-10/-. Went to the Blind man's[2] for plants. I got such a load that I was obliged to leave my Basket in the Road and send Molly for it. Planted till after dinner when I was putting up vallances. Miss Simpson and her visitors called. I went with them to Brathay Bridge. We got Broom in returning, strawberries etc., came home by Ambleside. Grasmere looked divinely beautiful. Mr and Miss Simpson and Tommy[3] drank tea at 8 o'clock. I walked to the Potters with them.

Sunday June 1st. Rain in the night—a sweet mild morning. Read Ballads; went to church. Singers from Wytheburn. Went part of the way home with Miss Simpson. Walked upon the hill above the house till dinner time—went again to church—a Christening and singing which kept us very late. The pew-side came down with me. Walked with Miss Simpson nearly home. After tea went to Ambleside, round the lakes—a very fine warm evening. I lay upon the steep of Loughrigg my heart dissolved in what I saw when I was not startled but re-called from my reverie by a noise as of a child paddling without shoes. I looked up and saw a lamb close to me. It approached nearer and nearer as if to examine me and stood a long time. I did not move. At last it ran past me and went bleating along the pathway seeming to be seeking its mother. I saw a hare in the

---

[1] The Olliffs or Olives lived a little further up the Keswick road, at The Hollins. They left Grasmere in 1802. See *E. T.*, p. 351.

[2] Matthew Newton. See under 16 January 1803.

[3] A grandson of Mr. Simpson.

high road. The post was not come in; waited in the Road till John's apprentice came with a letter from Coleridge and 3 papers. The moon shone upon the water—reached home at 10 o'clock—went to bed immediately. Molly brought Daisies etc. which we planted.

Monday [*2nd*]. A cold dry windy morning. I worked in the garden and planted flowers, etc. Sate under the trees after dinner till tea time. John Fisher stuck the peas, Molly weeded and washed. I went to Ambleside after tea, crossed the stepping-stones at the foot of Grasmere and pursued my way on the other side of Rydale and by Clappersgate. I sate a long time to watch the hurrying waves and to hear the regularly irregular sound of the dashing waters. The waves round about the little [Island] seemed like a dance of spirits that rose out of the water, round its small circumference of shore. Inquired about lodgings for Coleridge, and was accompanied by Mrs Nicholson[1] as far as Rydale. This was very kind, but God be thanked I want not society by a moonlight lake—It was near 11 when I reached home. I wrote to Coleridge and went late to bed.

Tuesday [*3rd*]. Sent off my letter by the Butcher—a boisterous drying day. I worked in the garden before dinner. Read R[ichar]d Second—was not well after dinner and lay down. Mrs Simpson's grandson brought me some gooseberries. I got up and walked with him part of the way home, afterwards went down rambling by the lake side—got Lockety[2] Goldings, strawberries etc., and planted. After tea the wind fell. I walked towards Mr Simpson's. Gave the newspapers to the Girl, reached home at 10. No letter, no William—a letter from R[ichar]d to John.

Wednesday [*4th*]. A very fine day. I sate out of doors most of the day, wrote to Mr Jackson.[3] Ambleside fair. I walked to the lake-side in the morning, took up plants and sate upon a stone reading Ballads. In the Evening I was watering plants when Mr and Miss Simpson called. I accompanied them home, and we went to the waterfall at the head of the valley. It was very interesting in the Twilight. I brought home lemon thyme and several other plants, and planted them by moonlight. I

---

[1] The postmistress at Ambleside.   [2] The globe-flower (Westmorland dialect).

[3] The owner of Greta Hall, Keswick. Dorothy was negotiating with him to let the house to the Coleridges. He was also the employer of 'Benjamin the waggoner', hero of Wordsworth's poem *The Waggoner*.

lingered out of doors in the hope of hearing my Brothers tread.

Thursday [5th]. I sate out of doors great part of the day and worked in the garden—had a letter from Mr Jackson, and wrote an answer to Coleridge. The little birds busy making love and pecking the blossoms and bits of moss off the trees, they flutter about and about and thrid the trees as I lie under them. Molly went out to tea, I would not go far from home, expecting my Brothers. I rambled on the hill above the house gathered wild thyme and took up roots of wild Columbine. Just as I was returning with my 'load', Mr and Miss Simpson called. We went again upon the hill, got more plants, set them, and then went to the Blind Man's for London Pride for Miss Simpson. I went up with them as far as the Blacksmith's.[1] A fine lovely moonlight night.

Friday [6th]. Sate out of doors reading the whole afternoon, but in the morning I wrote to my aunt Cookson.[2] In the evening I went to Ambleside with Coleridge's letter—it was a lovely night as the day had been. I went by Loughrigg and Clappersgate and just met the post at the turnpike—he told me there were two letters but none for me. So I was in no hurry and went round again by Clappersgate, crossed the stepping-stones and entered Ambleside at Matthew Harrison's. A letter from Jack Hutchinson,[3] and one from Montagu[4] enclosing a 3£ note. No William! I slackened my pace as I came near home fearing to hear that he was not come. I listened till after one o'clock to every barking dog, cock fighting, and other sports: it was Mr Borrick's opening. Foxgloves just coming into blossom.

Saturday [7th]. A very warm cloudy morning, threatening to rain. I walked up to Mr Simpson's to gather gooseberries—it was a very fine afternoon. Little Tommy came down with me, ate gooseberry pudding and drank tea with me. We went up

[1] John Watson, who lived at Winterseeds, and had his forge where Tongue Ghyll crosses the Keswick road. (G. G. W.)

[2] Wife of the Wordsworths' maternal uncle, the Revd. William Cookson, rector of Forncett, Norfolk, later a Canon of Windsor. D. W. had lived with the Cooksons for seven years, 1788–95.

[3] M. H.'s eldest brother, who lived at Stockton-on-Tees.

[4] Basil Montagu (1770–1850), one of W. W.'s earliest and most intimate friends. He was a barrister and did much in later years to reform the criminal law. In 1796 W. had lent him on annuity £300.

the hill to gather sods and plants and went down to the lake side and took up orchises etc. I watered the garden and weeded. I did not leave home in the expectation of Wm and John, and sitting at work till after 11 o'clock I heard a foot go to the front of the house, turn round, and open the gate. It was William— —After our first joy was over, we got some tea. We did not go to bed till 4 o'clock in the morning so he had an opportunity of seeing our improvements. The birds were singing, and all looked fresh, though not gay. There was a greyness on earth and sky. We did not rise till near 10 in the morning [Sunday]. We were busy all day in writing letters to Coleridge, Montagu, Douglass, Richard. Mr and Miss Simpson called in the evening, the little Boy carried our letters to Ambleside. We walked with Mr and Miss S. home, on their return. The evening was cold and I was afraid of the tooth-ach for William. We met John on our return home.

Monday 9th. In the morning W. cut down the winter cherry tree. I sowed French Beans and weeded. A coronetted Landau went by when we were sitting upon the sodded wall. The ladies (evidently Tourists) turned an eye of interest upon our little garden and cottage. We went to R. Newton's[1] for pike-floats and went round to Mr Gell's Boat and on to the Lake to fish. We caught nothing—it was extremely cold. The Reeds and Bulrushes or Bullpipes of a tender soft green, making a plain whose surface moved with the wind. The reeds not yet tall. The lake clear to the Bottom, but saw no fish. In the evening I stuck peas, watered the garden and planted Brocoli. Did not walk for it was very cold. A poor Girl called to beg who had no work at home and was going in search of it to Kendal. She slept in Mr Benson's Lathe,[2] and went off after Breakfast in the morning with 7d and a letter to the Mayor of Kendal.[3]

Tuesday 10th. A cold, yet sunshiny morning. John carried letters to Ambleside. I made tarts, pies etc. Wm stuck peas. After dinner he lay down. John not at home. I stuck peas alone. Molly washing. Cold showers with hail and rain, but at half-

---

[1] Robert Newton was proprietor of the village inn opposite the church, now Church Stile. Wordsworth and Coleridge stayed there in November 1799.

[2] North Country dialect for 'barn.'

[3] Thomas Maude, a former school-fellow of W. W. at Hawkshead.

past five after a heavy rain the lake became calm—and very beautiful. Those parts of the water which were perfectly un-ruffled lay like green islands of various shapes. W. and I walked to Ambleside to seek lodgings for C. No letters. No papers. It was a very cold cheerless evening. John had been fishing in Langdale and was gone to bed.

On Tuesday, May 27th, a very tall woman,[1] tall much be-yond the measure of tall women, called at the door. She had on a very long brown cloak, and a very white cap without Bonnet—her face was excessively brown, but it had plainly once been fair. She led a little bare-footed child about 2 years old by the hand and said her husband who was a tinker was gone before with the other children. I gave her a piece of Bread. After-wards on my road to Ambleside, beside the Bridge at Rydale, I saw her husband sitting by the roadside, his two asses feeding beside him and the two young children at play upon the grass. The man did not beg. I passed on and about $\frac{1}{4}$ of a mile further I saw two boys before me, one about 10 the other about 8 years old at play chasing a butterfly. They were wild figures, not very ragged, but without shoes and stockings; the hat of the elder was wreathed round with yellow flowers, the younger whose hat was only a rimless crown, had stuck it round with laurel leaves. They continued at play till I drew very near and then they addressed me with the Beggars' cant and the whining voice of sorrow. I said I served your mother this morning. (The Boys were so like the woman who had called at the door that I could not be mistaken.) O! says the elder you could not serve my mother for she's dead and my father's on at the next town—he's a potter. I persisted in my assertion and that I would give them nothing. Says the elder Come, let's away, and away they flew like lightning. They had however sauntered so long in their road that they did not reach Ambleside before me, and I saw them go up to Matthew Harrison's house with their wallet upon the elder's shoulder, and creeping with a Beggar's complaining foot. On my return through Ambleside I met in the street the mother driving her asses; in the two Panniers of one of which were the two little children whom she was chiding and threatening with a wand which she used to drive on her asses, while the little things hung in wantonness

[1] See W. W.'s poem 'Beggars', p. 176.

over the Pannier's edge. The woman had told me in the
morning that she was of Scotland, which her accent fully
proved, but that she had lived (I think at Wigton), that they
could not keep a house and so they travelled.

Wednesday 13th June.[1] A very cold morning—we went on the
lake to set pike floats with John's fish. W. and J. went first
alone. Mr Simpson called, and I accompanied him to the Lake
side. My Brothers and I again went upon the water, and returned to dinner. We landed upon the Island where I saw the
whitest Hawthorn I have seen this year, the generality of hawthorns are bloomless. I saw wild roses in the hedges. Went to
bed in the afternoon and slept till after six—a threatening of the
tooth-ach. Wm and John went to the pike floats—they brought
in 2 pikes. I sowed Kidney-beans and spinnach. A cold evening.
Molly stuck the peas. I weeded a little. Did not walk.

Thursday 14th June.[1] William and I went upon the water to
set pike floats. John fished under Loughrigg. We returned to
dinner, 2 pikes boiled and roasted. Very cold air but warm
sun. W. and I again went upon the water. We walked to
Rydale after tea, and up to the potter's. A cold night, but
warmer.

Friday [13th]. A rainy morning. W. and J. went upon the
Lake. Very warm, and pleasant gleams of sunshine. Went upon
the water after tea, caught a pike 7½ [lbs.]. Mr Simpson
trolling.[2] Mr Gell and his party came.

Saturday [14th]. A fine morning but cloudy. W. and John
went upon the lake. I staid at home. We drank tea at Mr
Simpson's. Stayed till after 10 o'clock.

Sunday [15th]. John walked to Coniston. W. and I sauntered
in the garden. Afterwards walked by the lake side: a cold air.
We pushed through the wood. Walked behind the fir grove
and returned to dinner. We lay down after dinner. Parker, the
Tanner and the Blacksmith from Hawkshead called.

Monday [16th]. Wm and I went to Brathay by Little Langdale and Collath and Skelleth.[3] It was a warm mild morning
with threatening of rain. The vale of Little Langdale looked

[1] Here D. W.'s dates are two days ahead of the actual dates; Wednesday was the
11th, Thursday the 12th June.
[2] Fishing from a boat with a running line.
[3] i.e. Colwith and Skelwith. They probably walked to Elterwater, and thence by
the narrow road over the lower end of Lingmoor Fell into Little Langdale.

bare and unlovely. Collath was wild and interesting, from the Peat carts and peat gatherers—the valley all perfumed with the Gale[1] and wild thyme. The woods about the waterfall veined with rich yellow Broom. A succession of delicious views from Skelleth to Brathay. We met near Skelleth a pretty little Boy with a wallet over his shoulder—he came from Hawkshead and was going to 'late' a lock[2] of meal. He spoke gently and without complaint. When I asked him if he got enough to eat he looked surprized and said 'Nay'. He was 7 years old but seemed not more than 5. We drank tea at Mr Ibbetson's,[3] and returned by Ambleside. Lent 3–9–0 to the Potter at Kendal. Met John on our return home at about 10 o'clock. Saw a primrose in blossom.

Tuesday [*17th*]. We put the new window in. I ironed and worked about a good deal in house and garden. In the Evening we walked for letters. Found one for Coleridge at Rydale, and I returned much tired.

Wednesday [*18th*]. We walked round the lake in the morning and in the evening to the lower waterfall at Rydale. It was a warm dark, lowering evening.

Thursday [*19th*]. A very hot morning. W. and I walked up to Mr Simpson's. W. and old Mr S. went to fish in Wytheburn water.[4] I dined with John, and lay under the trees. The after-noon changed from clear to cloudy and to clear again. John and I walked up to the waterfall and to Mr Simpson's, and with Miss Simpson met the fishers. W. caught a pike weighing 4¾ lbs. There was a gloom almost terrible over Grasmere water and vale. A few drops fell but not much rain. No Coleridge whom we fully expected.

Friday [*20th*]. I worked in the garden in the morning. Wm prepared Pea sticks. Threatening for rain but yet it comes not. On Wednesday evening a poor man called, a hatter—he had been long ill, but was now recovered and his wife was lying in of her 4th child. The parish would not help him because he had implements of trade etc. etc. We gave him 6d.

Saturday [*21st*]. In the morning W. and I went to Ambleside

[1] Bog-myrtle.
[2] Seek a measure (dialect).
[3] Julius Caesar Ibbetson (1759–1817), the painter, at that time living in Clappers-gate village.
[4] Now called Thirlmere. At that time it was also known as Leathes Water.

to get his tooth drawn, and put in. A fine clear morning but cold. W.'s tooth drawn with very little pain—he slept till 3 o'clock. Young Mr S.[1] drank tea and supped with us then fished in Rydale water and they caught 2 small fishes—W. no bite—John 3. Miss Simpson and 3 children called—I walked with them to Rydale. The evening cold and clear and frosty, but the wind was falling as I returned. I staid at home about an hour and then walked up the hill to Rydale lake. Grasmere looked so beautiful that my heart was almost melted away. It was quite calm only spotted with sparkles of light. The church visible. On our return all distant objects had faded away—all but the hills. The reflection of the light bright sky above Black quarter was very solemn. Mr S. did not go till 12 o'clock.

Sunday [22nd]. In the morning W. and I walked towards Rydale and up into the wood but finding it not very pleasant we returned—sauntered in the garden—a showery day. In the evening I planted a honeysuckle round the yew tree. In the evening we walked for letters. No letters: no news of Coleridge. Jimmy Benson came home drunk beside us.

Monday [23rd]. Mr Simpson called in the morning. Tommy's Father[2] dead. W. and I went into Langdale to fish. The morning was very cold. I sate at the foot of the lake till my head ached with cold. The view exquisitely beautiful, through a gate and under a sycamore tree beside the first house going into Loughrigg. Elter water looked barren, and the view from the church less beautiful than in winter. When W. went down to the water to fish I lay under the wind my head pillowed upon a mossy rock and slept about 10 minutes, which relieved my headach. We ate our dinner together and parted again. Wm was afraid he had lost his line and sought me. An old man saw me just after I had crossed the stepping stones and was going through a copse—Ho, where were you going? To Elterwater Bridge—Why says he it's well I saw you ye were gane to Little Langdale by Wrynose, and several other places, which he ran over with a mixture of triumph, good-nature, and wit—It's well I saw you or you'd ha' been lost. The evening grew very pleasant—we sate on the side of the hill looking to

[1] See p. 32 n. 5.
[2] Probably a son-in-law of Mr. Simpson, perhaps Mr. Jameson. See under 7 October.

Elterwater. I was much tired and returned home to tea. W. went to fish for pike in Rydale. John came in when I had done tea, and he and I carried a jug of tea to William. We met him in the old road from Rydale. He drank his tea upon the turf. The setting sun threw a red purple light upon the rocks and stone walls of Rydale which gave them a most interesting and beautiful appearance.

Tuesday [*24th*]. W. went to Ambleside. John walked out. I made tarts etc. Mr B. Simpson called and asked us to tea. I went to the view of Rydale to meet William. John went to him —I returned. W. and I drank tea at Mr Simpson's. Brought down Lemon Thyme, greens etc. The old woman was very happy to see us and we were so in the pleasure we gave. She was an affecting picture of patient disappointment, suffering under no particular affliction.

Wednesday [*25th*]. A very rainy day. I made a shoe. Wm and John went to fish in Langdale. In the evening I went above the house, and gathered flowers which I planted, fox-gloves, etc. On Sunday [29 June] Mr and Mrs Coleridge and Hartley came.[1] The day was very warm. We sailed to the foot of Loughrigg. They staid with us three weeks and till the Thursday following, i.e. till the 23 [24th] of July. On the Friday preceding their departure we drank tea at the island. The weather very delightful, and on the Sunday we made a great fire, and drank tea in Bainriggs with the Simpsons. I accompanied Mrs C. to Wytheburne, and returned with W.—to tea at Mr Simpson's—it was excessively hot, but the day after Friday July 24th [25th] still hotter. All the morning I was engaged in unpacking our Somersetshire goods[2] and in making pies. The house was a hot oven but yet we could not bake the pies. I was so weary I could not walk, so I went and sate with Wm in the orchard. We had a delightful half hour in the warm still evening.

Saturday 25th.[3] Still hotter. I sate with W. in the orchard all the morning and made my shoes. In the afternoon from

---

[1] The arrival of the Coleridges interrupted the regular writing of the journal. The brief summary of their three weeks' visit was not written until after their departure.

[2] Evidently some possessions which had been stored since the departure from Alfoxden two years before.

[3] Saturday was the 26th.

excessive heat I was ill in the headach and toothach and went to bed—I was refreshed with washing myself after I got up, but it was too hot to walk till near dark, and then I sate upon the wall finishing my shoes.

Sunday Mor. 26th.[1] Very warm. Molly ill. John bathed in the lake. I wrote out Ruth in the afternoon, in the morning I read Mr Knight's Landscape.[2] After tea we rowed down to Loughrigg Fell, visited the white foxglove, gathered wild strawberries, and walked up to view Rydale. We lay a long time looking at the lake, the shores all embrowned with the scorching sun. The Ferns were turning yellow, that is here and there one was quite turned. We walked round by Benson's wood home. The lake was now most still and reflected the beautiful yellow and blue and purple and grey colours of the sky. We heard a strange sound in the Bainriggs wood as we were floating on the water it *seemed* in the wood, but it must have been above it, for presently we saw a raven very high above us—it called out and the Dome of the sky seemed to echo the sound—it called again and again as it flew onwards, and the mountains gave back the sound, seeming as if from their center a musical bell-like answering to the bird's hoarse voice. We heard both the call of the bird and the echo after we could see him no longer.[3] We walked up to the top of the hill again in view of Rydale. Met Mr and Miss Simpson on horseback. The crescent moon which had shone upon the water was now gone down. Returned to supper at 10 o'clock.

Monday morning [*28th*]. Received a letter from Coleridge enclosing one from Mr Davy[4] about the Lyrical Ballads. Intensely hot. I made pies in the morning. Wm went into the wood and altered his poems. In the Evening it was so very warm that I was too much tired to walk.

Tuesday [*29th*]. Still very hot. We gathered peas for dinner.[5]

---

[1] Sunday was the 27th.

[2] *The Landscape: a Didactic Poem in Three Books,* by Richard Payne Knight (1794).

[3] Cf. *The Excursion,* IV. 1177–87.

[4] Humphry Davy (1778–1829), the scientist, of Bristol, was correcting the proofs of the second volume of *Lyrical Ballads* (published January 1801). He was a friend of Joseph Cottle, and himself a writer of verse, but is chiefly famous for his discoveries in chemistry for which he was knighted in 1812.

[5] Here two sentences are crossed out, but are repeated under the next entry (Wednesday) after 'excessive heat and headach'. This is one of several instances showing that D. W. did not write her journal every day.

We walked up in the Evening to find out Hewetson's cottage but it was too dark. I was sick and weary.

Wednesday [30th]. Gathered peas for Mrs Simpson—John and I walked up with them—very hot—Wm had intended going to Keswick. I was obliged to lie down after dinner from excessive heat and headach. The Evening excessively beautiful—a rich reflection of the moon, the moonlight clouds and the hills, and from the Rays gap[1] a huge rainbow pillar. We sailed upon the lake till it was 10 o'clock.

Thursday [31st]. All the morning I was busy copying poems. Gathered peas, and in the afternoon Coleridge came, very hot, he brought the 2nd volume of the Anthology.[2] The men went to bathe, and we afterwards sailed down to Loughrigg. Read poems on the water, and let the boat take its own course. We walked a long time upon Loughrigg and returned in the grey twilight. The moon just setting as we reached home.

Friday 1st August. In the morning I copied The Brothers. Coleridge and Wm went down to the lake. They returned and we all went together to Mary Point[3] where we sate in the breeze and the shade, and read Wm's poems. Altered The Whirlblast[4] etc. Mr Simpson came to tea and Mr B. Simpson[5] afterwards. We drank tea in the orchard.

Saturday Morning 2nd. Wm and Coleridge went to Keswick. John went with them to Wytheburn and staid all day fishing and brought home 2 small pikes at night. I accompanied them to Lewthwaite's cottage[6] and on my return papered Wm's room. I afterwards lay down till tea time and after tea worked at my shifts in the orchard. A grey evening. About 8 o'clock it gathered for rain and I had the scatterings of a shower, but afterwards the lake became of a glassy calmness and all was still. I sate till I could see no longer and then continued my work in the house.

[1] i.e. Dunmail Raise.

[2] The *Annual Anthology*, edited by Southey.

[3] One of the 'twin' heath-clad rocks in Bainriggs Wood, called after Mary and Sara Hutchinson. See *P.W.*, vol. II, p. 123, 'Forth from a jutting ridge.'

[4] Written at Alfoxden in 1798. See p. 175.

[5] Bartholomew Simpson, son of the Revd. Joseph Simpson, of Broadrain. See D. W.'s description of him and other members of the family in a letter to Jane Marshall, 10 September 1800, *E.T.*, p. 299.

[6] i.e. Grove Cottage, situated between Town End and the Swan, midway between The Hollins and Forest Side. (G. G. W.)

Sunday Morning 3rd. I made pies and stuffed the pike—baked a loaf. Headach after dinner—I lay down. A letter from Wm rouzed me, desiring us to go to Keswick. After writing to Wm we walked as far as Mr Simpson's and ate black cherries. A Heavenly warm evening with scattered clouds upon the hills. There was a vernal greenness upon the grass from the rains of the morning and afternoon. Peas for dinner.

Monday 4th. Rain in the night. I tied up Scarlet beans, nailed the honeysuckles etc. etc. John was prepared to walk to Keswick all the morning. He seized a returned chaise and went after dinner. I pulled a large basket of peas and sent to Keswick by a returned chaise. A very cold evening. Assisted to spread out linen in the morning.

Tuesday 5th. Dried the linen in the morning, the air still cold. I pulled a bag full of peas for Mrs Simpson. Miss Simpson drank tea with me and supped on her return from Ambleside. A very fine evening. I sate on the wall making my shifts till I could see no longer. Walked half-way home with Miss Simpson.

Wednesday 6th August. A rainy morning. I ironed till dinner time—sewed till near dark—then pulled a basket of peas, and afterwards boiled and picked gooseberries. William came home from Keswick at 11 o'clock. A very fine night.

Thursday Morning 7th August. Packed up the mattrass, and sent to Keswick. Boiled gooseberries—N.B. 2 lbs of sugar in the first panfull, 3 quarts all good measure—3 lbs in the 2nd 4 quarts—$2\frac{1}{2}$ lbs in the 3rd. A very fine day. William composing in the wood in the morning. In the evening we walked to Mary Point. A very fine sunset.

Friday Morning [8th]. We intended going to Keswick, but were prevented by the excessive heat. Nailed up scarlet beans in the morning. Drank tea at Mr Simpson's, and walked over the mountains by Wattenlath.[1] Very fine gooseberries at Mr S.'s. A most enchanting walk. Wattenlath a heavenly scene. Reached Coleridge's at 11 o'clock.

Saturday Morning [9th]. I walked with Coleridge in the Windy Brow[2] woods.

[1] A small tarn lying in a cradle of the mountains between Thirlmere and Borrowdale.
[2] Windy Brow was a house belonging to William Calvert where W. W. and D. W. had stayed in 1794.

Sunday [10th]. Very hot. The C.s went to church. We sailed upon Derwent in the evening.

Monday afternoon [11th]. Walked with C. to Windy Brow.

Tuesday [12th]. Drank tea with the Cockins—Wm and I walked along the Cockermouth road. He was altering his poems.

Wednesday [13th]. Made the Windy Brow seat.[1]

Thursday Morning [14th]. Called at the Speddings.[2] In the Evening walked in the wood with W. Very very beautiful the moon.

Friday Morning [15th]. W. in the wood—I went with Hartley to see the Cockins and to buy Bacon. In the evening we walked to Water End—feasted on gooseberries at Silver Hill.[3]

Saturday Morning [16th]. Worked for Mrs C.—and walked with Coleridge intending to gather Raspberries—joined by Miss Spedding.

Sunday 16th August.[4] Came home. Dined in Bòrrowdale. A rainy morning but a fine evening—saw the Bristol prison [5] and Bassenthwaite at the same time—Wm read us the 7 Sisters[6] on a stone.

Monday [18th]. Putting linen by and mending. Walked with John to Mr Simpson's and met Wm in returning. A fine warm day.

Tuesday [19th]. Mr and Mrs Simpson dined with us—Miss S. and Brother drank tea in the orchard.

Wednesday [20th]. I worked in the morning. Cold in the evening and rainy. Did not walk.

Thursday [21st]. Read Wallenstein[7] and sent it off—worked

[1] W. W. had written a poem called 'Inscription for a Seat by the Pathway Side ascending to Windy Brow' in 1794, while staying at Windy Brow, and rewritten it (in blank verse) in 1797. In October 1800, probably as a result of the incident recorded by D. W., he sent the poem to the *Morning Post*, where it appeared on 21 October, with some alterations which are possibly in part the work of Coleridge. See *P.W.*, vol. 1, pp. 300–1 and 372.

[2] Of Mirehouse on Bassenthwaite, formerly of Armathwaite Hall. John Spedding had been at Hawkshead school during part of the time W. W. was there. His two sisters Margaret (later Mrs. Froude) and Maria (mentioned below, 16 August) and their mother had made D. W.'s acquaintance in 1794 when D. W. and W. W. were living at Windy Brow.

[3] On the west side of Derwent Water.   [4] Actually the 17th.

[5] Not identified. Probably their nickname for a rock or possibly a building.

[6] See *P.W.*, vol. II, p. 146.

[7] In Coleridge's translation.

in the morning—walked with John round the two lakes—gathered white foxglove seeds and found Wm in Bainriggs at our return.

Friday 21st.[1] Very cold. Baking in the morning, gathered pea seeds and took up—lighted a fire upstairs. Walked as far as Rydale with John intending to have gone on to Ambleside but we found the papers at Rydale—Wm walking in the wood all the time. John and he went out after our return—I mended stockings. Wind very high shaking the corn.

Saturday 22nd. A very fine morning. Wm was composing all the morning. I shelled peas, gathered beans, and worked in the garden till ½ past 12 then walked with William in the wood. The Gleams of sunshine and the stirring trees and gleaming boughs, chearful lake, most delightful. After dinner we walked to Ambleside—showery—went to see Mr Partridge's house. Came home by Clappersgate. We had intended going by Rydale woods, but it was cold—I was not well, and tired. Got tea immediately and had a fire. Did not reach home till 7 o'clock—mended stockings—and W. read Peter Bell. He read us the Poem of Joanna[2] beside the Rothay by the roadside.

Sunday 23rd. A fine cool pleasant breezy day—walked in the wood in the morning. Mr Twining called. John walked up to Mr Simpson's in the evening. I staid at home and wrote to Mrs Rawson[3] and my aunt Cookson—I was ill in the afternoon and lay down—got up restored by a sound sleep.

Monday 24th. A fine day—walked in the wood in the morning and to the firgrove—walked up to Mr Simpson's in the evening.

Tuesday 25th. We walked in the evening to Ambleside. Wm not quite well. I bought sacking for the mattrass. A very fine solemn evening. The wind blew very free from the island and at Rydale. We went on the other side of Rydale, and sate a long time looking at the mountains, which were all black at Grasmere and very bright in Rydale—Grasmere exceedingly dark and Rydale of a light yellow green.

Wednesday 27th. In the morning we walked. Mr Palmer passed

[1] For this and the following four days, D. W.'s dates are one day behind the actual dates.

[2] 'To Joanna', published in *Lyrical Ballads*, 1800, among the series *Poems on the Naming of Places*. Joanna was M. H.'s youngest sister, but in fact the poem does not concern her. See p. 177.

[3] The Wordsworths' cousin at Halifax, with whom D. W. had lived as a child.

us.[1] We walked along the shore of the lake in the Evening, and went over into Langdale and down to Loughrigg Tarn—a very fine evening calm and still.

Thursday 27 August.[2] Still very fine weather. I baked bread and cakes. In the Evening we walked round the Lake by Rydale. Mr Simpson came to fish.

Friday evening [29th]. We walked to Rydale to inquire for letters. We walked over the hill by the Firgrove. I sate upon a rock and observed a flight of swallows gathering together high above my head they flew towards Rydale. We walked through the wood over the stepping stones. The lake of Rydale very beautiful, partly still. John and I left Wm to compose an Inscription—that about the path.[3] We had a very fine walk by the gloomy lake. There was a curious yellow reflection in the water as of corn fields. There was no light in the clouds from which it appeared to come.

Saturday Morning 28th August. I was baking Bread, pies and dinner. It was very warm. Wm finished his Inscription of the Pathway, then walked in the wood and when John returned he sought him and they bathed together. I read a little of Boswell's Life of Johnson. I had a headache and went to lie down in the orchard. I was rouzed by a shout that Anthony Harrison[4] was come. We sate in the orchard till tea time, drank tea early and rowed down the lake which was stirred by Breezes. We looked at Rydale which was soft, chearful, and beautiful. We then went to peep into Langdale. The Pikes were very grand. We walked back to the view of Rydale, which was now a dark mirror. We rowed home over a lake still as glass and then went to George Mackareth's to hire a horse for John. A fine moonlight night. The beauty of the Moon was startling as it rose to us over Loughrigg Fell. We returned to supper at 10 o'clock. Thomas Ashburner brought us our 8th cart of coals since 17th May.

[1] This sentence has been omitted in previous editions.

[2] Her dates are again wrong until Monday 1st September. Thursday was the 28th, Saturday the 30th, Sunday the 31st August.

[3] Probably (as suggested by de Selincourt) the poem beginning 'When, to the attractions of the busy world' (see p. 180), though it is somewhat strange that D. W. describes it as an 'Inscription'. See under 1 September where she mentions a poem which she calls 'The Firgrove', probably the same.

[4] A Penrith friend. He published in 1806 *Poetical Recreations* in 2 vols.

Sunday 29th. Anthony Harrison and John left us at ½ past seven—a very fine morning. A great deal of corn is cut in the vale, and the whole prospect though not tinged with a general autumnal yellow, yet softened down into a mellowness of colouring which seems to impart softness to the forms of hills and mountains. At 11 o'clock Coleridge came when I was walking in the still clear moonshine in the garden. He came over Helvellyn. Wm was gone to bed and John also, worn out with his ride round Coniston. We sate and chatted till ½-past three, W. in his dressing gown. Coleridge read us a part of Christabel. Talked much about the mountains, etc. etc. Mrs Thrale's [? matter]—Losh's[1] opinion of Southey—the first of poets.

Monday Morning 1st September. We walked in the wood by the Lake. W. read Joanna and the Firgrove[2] to Coleridge. They bathed. The morning was delightful with somewhat of an autumnal freshness. After dinner Coleridge discovered a rock-seat in the orchard. Cleared away the brambles. Coleridge obliged to go to bed after tea. John and I followed Wm up the hill and then returned to go to Mr Simpson's. We borrowed some bottles for bottling rum. The evening somewhat frosty and grey but very pleasant. I broiled Coleridge a mutton chop which he ate in bed. Wm was gone to bed. I chatted with John and Coleridge till near 12.

Tuesday 2nd. In the morning they all went to Stickel Tarn.[3] A very fine, warm sunny beautiful morning. I baked a pie etc. for dinner—little Sally[4] was with me. The fair-day. Miss Simpson and Mr came down to tea—we walked to the fair. There seem'd very few people and very few stalls yet I believe there were many cakes and much beer sold. My Brothers came home to dinner at 6 o'clock. We drank Tea immediately after by

---

[1] James Losh (1763–1833) of Woodside, near Carlisle, an early friend of W.; a Unitarian and advanced radical, he had often lent W. books and papers in the Racedown and Alfoxden days.

[2] 'The Firgrove' is almost certainly an early and unfinished draft of 'When, to the attractions of the busy world'. The grove, then a thick fir wood, is on the left of the road from How Top, going towards Ambleside, opposite the Wishing Gate. Afterwards they referred to it as 'John's grove', after their brother John, whose favourite haunt it was.

[3] The tarn under the great precipice Pavey Ark on the way up the Langdale Pikes.

[4] Sally Ashburner, one of the daughters of the Wordsworths' neighbour, Thomas Ashburner, whose second wife, Peggy, is often mentioned in the journal.

candlelight. It was a lovely moonlight night. We talked much about a house on Helvellyn. The moonlight shone only upon the village it did not eclipse the village lights and the sound of dancing and merriment came along the still air. I walked with Coleridge and Wm up the Lane and by the Church, and then lingered with Coleridge in the garden. John and Wm were both gone to bed, and all the lights out.

Wednesday 3rd September. Coleridge Wm and John went from home to go upon Helvellyn with Mr Simpson. They set out after breakfast. I accompanied them up near the Blacksmith's. A fine coolish morning. I ironed till ½ past three—now very hot. I then went to a funeral at John Dawson's.[1] About 10 men and 4 women. Bread cheese and ale. They talked sensibly and chearfully about common things. The dead person 56 years of age buried by the parish. The coffin was neatly lettered and painted black and covered with a decent cloth. They set the corpse down at the door and while we stood within the threshold the men with their hats off sang with decent and solemn countenances a verse of a funeral psalm. The corpse was then borne down the hill and they sang till they had got past the Town-end. I was affected to tears while we stood in the house, the coffin lying before me. There were no near kindred, no children. When we got out of the dark house the sun was shining and the prospect looked so divinely beautiful as I never saw it. It seemed more sacred than I had ever seen it, and yet more allied to human life. The green fields, neighbours of the churchyard, were as green as possible and with the brightness of the sunshine looked quite gay. I thought she was going to a quiet spot and I could not help weeping very much. When we came to the bridge they began to sing again and stopped during 4 lines before they entered the churchyard. The priest[2] met us—he did not look as a man ought to do on such an occasion—I had seen him half-drunk the day before in a pot-house. Before we came with the corpse one of the company observed he wondered what sort of cue 'our Parson would be in.' N.B. it was the day after the Fair. I had

[1] John Dawson lived at How Top, between Dove Cottage and White Moss Common, near the Firgrove (see 9 September). For the funeral cf. *The Excursion*, II. 370–402 and 546–66.
[2] Edward Rowlandson, curate for the absentee rector, John Craik. See *P.W.*, vol. IV, p. 434, for Wordsworth's own description of him.

not finished ironing till 7 o'clock. The wind was now high
I did not walk—writing my journal now at 8 o'clock. Wm
John came home at 10 o'clock.

Thursday 4th September. A fine warm day. I was busy all the
morning making a mattrass. Mr Simpson called in the afternoon. Wm walked in the wood in the morning, and in the
evening as we set forward to walk a letter from Mrs Clarkson.[1]
We walked into the black quarter. The patches of corn very
interesting.

Friday Morning [*5th*]. Finished the mattrass, ironed the white
bed in the afternoon. When I was putting it up Mr and Mrs
Losh[2] arrived while Wm and John were walking.

Saturday Morning 6th September. Breakfasted with the Loshes
—very warm—returned through Rydale woods. The Clarksons
dined. After tea we walked round Rydale—a little rain.

Sunday Morning 7th. Rainy. Walked before dinner over the
stepping stones to Langdale and home on the other side of the
lake. I lay down after dinner. Wm poorly. Walked into the
Black quarter.

Monday Morning 8th September. Very rainy. The Clarksons
left us after dinner—still rainy. We walked towards Rydale,
and then to Mr Olliff's gate. A fine evening.

Tuesday Morning 9th. Mr Marshall[3] came—he dined with us.
My Brothers walked with him round the lakes after dinner—
windy—we went to the island. W. and I after to tea. John and I
went to the B. quarter, before supper went to seek a horse at
Dawson's—fir grove. After supper, talked of Wm's Poems.

Wednesday Sept. 10th. After Breakfast Mr Marshall, Wm
and John went on horseback to Keswick—I wrote to Mrs
Marshall[4]—a fine autumn day. I had a fire. Paid Mr Bousfield
8–2–11. After tea walked with French Beans to Mr Simpson's—
went up to the Forest side above a deserted house, sat till

[1] Catherine Clarkson (1772–1856), wife of Thomas Clarkson who devoted his
life to the abolition of the slave trade. They lived at Eusemere at the foot of Ullswater. Mrs. Clarkson became D. W.'s most intimate friend and correspondent.

[2] Mrs. James Losh was Cecilia Baldwin of Aldingham, near Ulverston, whose
brother John Baldwin had been a Cambridge friend of W.'s.

[3] John Marshall of Leeds, who had married Jane Pollard, D. W.'s early friend
at Halifax.

[4] For this letter see *E.T.*, p. 293. According to the letter, the walk round the
lakes on Tuesday took place before dinner, not after, and Mr. Marshall accompanied John and D. W. to 'the Black quarter'.

on. Mr and Miss S. came down with me and

. All the morning mending white gown—
—Molly washing. Drank tea at Mr Simpson's.
at home at my return—he was unable to go on with
Marshall and parted from him in Borrowdale. Made tea
after my return.

Friday 12th Sept. I worked in the morning cut my thumb.
Walked in the Fir-grove before dinner—after dinner sate
under the trees in the orchard. A rainy morning but very fine
afternoon. Miss Simpson called for my packing needle. The
Fern of the mountains now spreads yellow veins among the
trees. The coppice wood turns brown. William observed some
affecting little things in Borrowdale. A decayed house with
this inscription [*blank space in MS*.] in the church-yard, the tall
silent rocks seen thro' the broken windows. A kind of rough
column put upon the gavel end of a house with a ball stone
smooth from the river placed upon it for ornament. Near it
one stone like it upon an old mansion carefully hewn.

Saturday Morning 13th September. William writing his preface[1] did not walk. Jones[2] and Mr Palmer came to tea. We
walked with them to Borricks—a lovely evening but the air
frosty—worked when I returned home. Wm walked out. John
came home from Mr Marshall. Sent back word to Mrs Clarkson.

Sunday Morning 14th. Made bread. A sore thumb from a cut.
A lovely day—read Boswell in the house in the morning and
after dinner under the bright yellow leaves of the orchard. The
pear trees a bright yellow, the apple trees green still. A sweet
lovely afternoon.

Here I have long neglected my Journal. John came home in
the evening after Jones left us. Jones returned again on the
Friday, the 19th September. Jones stayed with us till Friday,
26th September. Coleridge came on Tuesday 23rd and went
home with Jones. Charles Lloyd called on Tuesday 23rd, and

[1] The Preface to the second edition of *Lyrical Ballads*, 1800.
[2] Revd. Robert Jones, W.'s college friend, who accompanied him on his con-
tinental tour in 1790.

on Sunday 27th we drank tea and supped with him, and on that day heard of the Abergavenny's[1] arrival. While Jones was with us we had much rainy weather. On Sunday the 21st Tom Myers[2] and Father called, and on the 28th Mr and Miss Smith.[3]

On Monday 29th John left us. Wm and I parted with him in sight of Ulswater.[4] It was a fine day, showery but with sunshine and fine clouds. Poor fellow, my heart was right sad—I could not help thinking we should see him again because he was only going to Penrith.

On Tuesday 30th September Charles Lloyd dined with us. We walked homewards with him after dinner. It rained very hard. Rydale was extremely wild and we had a fine walk. We sate quietly and comfortably by the fire. I wrote—the last sheet of notes and preface.[5] Went to bed at 12 o'clock.

Wednesday 1st October. A fine morning—a showery night. The lake still in the morning—in the forenoon flashing light from the beams of the sun, as it was ruffled by the wind. We corrected the last sheet.

Thursday 2nd October. A very rainy morning. We walked after dinner to observe the torrents. I followed Wm to Rydale, he afterwards went to Butterlip How. I came home to receive the Lloyds. They walked with us to see Churnmilk force[6] and the Black quarter. The black quarter looked marshy, and the general prospect was cold, but the Force was very grand. The Lychens are now coming out afresh, I carried home a collection in the afternoon. We had a pleasant conversation about the manners of the rich—avarice, inordinate desires, and the effeminacy unnaturalness and the unworthy objects of education. After the Lloyds were gone we walked—a showery evening. The moonlight lay upon the hills like snow.

Friday 3rd October. Very rainy all the morning. Little Sally learning to mark. Wm walked to Ambleside after dinner. I went with him part of the way—he talked much about the

---

[1] The ship of which J. W. had just been made captain.

[2] W.'s cousin; his father, the Revd. Thomas Myers (1735–1826), had married W.'s aunt, Anne W.

[3] Probably the Smiths of Coniston. Elizabeth Smith (1776–1806) was a gifted self-taught linguist, translating from German and even Hebrew. She was a friend of Thomas Wilkinson of Yanwath (see p. 76).

[4] i.e. at Grisedale Tarn. See *P.W.*, vol. IV, p. 263.

[5] i.e. of the Notes and Preface to the second edition of *Lyrical Ballads*.

[6] Now known as Sour Milk Ghyll.

object of his Essay for the 2nd volume of LB. I returned expecting the Simpsons—they did not come. I should have met Wm but my teeth ached and it was showery and late—he returned after 10. Amos Cottle's[1] death in the Morning Post. Wrote to S. Lowthian.[2]

N.B. When Wm and I returned from accompanying Jones we met an old man almost double,[3] he had on a coat thrown over his shoulders above his waistcoat and coat. Under this he carried a bundle and had an apron on and a night cap. His face was interesting. He had dark eyes and a long nose. John who afterwards met him at Wythburn took him for a Jew. He was of Scotch parents but had been born in the army. He had had a wife 'and a good woman and it pleased God to bless us with ten children'. All these were dead but one of whom he had not heard for many years, a sailor. His trade was to gather leeches, but now leeches are scarce and he had not strength for it. He lived by begging and was making his way to Carlisle where he should buy a few godly books to sell. He said leeches were very scarce partly owing to this dry season, but many years they have been scarce—he supposed it owing to their being much sought after, that they did not breed fast, and were of slow growth. Leeches were formerly 2/6 [per] 100; they are now 30/. He had been hurt in driving a cart, his leg broke his body driven over his skull fractured. He felt no pain till he recovered from his first insensibility. It was then late in the evening, when the light was just going away.

Saturday October 4th [1800]. A very rainy, or rather showery and gusty morning for often the sun shines. Thomas Ashburner could not go to Keswick. Read a part of Lamb's play.[4] The language is often very beautiful, but too imitative in particular phrases, words etc. The characters except Margaret's unintelligible, and except Margaret's do not shew themselves in action. Coleridge came in while we were at dinner very wet. —We talked till 12 o'clock. He had sate up all the night before

[1] Brother of Joseph Cottle.
[2] Sally Lowthian, one of the household staff of John Wordsworth of Cockermouth, father of W. W. and D. W.
[3] The following description of the old leech-gatherer was partly used, eighteen months later, in 'Resolution and Independence', called 'The Leech-Gatherer' before its publication in 1807. See p. 183.
[4] *Pride's Cure*, a title afterwards changed to *John Woodvill*.

writing Essays for the newspaper.—His youngest child had been very ill in convulsion fits. Exceedingly delighted with the 2nd part of Christabel.

Sunday Morning 5th October. Coleridge read a 2nd time Christabel—we had increasing pleasure. A delicious morning. Wm and I were employed all the morning in writing an addition to the preface. Wm went to bed very ill after working after dinner. Coleridge and I walked to Ambleside after dark with the letter. Returned to tea at 9 o'clock. Wm still in bed and very ill. Silver How in both lakes.[1]

Monday [6th]. A rainy day. Coleridge intending to go but did not get off. We walked after dinner to Rydale. After tea read The Pedlar.[2] Determined not to print Christabel with the LB.

Tuesday [7th]. Coleridge went off at 11 o'clock.—I went as far as Mr Simpson's returned with Mary.[3] She drank tea here. I was very ill in the evening at the Simpsons—went to bed —supped there. Returned with Miss S. and Mrs J.[4]—heavy showers. Found Wm at home. I was still weak and unwell— went to bed immediately.

Wednesday [8th]. A threatening bad morning—We dried the Linen frequent threatening of showers. Received a 5£ note from Montagu. Wm walked to Rydale. I copied a part of The Beggar in the morning—I was not quite well in the evening therefore I did not walk—Wm walked. A very mild moonlight night. Glowworms everywhere.

Thursday [9th]. I was ironing all the day till tea-time. Very rainy. Wm and I walked in the evening—intending to go to Lloyd's but it came on so very rainy that we were obliged to shelter at Fleming's. A grand Ball at Rydale. After sitting some time we went homewards and were again caught by a shower and sheltered under the sycamores at the boat house—a very cold snowlike rain. A man called in a soldier's dress—he was

---

[1] i.e. the reflection.

[2] Begun at Alfoxden in the early spring of 1798, and revised and altered in the early spring of 1802. With *The Ruined Cottage* it ultimately became partly incorporated in *The Excursion*; but some of it also in the second and third books of *The Prelude*.

[3] Probably a daughter of Mrs. Jameson. See note 4 and entry for 12 October.

[4] Miss Simpson and Mrs. Jameson. See under 10 October. Mrs. Jameson was probably another daughter of the Simpsons of Broadrain. See under 23 July.

thirty years old, of Cockermouth, had lost a leg and thigh in battle was going to his home. He could earn more money in travelling with his ass than at home.

Friday 10th October. In the morning when I arose the mists were hanging over the opposite hills and the tops of the highest hills were covered with snow. There was a most lovely combination at the head of the vale—of the yellow autumnal hills wrapped in sunshine, and overhung with partial mists, the green and yellow trees and the distant snow-topped mountains. It was a most heavenly morning. The Cockermouth traveller came with thread hardware mustard, etc. She is very healthy; has travelled over the mountains these thirty years. She does not mind the storms if she can keep her goods dry. Her husband will not travel with an ass, because it is the tramper's badge—she would have one to relieve her from the weary load. She was going to Ulverston and was to return to Ambleside Fair. After I had finished baking I went out with Wm Mrs Jameson and Miss Simpson towards Rydale—the fern among the Rocks exquisitely beautiful. We turned home and walked to Mr Gell's. After dinner Wm went to bed—I read Southey's letter. Miss Simpson and Mrs Jameson came to tea. After tea we went to Lloyd's—a fine Evening as we went but rained in returning—we were wet—found them not at home. I wrote to Mrs Clarkson—sent off The Beggar etc. by Thomas Ashburner who went to fetch our 9th cart of coals. William sat up after me writing Point Rash judgment.[1]

Saturday 11th. A fine October morning. Sat in the house working all the morning. Wm composing—Sally Ashburner learning to mark. After Dinner we walked up Greenhead Gill in search of a sheepfold.[2] We went by Mr Ollif's and through his woods. It was a delightful day and the views looked excessively chearful and beautiful chiefly that from Mr Oliff's field where our house is to be built. The colours of the mountains soft and rich, with orange fern—the Cattle pasturing upon the hill-tops Kites sailing in the sky above our heads— Sheep bleating and in lines and chains and patterns scattered

[1] i.e. *Poems on the Naming of Places*, IV. See p. 187. It was published in the second volume of *Lyrical Ballads*.

[2] The long blank-verse poem 'Michael' is called throughout D. W.'s journal entries, 'The Sheepfold', and probably the words 'Wm composing' refer to a first draft or sketch of the poem.

over the mountains. They come down and feed on the little green islands in the beds of the torrents and so may be swept away. The Sheepfold is falling away it is built nearly in the form of a heart unequally divided. Look down the brook and see the drops rise upwards and sparkle in the air, at the little falls the higher sparkles the tallest. We walked along the turf of the mountain till we came to a Cattle track—made by the cattle which come upon the hills. We drank tea at Mr Simpson's returned at about nine—a fine mild night.

Sunday 12th October. Beautiful day. Sate in the house writing in the morning while Wm went into the Wood to compose. Wrote to John in the morning—copied poems for the LB,[1] in the evening wrote to Mrs Rawson. Mary Jameson[2] and Sally Ashburner dined. We pulled apples after dinner, a large basket full. We walked before tea by Bainriggs to observe the many coloured foliage the oaks dark green with yellow leaves, the birches generally still green, some near the water yellowish. The Sycamore crimson and crimson-tufted, the mountain ash a deep orange, the common ash Lemon colour but many ashes still fresh in their summer green. Those that were discoloured chiefly near the water. William composing in the Evening. Went to bed at 12 o'clock.

Monday October 13th. A grey day. Mists on the hills. We did not walk in the morning. I copied poems on the naming of places at night. A fair at Ambleside. Walked in the black quarter.

Tuesday 14th. Wm lay down after dinner—I read Southey's Spain.[3] The wind rose very high at Evening. Wm walked out just at bedtime—I went to bed early. We walked before dinner to Rydale.

Wednesday [15th]. A very fine clear morning. After Wm had composed a little, I persuaded him to go into the orchard. We walked backwards and forwards. The prospect most divinely beautiful from the seat—all colours, all melting into each other. I went in to put bread in the oven and we both walked within view of Rydale. Wm again composed at the sheep-fold[4] after

[1] i.e. for the second volume of *Lyrical Ballads*, published the following January.
[2] See under 7 October.
[3] *Letters written during a Short Residence in Spain and Portugal*, published by Cottle, 1797.
[4] i.e. 'Michael'. See n. 2, p. 44.

dinner. I walked with him to Wytheburn, and he went on to Keswick. I drank tea and supped at Mr Simpson's—a very cold frosty air, and a spangled sky in returning. Mr and Miss S. came with me. Wytheburn looked very wintry but yet there was a foxglove blossoming by the road-side.

Thursday 16th October. A very fine morning—starched and hung out linen a very fine day. John Fisher, T. A., S. A. and Molly working in the garden. Wrote to Miss Nicholson.[1] I walked as far as Rydale between 3 and 4—Ironed till six—got tea and wrote to Mr Griffith.[2] A letter from Mr Clarkson.

Friday 17th. A very fine grey morning. The swan hunt. Sally working in the garden. I walked round the lake between ¼ past 12 and ½ past one. Wrote to M. H. After dinner I walked to Lloyd's—carried my letters to Miss N. and M. H. The Lloyds not in—I waited for them. Charles not well. Letters from M. H., Biggs[3] and John. In my walk in the morning, I observed Benson's Honeysuckles in flower, and great beauty. It was a very fine mild evening. Ll.'s servants came with me to Parke's.[4] I found Wm at home where he had been almost ever since my departure. Coleridge had done nothing for the L. B. Working hard for Stuart.[5] Glowworms in abundance.

Saturday [18th]. A very fine October morning. William worked all the morning at the Sheep-fold but in vain. He lay down in the afternoon till 7 o'clock but could not sleep—I slept. My head better—he unable to work. We did not walk all day.

Sunday Morning [19th]. We rose late and walked directly after breakfast. The tops of G[ras]mere mountains cut off. Rydale was very very beautiful the surface of the water quite still like a dim mirror. The colours of the large island exquisitely beautiful and the trees still fresh and green were magnified by the mists. The prospects on the west side of the Lake were very beautiful. We sate at the two points looking up to Park's. The lowing of the Cattle was echoed by a hollow voice in Knab

---

[1] Probably Caroline, eldest daughter of Samuel Nicholson of Cateaton Street, London, and also of Halifax. See *E.Y. passim.*

[2] A cousin of D. W.'s mother, living in America.

[3] Joseph Cottle's partner in the Bristol publishing business.

[4] Nab Cottage, on Rydal Lake, the house where, later, Hartley Coleridge lodged.

[5] Daniel Stuart (1766–1846), editor of the *Morning Post* and later of the *Courier.*

Scar. We went upon Loughrigg Fell—and were disappointed with G[ras]mere, it did not look near so beautiful as Rydale. We returned home over the stepping-stones. Wm got to work. We are not to dine till 4 o'clock.—Dined at ½ past 5—Mr Simpson dined and drank tea with us. We went to bed immediately after he left us.

Monday 20th. William worked in the morning at the sheepfold. After dinner we walked to Rydale crossed the stepping stones and while we were walking under the tall oak trees the Lloyds called out to us. They went with us on the western side of Rydale. The lights were very grand upon the woody Rydale Hills. Those behind dark and topp'd with clouds. The two lakes were divinely beautiful. Grasmere excessively solemn and the whole lake was calm and dappled with soft grey ripples. The Lloyds stayed with us till 8 o'clock. We then walked to the top of the hill at Rydale. Very mild and warm. About 6 glowworms shining faintly. We went up as far as the grove. When we came home the fire was out. We ate our supper in the dark and went to bed immediately. William was disturbed in the night by the rain coming into his room, for it was a very rainy night. The Ash leaves lay across the Road.

Tuesday 21st. We walked in the morning past Mr Gell's—a very fine clear sharp sunny morning. We drank tea at the Lloyds. It was very cold in the evening, quite frosty, and starlight. Wm had been unsuccessful in the morning at the sheepfold. The reflection of the ash scattered, and the tree stripped.

Wednesday Morning [22nd]. We walked to Mr Gell's a very fine morning. Wm composed without much success at the Sheepfold. Coleridge came in to dinner. He had done nothing.[1] We were very merry. C. and I went to look at the prospect from his seat. In the evening Stoddart[2] came in when we were at tea, and after tea Mr and Miss Simpson with large potatoes and plumbs. Wm read after supper, Ruth etc.—Coleridge Christabel.

Thursday 23rd. Coleridge and Stoddart went to Keswick. We accompanied them to Wytheburn. A wintry grey morning— from the top of the Rays Grasmere looked like winter and

---

[1] i.e. for the *Lyrical Ballads*.

[2] Sir John Stoddart (1773–1856), a prominent journalist, and from 1803 to 1807 King's Advocate at Malta. In 1808 Hazlitt married Stoddart's sister.

Wytheburn still more so. We called upon Mrs Simpson and sate 10 minutes in returning. Wm was not successful in composition in the Evening.

Friday 24th. A very fine morning. We walked before Wm began to work to the top of the Rydale Hill. He was afterwards only partly successful in composition. After dinner we walked round Rydale Lake, rich, calm, streaked, very beautiful. We went to the top of Loughrigg. Grasmere sadly inferior. We were much tired Wm went to bed till ½ past seven. The ash in our garden green, one close to it bare, the next nearly so.

Saturday [25th]. A very rainy day. Wm again unsuccessful. We could not walk it was so very rainy. We read Rogers, Miss Seward,[1] Cowper etc.

Sunday [26th]. Heavy rain all night. A fine morning after 10 o'clock. Wm composed a good deal—in the morning. The Lloyds came to dinner and were caught in a shower. Wm read some of his poems after dinner. A terrible night. I went with Mrs Lloyd to Newton's to see for Lodgings. Mr Simpson in coming from Ambleside called in for a glass of rum, just before we went to bed.

28th October, Monday.[2] Not fine[3] a rainy morning. The Hill tops covered with snow. Charles Lloyd came for his wife's glass. I walked home with him past Rydale. When he came I met him as I was carrying some cold meat to Wm in the Fir-grove. I had before walked with him there for some time. It was a fine shelter from the wind. The Coppices now nearly of one brown. An oak tree in a sheltered place near John Fisher's—not having lost any of its leaves was quite brown and dry. We did not walk after dinner. It was a fine wild moonlight night. Wm could not compose much fatigued himself with altering.

Tuesday 29th. A very rainy night. I was baking bread in the morning and made a giblet pie. We walked out before dinner to our favourite field. The mists sailed along the mountains and rested upon them enclosing the whole vale.[4] In the evening the Lloyds came. We drank tea with them at Borrick's and played

---

[1] Anna Seward, of Lichfield (1747–1809), a friend of Walter Scott and Erasmus Darwin. She had published since about 1782 several volumes of poems.

[2] Here D. W.'s dates are one day ahead of the actual ones until the following Wednesday, when she ceases for some time to put dates.

[3] The word 'fine' is erased.

[4] Here D. W. writes 'Wednesday 30th A cold and rainy'—but crosses it out and continues 'In the evening', etc.

a rubber at whist—stayed supper. Wm looked very well. A
fine moonlight night when we came home.

Wednesday [29th]. William working at his poem all the morning. After dinner Mr Clarkson called. We went down to Borrick's and he and the Lloyds and Priscilla[1] came back to drink
tea with us. We met Stoddart upon the Bridge..Played at cards.
The Lloyds etc. went home to supper—Mr Clarkson slept here.

Thursday [30th]. A rainy morning. Mr C. went over Kirk-
stone. Wm talked all day and almost all night with Stoddart.
Mrs and Miss Ll. called in the morning. I walked with them to
Tail End.[2] A fine pleasant morning but a very rainy afternoon.
W. and S. in the house all day.

Friday [31st]. W. and S. did not rise till 1 o'clock. W. very
sick and very ill. S. and I drank tea at Lloyds and came home
immediately after. [A very fine moonlight night—The moon
shone like herrings in the water.]

Saturday [1st]. William better. We met as we walked to
Rydale a Boy from Lloyds, coming for Don Quixote. Talk in
the evening. Tom Ashburner brought our 10th cart of coals.

Sunday Morning [2nd]. We (walked) into the Black Quarter.
A very fine morning. [A succession of beautiful views mists etc.   *etc.*
etc.] Much rain in the night. In the Evening drank tea at Lloyds
—found them all ill in colds. Came home to supper.

Monday Morning [3rd]. Walked to Rydale. A cold day. Wm
and Stoddart still talking, frequent showers in our walk. In the
evening we talked merrily over the fire. The Speddings[3]
stopped at the door.

Tuesday [4th]. Stoddart left us—I walked a little way with
W. and him, W. went to the Tarn[4] afterwards to the top of
Seat Sandal. He was obliged to lie down in the tremendous
wind. The snow blew from Helvellyn horizontally like smoke—
the Spray of the unseen Waterfall like smoke.—Miss Lloyd
called upon me—I walked with her past Rydale. Wm sadly
tired, threatenings of the piles.

Wednesday [5th]. Wm not well. A very fine beautiful clear
winter's day. I walked after dinner to Lloyds—drank tea and

[1] Priscilla, sister of Charles Lloyd. In 1804 she married W. W.'s youngest
brother, Christopher.
[2] See above, p. 19.
[3] See above, p. 34.
[4] Grisedale Tarn.

Mrs and Miss Lloyd came to Rydale with me. The moon was rising but the sky all over cloud. I made tea for William. Piles.

Thursday 6th November. A very rainy morning and night. I was baking bread dinner and parkins. Charles and P. Lloyd called. Wm somewhat better read Point Rash Judgment. The lake calm and very beautiful. A very rainy afternoon and night.

Friday 7th November. A cold rainy morning. Wm still unwell. I working and reading Amelia. The Michaelmas daisy droops, the pansies are full of flowers. The Ashes opposite are green all but one but they have lost many of their leaves. The copses are quite brown. The poor woman and child from White-haven drank tea—nothing warm that day. Friday 7th.[1] A very rainy morning. It cleared up in the afternoon. We expected the Lloyds but they did not come. Wm still unwell.[2] A rainy night.

Saturday 8th November. A rainy morning. A whirlwind came that tossed about the leaves and tore off the still green leaves of the Ashes. A fine afternoon. Wm and I walked out at 4 o'clock. Went as far as Rothay Bridge. Met the Butcher's man with a l[ette]r from Monk Lewis.[3] The country very wintry—some oaks quite bare—others more sheltered with a few green leaves others with brown leaves, but the whole face of the country in a winter covering. We went early to bed.

Sunday [9th] Wm slept tolerably—better this morning. It was a frosty night. We walked to Rydale after dinner, partly expecting to meet the Lloyds. Mr Simpson brought newspapers but met Molly with them. W. [?] burnt[4] the sheep fold. A rainy night.

Monday [10th]. I baked bread. A fine clear frosty morning. We walked after dinner—to Rydale village. Jupiter over the Hill-tops, the only star like a sun flashed out at intervals from behind a black cloud.

Tuesday Morning [11th]. Walked to Rydale before dinner for letters. William had been working at the sheep-fold. They were salving sheep. A rainy morning. The Lloyds drank tea with us.

---

[1] D. W. forgetfully re-begins her entry for the day.

[2] Two words are here erased. They seem to be 'and melancholy'.

[3] Matthew Gregory Lewis (1775–1818), author of the sensational novel, *The Monk*, from which he took this nickname, and of various dramas.

[4] This word is not erased but difficult to read.

Played at cards—Priscilla not well. We walked after they left us to the top of the Rydale Hill then towards Mr Ollif's and towards the village. A mild night partly cloudy partly starlight. The cottage lights, the mountains not very distinct.

Wednesday [12th]. We sate in the house all the day. Mr Simpson called and found us at dinner—a rainy evening—he staid the evening and supper. I lay down after dinner with a headach.

Thursday [13th]. A stormy night. We sate in the house all the morning. Rainy weather. Old Mr Simpson, Mrs J. and Miss S. drank tea and supped, played at cards, found us at dinner. A poor woman from Hawkshead begged, a widow of Grasmere, a merry African from Longtown.

Friday [14th]. I had a bad head-ach. Much wind but a sweet mild morning. I nailed up trees. Sent Molly Ashburner to excuse us to Lloyds. 2 letters from Coleridge—very ill. One from Sara H., one from S. Lothian—I wrote to S. Hutchinson[1] and received 3£ from her.

Saturday Morning [15th]. A terrible rain so Wm prevented from going to Coleridge's. The afternoon fine and mild I walked to the top of the hill for a head-ach. We both set forward at 5 o'clock after tea. A fine wild but not cold night. I walked with him over the Rays—it was starlight. I parted with him very sad unwilling not to go on. The hills and the stars and the white waters with their ever varying yet ceaseless sound were very impressive. I supped at the Simpsons. Mr P. walked home with me.

Sunday 16th November. A very fine warm sunny morning. A Letter from Coleridge and one from Stoddart. Coleridge better — —My head aching very much I sent to excuse myself to Lloyds—then walked to the Cottage beyond Mr Gell's. One beautiful ash tree sheltered with yellow leaves—one low one quite green. Some low ashes green—A noise of boys in the rocks hunting some animal. Walked a little in the garden when I came home, very pleasant. Now rain came on. Mr Jackson called in the evening when I was at tea brought me a letter from C. and W. C. better.

Monday Morning [17th]. A fine clear frosty morning with a sharp wind. I walked to Keswick. Set off at 5 minutes past 10, and arrived at ½ past 2. I found them all well.

[1] M. H.'s favourite sister.

On Tuesday morning W. and C. set off towards Penrith. Wm met Sara Hutchinson at Threlkeld. They arrived at Keswick at tea-time.

Wednesday [*19th*]. We walked by the lake side and they went to Mr Denton's. I called upon the Miss Cockyns.

Thursday [*20th*]. We spent the morning in the Town. Mr Jackson and Mr Peach[1] dined with us.

Friday [*21st*]. A very fine day. Went to Mrs Greaves. Mrs C. and I called upon the Speddings. A beautiful Crescent moon.

Saturday Morning [*22nd*]. After visiting Mr Peach's Chinese pictures we set off to Grasmere. A threatening and rather rainy morning. Arrived at G. very dirty and a little wet at the closing in of Evening. Wm not quite well.

Sunday [*23rd*]. Wm not well. I baked bread and pie for dinner. Sarah and I walked after dinner and met Mr Gawthorpe, paid his bill and he drank tea with us paid 5£ for Mr Bousfield.

Monday [*24th*]. A fine morning. Sara and I walked to Rydale. After dinner we went to Lloyds and drank tea, and supped. A sharp cold night with sleet and snow. I had the tooth-ach in the night. Took Laudanum.

Tuesday [*25th*]. Very ill—in bed all day—better in the Evening. Read Tom Jones—very sleepy slept all night.

Wednesday [*26th*]. Well in the morning. Wm very well. We had a delightful walk up into Eastdale. The tops of the Mountains covered with snow—frosty and sunny—the roads slippery. A letter from Mary. The Lloyds drank tea. We walked with them near to Ambleside. A beautiful moonlight night. Sara and I walked before dinner. William very well and highly poetical.

Thursday 27th November. Wrote to Tom Hutchinson[2] to desire him to bring Mary with him from Stockton. A thaw and the ground covered with snow. Sara and I walked before dinner.

Friday [*28th*]. Coleridge walked over. Miss Simpson drank tea with us. William walked home with her. Coleridge was very unwell. He went to bed before Wm's return. Great Boils upon his neck.

---

[1] Apparently a friend of Coleridge's landlord Mr. Jackson. He lived in a part of Greta Hall.

[2] M. H.'s second and favourite brother with whom she was living at Gallow Hill.

Saturday [29th]. A fine day.

Sunday 29th November.[1] A very fine clear morning. Snow upon the ground everywhere. Sara and I walked towards Rydale by the upper road and were obliged to return because of the snow:[2] walked by moonlight.

Monday [1st]. A thaw in the night and the snow was entirely gone. Sara and I had a delightful walk by the upper Rydale Road and Mr King's. Coleridge unable to go home for his health. We walked by moonlight. Baking day little loaves.[3]

Tuesday December 2nd.—A rainy morning. Coleridge was obliged to set off. Sara and I met C. Lloyd and P.[4]—turned back with them. I walked round the 2 lakes with Charles very pleasant—passing lights—I was sadly wet when we came home and very cold. Priscilla drank tea with us. We all walked to Ambleside. A pleasant moonlight evening but not clear. Supped upon a hare. It came on a terrible evening hail and wind and cold and rain.

Wednesday December 3rd. We lay in bed till 11 o'clock. Wrote to John, and M. H. William and Sara and I walked to Rydale after tea—a very fine frosty night. Sara and W. walked round the other side. I was tired and returned home. We went to bed early.

Thursday [4th]. Coleridge came in just as we finished dinner— Pork from the Simpsons. Sara and I walked round the 2 lakes— a very fine morning. C. ate nothing to cure his boils. We walked after tea by moonlight to look at Langdale covered with snow—the pikes not grand, but the old man very impressive. Cold and slippery but exceedingly pleasant. Sat up till ½ past one.

Friday Morning [5th]. Terribly cold and rainy. Coleridge and Wm set forward towards Keswick but the wind in Coleridge's eyes made him turn back. Sara and I had a grand bread and cake baking. We were very merry in the evening but grew sleepy soon though we did not go to bed till 12 o'clock.

Saturday [6th]. Wm accompanied Coleridge to the foot of the Rays. A very pleasant morning. Sara and I accompanied him

---

[1] D. W. dates wrongly here; Sunday was the 30th.

[2] MS. has colon after 'return'; clearly a slip.

[3] This sentence, though not erased, has not been previously printed.

[4] Priscilla, sister of Charles Lloyd. See above, p. 49.

half way to Keswick. Thirlemere was very beautiful—even more so than in summer. William was not well had laboured unsuccessfully. Charles Lloyd had called. Sara and I drank tea with Mrs Simpson. A sharp shower met us—it rained a little when we came home. Mr B. S. accompanied us. Miss S. at Ambleside. William tired and not well. A letter from M. H.

Sunday [*7th*]. A fine morning. I read. Sara wrote to Hartley, Wm to Mary, I to Mrs C. We walked just before dinner to the Lake-side and found out a seat in a tree windy but pleasant. Sara and Wm walked to the waterfalls at Rydale. I was unwell and went to bed till 8 o'clock—a pleasant mild evening. Went to bed at 12. Miss Simpson called.

Monday 8th December. A sweet mild morning.—I wrote to Mrs Cookson[1] and Miss Griffith.[2]

Tuesday 9th. I dined at Lloyds. Wm drank tea. Walked home. A pleasant starlight frosty evening. Reached home at one o'clock. Wm finished his poem today.[3]

Wednesday 10th. Walked to Keswick. Snow upon the ground. A very fine day. Ate bread and ale at John Stanley's.[4] Found Coleridge better. Stayed at Keswick till Sunday 14th December.

Monday [*15th*]. Baking and starching.

Tuesday [*16th*]. Ironing—the Lloyds called.

Wednesday [*17th*]. A very fine day. Writing all the morning for William.

Thursday [*18th*]. Mrs Coleridge and Derwent came. Sweeping chimneys.

Friday [*19th*]. Baking.

Saturday [*20th*]. Coleridge came. Very ill rheumatic, feverish. Rain incessantly.

Monday [*22nd*]. S. and Wm went to Lloyds. Wm dined, it rained very hard when he came home at . . .[5]

---

[1] See above, p. 24.

[2] One of the Griffiths of Newcastle.

[3] i.e. 'Michael'.

[4] Landlord of the King's Head at Thirlspot on the way to Keswick.

[5] The notebook containing this part of the journal ends in the middle of a sentence. Another notebook, now lost, must have contained entries from 23 December 1800 to 9 October 1801.

This notebook also contains five stanzas in D. W.' s hand, never printed by W. W., of 'The Complaint of a Forsaken Indian Woman'.

II. *10 October 1801 to 14 February 1802*[1]

Penshurst—Pedlar—Mary H.—Grasmere & Keswick—Sara's waistcoats—Fable of the Dogs—Cows—Lamb's Londoner—Lucy Aikin's poems—Mr Graham—Mrs Clarkson health—My German—our Riches—Miss Simpson—The poor woman who was drowned—William's health—medicines—The garden —Wm working there—quietness from company—Letting our house—keeping it—Books that we are to carry—L. degrades himself—narrow minded bigotry—unfortunate quotation—Letter from Sara—Montagu—Dr Dodd—Rubbing tables.[2]

Saturday 10th October 1801. Coleridge went to Keswick after we had built Sara's seat.[3]

Sunday 11th. Mr and Miss Simpson came in after tea and supped with us.

Monday 12th. We drank tea at Mr Simpson's.

Tuesday 13th. A thorough wet day.[4]

Thursday 15th. We dined at Mr Luff's.[5] A rainy morning. Coleridge came into Mr L.'s while we were at dinner. Wm and I walked up Loughrigg Fell then by the waterside. I held my head under a spout. Very sick and ill when I got home— went to bed in the sitting room—took laudanum.

[1] This volume is written in a notebook bound in blue marbled board. It contains also D. W.'s Hamburgh Journal, 14 September–1 October 1798, and drafts in W. W.'s hand of 'The Brothers' and 'Emma's Dell'.

[2] These notes are roughly and irregularly written on the first page of this notebook. It seems that she is noting down subjects for recording in the journal. Most of them can be traced between 22 December 1801 and mid-February 1802. But there is no mention in the journal of 'letting our house' or 'books that we are to carry', which probably refer to the project of going to live in France. There is also no mention of 'Dr Dodd'. 'L' probably stands for 'Lloyd'. 'Lamb's Londoner' (also not mentioned in the journal) was an essay published 1 February 1802 in the *Morning Post*, a passionate outburst in praise of London, which Lamb transcribed in a letter to Manning of 15 February 1802. Lucy Aikin, a niece of Mrs. Anna Letitia Barbauld, published no poems before 1810.

[3] Coleridge records a detailed description of the building of the seat, of which 'Sara had layed the first stone so long back as Thursday March 26th 1801', on the fly-leaf of his copy of Matthison's *Gedichte*. See G. Whalley, *Coleridge and Sara Hutchinson and the Asra Poems*, p. 123 n.

[4] In the same line, partially erased: 'Wednesday 14th omitted.'

[5] Captain and Mrs. Luff, friends of the Clarksons, were at present living in Ambleside. They also had a house at Patterdale.

Friday 16th. Tom Hutchinson came. It rained almost all day. Coleridge poorly.

Saturday 17th. We walked into Easedale. Coleridge poorly after dinner.

Sunday 18th. I have forgotten.

Monday 19th. Coleridge went home. Tom and William walked to Rydale—a very fine day. I was ill in bed all day. Mr Simpson tea and supper.

Tuesday 20th. We went to the Langdales and Colleth—a very fine day; a heavy shower in the afternoon in Langdale.

Wednesday 21st. Dined at Bowness, slept at Penny Bridge—in danger of being cast away on Windermere. A very fine day, but windy a little—a moonlight night.

Thursday 22nd. Breakfasted at Penny Bridge—dined at Coniston—a grand stormy day—drank tea at home.

Friday 23rd. A sweet delightful morning. I planted all sorts of plants, Tom helped me. He and W. then rode to Hawkshead. I baked bread and pies. Tom brought me 2 shrubs from Mr Curwen's nursery.

Saturday 24th. Attempted Fairfield but misty and we went no further than Green Head Gill to the sheepfold. Mild misty beautiful soft. Wm and Tom put out the Boat—brought the coat from Mr Luff's. Mr Simpson came in at dinner-time—drank tea with us and played at cards.

Sunday 25th. Rode to Legberthwaite[1] with Tom—expecting Mary[2]—sweet day. Went upon Helvellyn, glorious glorious sights. The sea at Cartmel. The Scotch mountains beyond the sea to the right. Whiteside large and round and very soft and green behind us. Mists above and below and close to us, with the Sun amongst them—they shot down to the coves. Left John Stanley's at 10 minutes past 12. Returned thither $\frac{1}{4}$ past 4—drank tea ate heartily. Before we went on Helvellyn we got bread and cheese—paid 4/- for the whole—reached home at 9 o'clock. A soft grey evening—the light of the moon but she did not shine on us.

Monday 26th October. Omitted. They[3] went to Buttermere.

Tuesday 27th October. Omitted, drank tea at Mr Simpsons.

---

[1] A hamlet on the road to Keswick at the head of the Vale of St. John.
[2] M. H. reached Keswick on the 23rd. *CNB*, vol. 1, p. 999.
[3] i.e. W. W. and Tom Hutchinson.

Wednesday 28th. The Clarksons came.

Thursday 29th. Rain all day.

Friday 30th. Rain all day.

Saturday 31st. We walked to Rydale—a soft and mild morning but threatening for rain.

Sunday Nov[embe]r 1st. Very cold—we walked in the evening to Butterlip How.

Monday 2nd. Very rainy.

Tuesday 3rd. We dined at Lloyd's. Cold and clear day.

Wednesday 4th. Mr C. and Wm rode out—very cold.

Thursday [5th]. [The Clarksons] left us.[1]

Friday [6th]. Coleridge came.

[*Monday 9th.*] Walked with Coleridge to Keswick . . .[1] the mountains for ever varying, now hid in the Clouds and now with their tops visible while perhaps they were half concealed below—Legberthwaite beautiful. We ate Bread and Cheese at John Stanley's and reached Keswick without fatigue just before Dark. We enjoyed ourselves in the study and were *at home.* Supped at Mr Jackson's. Mary and I sate in C.'s room a while.[2]

Tuesday 10th. Poor C. left us[3] and we came home together. We left Keswick at 2 o'clock and did not arrive at G. till 9 o'clock. Drank tea at John Stanley's very comfortably. I burnt myself with Coleridge's Aquafortis. Mary's feet sore. C. had a sweet day for his ride. Every sight and every sound reminded me of him dear dear fellow—of his many walks to us by day and by night—of all dear things. I was melancholy and could not talk, but at last I eased my heart by weeping—nervous blubbering says William. It is not so. O how many, many reasons have I to be anxious for him.

Wednesday 11th. Baked bread and giblet pie—put books in

---

[1] A page is here torn out which contained entries from 5 November to the beginning of 9 November ('Walked with Coleridge to Keswick'), portions of which are recovered from C. W.'s *Memoirs*, vol. I, p. 177. See Preface, p. viii. The next page begins: 'the mountains for ever varying'. It is probable that M. H. arrived on 6 or 7 November.

[2] We learn from C.'s letter to Southey dated 9 November (Griggs, vol. II, p. 774) that Mrs. C. and the children were staying with the Clarksons at Eusemere. This accounts for the comfortable stay of the Wordsworths at Greta Hall, free from the unfriendly presence of Mrs. C.

[3] C. went to London for the winter, after first staying with the Clarksons; he spent the New Year with Thomas Poole at Stowey. In March 1802 he returned to Keswick. *CNB*, vol. I, p. 1020.

order—mended stockings. Put aside dearest C.'s letters, and now at about 7 o'clock we are all sitting by a nice fire—W. with his book and a candle and Mary writing to Sara.

Thursday 12th. A beautiful still sunshiny morning. We rose very late. I put the rag Boxes into order. We walked out while the Goose was roasting—we walked to the top of the Hill. M. and I followed Wm—he was walking upon the turf between John's Grove and the Lane. It was a most sweet noon. We did not go into John's Grove but we walked among the Rocks and there we sate. Mr Olliff passed Mary and me upon the Road —Wm still among the Rocks. The Lake beautiful from the Orchard. Wm and I walked out before tea—The Crescent moon—we sate in the slate quarry—I sate there a long time alone. Wm reached home before me—I found them at Tea. There were a thousand stars in the Sky.

Friday Morning [13th]. Dullish, damp and cloudy—a day that promises not to dry our clothes—We spent a happy evening— went to bed late, and had a restless night—Wm better than I expected.

Saturday Morning [14th]. Still a cloudy dull day, very dark. I lay in bed all the Day very unwell: they made me some broth and I rose better after it was dark. We spent a quiet evening by the fire.

Sunday [15th]. I walked in the morning to Churnmilk Force nearly, and went upon Heifer crags. The valley of its winter yellow, but the bed of the brook still in some places almost *shaded* with leaves—the oaks brown in general but one that might be almost called green—the whole prospect was very soft and the distant view down the vale very impressive, a long vale down to Ambleside—the hills at Ambleside in mist and sunshine—all else grey. We sate by the fire and read Chaucer (Thomson, Mary read) and Bishop Hall.[1] Letters from Sara and Mrs Clarkson late at night.

Monday 16th November. A very dankish misty wettish morning. Mary and Molly ironed all day. I made bread and called at Mr Olliff's—Mrs O. at home—the prospect soft from the windows. Mrs O. observed that it was beautiful *even* in winter! The Luffs passed us. We walked backwards and forwards in the

---

[1] Joseph Hall (1574–1656), Bishop of Exeter and then of Norwich, whence he was ejected during the Civil War. They read him in Anderson's *British Poets*.

Church field. Wm somewhat weakish, but upon the whole pretty well—he is now at 7 o'clock reading Spenser. Mary is writing beside me. The little syke[1] murmurs. We are quiet and happy, but poor Peggy Ashburner is very ill and in pain. She coughs as if she would cough her life away. I am going to write to Coleridge and Sara. Poor C.! I hope he was in London yesterday. Molly has been very witty with Mary all day. She says 'Ye may say what ye will but there's nothing like a gay auld man for behaving weel to a young wife. Ye may laugh but this wind blows no favour—and where there's no love there's no favour.' On Sunday I lectured little John Dawson[2] for telling lies. I told him I had heard that he charged Jenny Baty falsely with having beaten him. Says Molly: 'she says it's not so that she never lifted hand till him, and she *should* speak truth you would think in her condition'—she is with child. Two Beggars today.

Tuesday 17th. A very rainy morning we walked into Easedale before dinner. Miss S. came in at dinner time—we went to Mr Gell's cottage—then returned. The coppices a beautiful brown, the oaks having a very fine leafy shade. We stood a long time to look at the corner Birch tree. The wind was among the light thin twigs, and they yielded to it this way and that. Drank tea and supped at the Simpsons—a moonlight wettish night. Dirty roads.

Wednesday 18th. We sate in the house in the morning reading Spenser. I was unwell and lay in bed all the afternoon. Wm and Mary walked to Rydale. Very pleasant moonlight. The Lakes beautiful. The church an image of peace. Wm wrote some lines upon it.[3] I in bed when they came home. Mary and I walked as far as Sara's Gate[4] before Supper. We stood there a long time, the whole scene impressive, the mountains indistinct the Lake calm and partly ruffled—large Island, a sweet sound of water falling into the quiet Lake. A storm was gathering in Easedale so we returned but the moon came out and opened to us the Church and village. Helm Crag in shade, the larger Moun-

---

[1] A North Country word for a small stream.

[2] Probably the son of John Dawson of How Top, baptized 3 March 1799, and thus a precocious little sinner. (E. de S.)

[3] These lines have not been identified.

[4] The gate on the right of the road to Rydal, opposite 'John's Grove', also called 'the Wishing Gate'.

tains Dappled like a sky. We stood long upon the bridge. Wished for Wm, he had stayed at home being sickish—found him better. We went to bed.

Thursday 19th Nov[embe]r.—A beautiful sunny, frosty morning. We did not walk all day. Wm said he would put it off till the fine moonlight night and then it came on a heavy rain and wind. Charles and Olivia Lloyd called in the morning.

Friday 20th. I wrote to Coleridge in the morning. We walked in the morning to Easedale. In the evening we had chearful letters from Coleridge and Sara.

Saturday 21st. We walked in the morning and payed one pound and 4d for letters. William out of spirits. We had a pleasant walk and spent a pleasant evening. There was a furious wind and cold at night. Mr Simpson drank tea with us and helped William out with the Boat. Wm and Mary walked to the Swan homewards with him. A keen clear frosty night. I went into the orchard while they were out.

Sunday 22nd.—We wrote to Coleridge—sent our letter by the Boy. Mr and Miss Simpson came in at tea time. We went with them to the Blacksmith's and returned by Butterlip How—a frost and wind with bright moonshine. The vale looked spacious and very beautiful—the level meadows seemed very large, and some nearer us unequal ground heaving like sand, the Cottages beautiful and quiet. We passed one near which stood a cropped ash with upright forked Branches like the Devil's horns frightening a guilty conscience. We were happy and chearful when we came home—we went early to bed.

Monday 23rd. A beautiful frosty morning. Mary was making William's woollen waistcoat. Wm unwell and did not walk. Mary and I sate in our cloaks upon the Bench in the Orchard. After dinner I went to bed unwell. Mary had a head-ach at night. We all went to bed soon.

Tuesday 24th. A rainy morning. We all were well except that my head ached a little and I took my Breakfast in bed. I read a little of Chaucer, prepared the goose for dinner, and then we all walked out. I was obliged to return for my fur tippet and Spenser it was so cold. We had intended going to Easedale but we shaped our course to Mr Gell's cottage. It was very windy and we heard the wind everywhere about us as we went along the Lane but the walls sheltered us. John Green's house[1] looked pretty under Silver How. As we were going along we were stopped at once, at the distance perhaps of 50 yards from our favorite Birch tree. It was yielding to the gusty wind with all its tender twigs, the sun shone upon it and it glanced in the wind like a flying sunshiny shower. It was a tree in shape with stem and branches but it was like a Spirit of water. The sun went in and it resumed its purplish appearance the twigs still yielding to the wind but not so visibly to us. The other Birch trees that were near it looked bright and chearful, but it was a creature by its own self among them. We could not get into Mr Gell's grounds—the old tree fallen from its undue exaltation above the Gate. A shower came on when we were at Benson's. We went through the wood—it became fair—there was a rainbow which spanned the lake from the Island house to the foot of Bainriggs. The village looked populous and beautiful. Catkins are coming out palm trees budding—the alder with its plumb coloured buds. We came home over the stepping stones.[2] The Lake was foamy with white waves. I saw a solitary butter flower[3] in the wood. *I* found it not easy to get over the stepping stones. Reached home at dinner time. Sent Peggy Ashburner some goose. She sent me some honey with a thousand thanks. 'Alas! the gratitude of men has etc.'[4] I went in to set her right about this and sate a while with her. She talked about Thomas's having sold his land.[5] 'Ay,' says she I said many a time 'He's not come fra London to buy our Land however.' Then she told me with what pains and industry they had made up their taxes interest etc. etc.—how they all got up at 5 o'clock in the morning to spin and Thomas carded, and that they had paid off a hundred pound of the interest. She said she used to take such pleasure in the cattle and sheep. 'O how pleased I used to be when they fetched them down, and when I had been a bit poorly I would gang out upon a hill and look over t' fields and see them and it used to do me so much good you cannot think.' Molly said to me when I came in 'poor Body. She's very ill

---

[1] i.e. Pavement End; the family of the Greens are described in *The Excursion*, VII. 636–94. (G. G. W.)

[2] At the head of Rydal Water, now superseded by Slater's Bridge. (G. G. W.)

[3] A local name for buttercup.

[4] 'Simon Lee', ll. 95–6; *P.W.*, vol. IV, p. 60.

[5] See the poem 'Repentance', *P.W.*, vol. II, p. 46.

but one does not know how long she may last. Many a fair face may gang before her.' We sate by the fire without work for some time then Mary read a poem of Daniell upon Learning. After tea Wm read Spenser now and then a little aloud to us. We were making his waistcoat. We had a note from Mrs C., with bad news from poor C. very ill. William walked to John's Grove. I went to meet him—moonlight but it rained. I met him before I had got as far as John Baty's[1]—he had been surprized and terrified by a sudden rushing of winds which seemed to bring earth sky and lake together, as if the whole were going to enclose him in—he was glad he was in a high Road.

In speaking of our walk on Sunday Evening the 22nd November I forgot to notice one most impressive sight. It was the moon and the moonlight seen through hurrying driving clouds immediately behind the Stone man upon the top of the hill on the Forest side. Every tooth and every edge of Rock was visible, and the Man stood like a Giant watching from the Roof of a lofty castle. The hill seemed perpendicular from the darkness below it. It was a sight that I could call to mind at any time it was so distinct.

Wednesday 25th November. It was a showery morning and threatened to be a wettish day, but the sun shone once or twice. We were engaged to the Lloyds and Wm and Mary were determined to go that it might be over. I accompanied them to the Thorn beside Rydale Water. I parted from them first at the top of the hill and they called me back. It rained a little and rained afterwards all the afternoon. I baked pies and bread, and wrote to Sara Hutchinson and Coleridge. I passed a pleasant evening but the wind roared so and it was such a storm that I was afraid for them. They came in at nine o'clock no worse for their walk and chearful blooming and happy.

Thursday 26th. Mr Olliff called before Wm was up to say that they would drink tea with us this afternoon. We walked into Easedale to gather mosses and to fetch cream. I went for the cream and they sate under a wall. It was piercing cold and a hail storm came on in the afternoon. The Olliffs arrived at 5 o'clock. We played at cards and passed a decent evening. It

[1] The Batys (colloquial for Bateman) lived at one of the four cottages just above Sykeside, now the Wordsworth Museum, at right angles to the road. (G. G. W.)

was a very still night but piercing cold. When they went away at 11 o'clock, a shower came on.

Friday 27th. Snow upon the ground thinly scattered. It snowed after we got up and then the sun shone and it was very warm though frosty—now the sun shines sweetly. A woman came who was travelling with her husband—he had been wounded and was going with her to live at Whitehaven. She had been at Ambleside the night before, offered 4d at the Cock for a bed—they sent her to one Harrison's where she and her husband had slept upon the hearth and bought a penny-worth of chips for a fire. Her husband was gone before very lame—'Aye' says she 'I was once an officer's wife I, as you see me now. My first husband married me at Appleby. I had 18£ a year for teaching a school and because I had no fortune his father turned him out of doors. I have been in the West Indies. I lost the use of this Finger just before he died he came to me and said he must bid farewell to his dear children and me. I had a muslin gown on like yours—I seized hold of his coat as he went from me and slipped the joint of my finger. He was shot directly. I came to London and married this man. He was clerk to Judge Chambray, *that man*, that man that's going on the Road now. If he, Judge Chambray,[1] had been at Kendal he would [have] given us a guinea or two and made nought of it, for he is very generous.' Before dinner we set forward to walk intending to return to dinner. But as we had got as far as Rydale Wm thought he would go on to Mr Luff's. We accompanied him under Loughrigg, and parted near the stepping stones.[2] It was very cold. Mary and I walked quick home. There was a fine gleam of Sunshine upon the eastern side of Ambleside Vale. We came up the old road and turning round we were struck with the appearance. Mary wrote to her aunt.[3] We expected the Simpsons. I was sleepy and weary and went to bed—before tea. It came on wet in the evening and was very cold. We expected letters from C. and Sara—Sara's came by the Boy. But none from C.—a sad disappointment. We did not go

---

[1] Sir Alan Chambré (1793–1823), a Kendal man, Recorder of Lancaster, became a judge in 1800. He was a man of benevolent character.

[2] Not the stepping-stones at the head of Rydal, but those over the Rothay below Rydal village, where it runs through Ambleside Park.

[3] Miss Elizabeth Monkhouse (1750–1828) of Penrith.

to meet Wm as we had intended—Mary was at work at Wm's warm waistcoat.

Saturday 28th November.—A very fine sunny morning. Soldiers still going by. I should have mentioned that yesterday when we went with Wm to Mr Luff's we met a soldier and his wife, he with a child in his arms, she carrying a bundle and his gun—we gave them some halfpence it was such a pretty sight. William having slept ill lay in bed till after one o'clock. Mary and I walked up to Mr Simpson's between 20 minutes before 2 and 20 minutes before 3 to desire them not to come. We drank tea and supped at Mr Olliff's—a keen frost with sparkling stars when we came home at ½ past 11.

Sunday 29th. Baking bread apple pies, and giblet pie—a bad giblet pie. It was a most beautiful morning. George Olliff brought Wm's stick. The sun shone all the day, but we never walked. In the evening we had intended going for letters but the Lad said he would go. We sate up till after one—no letters! Very cold—hard frost.

Monday 30th. A fine sharp morning. The Lad brought us a Letter from Montague and a short one from Coleridge. C. very well—promised to write tomorrow. We walked round the Lake. Wm and Mary went first over the stepping stones. I remained after them and went into the prospect field above Benson's to sit—Mary joined me there. Clear and frosty without wind. William went before to look at Langdale. We saw the pikes and then came home. They have cropped the tree which over-shadowed the gate beside that cottage at the turning of the hill which used to make a frame for Loughrigg Tarn and Windermere. We came home and read. Mary wrote to Joanna—I wrote to Richard, and Mrs Coleridge.

Tuesday 1st December 1801. A fine sunny and frosty morning. Mary and I walked to Rydale for letters, William was not well and staid at home reading after having lain long in bed. We found a Letter from Coleridge, a short one—he was pretty well. We were overtaken by two soldiers on our return—one of them being very drunk we wished them to pass us, but they had too much liquor in them to go very fast so we contrived to pass them—they were very merry and very civil. They fought with the mountains with their sticks. Aye says one, that will [? fall] upon us. One might stride over that etc. They never

saw such a wild country though one of them was a Scotchman.
They were honest looking fellows. The Corporal said he was
frightened to see the Road before them. We met Wm at Sara's
gate. He went back intending to go round the lake but having
attempted to cross the water and not succeeding he came back.
The Simpsons Mr and Miss drank tea with us—Wm was very
poorly and out of spirits. They stayed supper.

Wednesday 2nd. A fine grey frosty morning. Wm rose late.
I read the tale of Phœbus and the Crow[1] which he afterwards
attempted to translate and did translate a large part of it today.
Mrs Olliff brought us some yeast and made us promise to go
there the next day to meet the Luffs. We were sitting by the
fire in the evening when Charles and Olivia Lloyd came in. I
had not been very well so I did not venture out with them when
they went away—Mary and William went as far as Rydale
village. It snowed after it was dark, and there was a thin covering over the ground which made it light and soft. They looked
fresh and well when they came in. I wrote part of a letter to
Coleridge. After his return William went on a little with
Chaucer.

Thursday 3rd December 1801. I was not well in the morning.
We baked bread—after dinner I went to bed—William walked
into Easedale. Rain, hail and snow. I rose at ½ past 7, got tea,
then went to sup at Mr Olliff's—I had a glorious sleep and was
quite well. A light night roads very slippery. We spent a
pleasant evening—Mr and Mrs Luff there—Mrs L. poorly. I
wrote a little bit of my letter to Coleridge before I went to Mr
O.'s. We went to bed immediately after our return—Molly gone.

Friday 4th. My head bad and I lay long. Mrs Luff called—
Mary went with her to the slate quarry. Mr Simpson and
Charles Lloyd called for the yeast Receipt. William translating
the Prioress's tale. William and Mary walked after tea to Ry-
dale. It snowed and rained and they came in wet. I finished the
Letter to Coleridge and we received a letter from him and
Sara. S.'s letter written in good spirits—C.'s also. A letter of
Lamb's about George Dyer[2] with it.

---

[1] i.e. Chaucer's *The Manciple's Tale.*

[2] George Dyer (1755–1841), poet, friend of Lamb and also formerly of Wordsworth's schoolmaster at Hawkshead, William Taylor. He wrote an illustrated
History of the University and Colleges of Cambridge, 1812.

Saturday 5th. My head bad and I lay long. Mr Luff called before I rose. We put off walking in the morning: dull and misty and grey—very rainy in the afternoon and we could not go out. William finished the Prioress's tale, and after tea Mary and he wrote it out. Wm not well.—No parcel from Mrs Coleridge.

Sunday 6th. A very fine beautiful sunshiny morning. William worked a while at Chaucer, then we set forward to walk into Easedale. We met Mr and Mrs Olliff who were going to call upon us. They turned back with us and we parted at the White Bridge. We went up in to Easedale and walked backwards and forwards in that flat field which makes the second circle of Easedale with that beautiful Rock in the field beside us and all the rocks and the woods and the mountains enclosing us round. The Sun was shining among them, the snow thinly scattered upon the tops of the mountains. In the afternoon we sate by the fire—I read Chaucer aloud, and Mary read the first Canto of the Fairy Queen. After tea Mary and I walked to Ambleside for letters—reached home by 11 o'clock. We had a sweet walk. It was a sober starlight evening, the stars not shining as it were with all their brightness when they were visible and sometimes hiding themselves behind small greyish clouds that passed soberly along. We opened C.'s letter at Wilcock's door we thought we saw that he wrote in good spirits so we came happily homewards where we arrived 2 hours after we left home. It was a sad melancholy letter and prevented us all from sleeping.

Monday Morning 7th. We rose by candlelight. A showery unpleasant morning after a downright rainy night. We determined however to go to Keswick if possible, and we set off at a little after 9 o'clock. When we were upon the Rays it snowed very much and the whole prospect closed in upon us like a moorland valley upon a moor—very wild—but when we were at the top of the Rays we saw the mountains before us. The sun shone upon them here and there and Wytheburn vale though wild looked soft. The day went on chearfully and pleasantly now and then a hail shower attacked us but we kept up a good heart for Mary is a famous Jockey. We met Miss Barcroft—she had been unwell in the '*Liverpool* complaint' and was riding out for the benefit of her health. She had not seen Mrs C. 'The weather had been such as to preclude all intercourse between neighbours!' We reached Greta Hall at about one o'clock. Met Mrs C. in the field. Derwent in the cradle asleep—Hartley at his dinner—Derwent pale, the image of his Father, Hartley well. We wrote to C. Mrs. C. left us at ½ past 2—we drank tea by ourselves, the children playing about us. Mary said to Hartley, Shall I take Derwent with me? No says H. I cannot spare my little Brother in the sweetest tone possible and he can't do without his Mama. Well says Mary, why cannot I be his Mama. Can't he have more Mamas than one? No says H. What for? Because they do not love as Mothers do. What is the difference between Mothers and Mamas? Looking at his sleeves, Mothers wear sleeves like this pulling his own tight down and Mamas (pulling them up and making a bustle about his shoulders) so—. We parted from them at 4 o'clock. It was a little of the dusk when we set off. Cotton mills lighted up. The first star at Nadel fell, but it was never dark. We rode very briskly. Snow upon the Rays— reached home far sooner than we expected, at 7 o'clock. William at work with Chaucer, The God of Love.[1] Sate latish. I wrote a little to C.

Tuesday 8th December 1801. A dullish rainyish morning. Wm at work with Chaucer. I read Bruce's Lochleven and Life.[2] Going to bake bread and pies. After dinner I felt myself unwell having not slept well in the night so, after we had put up the Book cases which Charles Lloyd sent us I lay down. I did not sleep much but I rose refreshed. Mary and William walked to the Boat house at Rydale while he[3] was in bed. It rained very hard all night. No company. Wm worked at the Cuckow and the Nightingale till he was tired. Mary very sleepy and not quite well. We both slept sound. Letter from R[ichar]d with news of John dated 7th August.

Wednesday Morning 9th December. William slept well but his tongue fev[er]ish. I read Palamon and Arcite. Mary read Bruce. William writing out his alteration of Chaucer's Cuckow and Nightingale. After dinner it was agreed that we should walk,

---

[1] i.e. 'The Cuckoo and the Nightingale', *P. W.*, vol. IV, p. 217.

[2] Michael Bruce (1746–67), Scottish poet, wrote *Lochleven* in 1766. D. W. probably read it in vol. IX of Anderson's *British Poets*, which the Wordsworths possessed and which also contains a memoir of him.

[3] D. W. wrote 'he' for 'I'.

when I had finished a letter to C., part of which I had written in the morning by the kitchen fire while the mutton was roasting. William did not go with us but Mary and I walked into Easedale and backwards and forwards in that large field under George Rawnson's[1] white cottage. We had intended gathering mosses and for that purpose we turned into the green Lane behind the Tailor's but it was too dark to see the mosses. The river came galloping past the church as fast as it could come and when we got into Easedale we saw Churn Milk force like a broad stream of snow. At the little foot-Bridge we stopped to look at the company of rivers which came hurrying down the vale this way and that; it was a valley of streams and Islands, with that great waterfall at the head and lesser falls in different parts of the mountains coming down to these Rivers. We could hear the sound of those lesser falls but we could not *see* them. We walked backwards and forwards till all distant objects except the white shape of the waterfall, and the lines of the mountains were gone. We had the Crescent Moon when we went out, and at our return there were a few stars that shone dimly, but it was a grey cloudy night.

Thursday 10th December. A very fine sunny morning—not frosty. We walked into Easedale to gather mosses, and then we went past to Aggy Fleming's and up the gill, beyond that little waterfall.[2] It was a wild scene of crag and mountain. One craggy point rose above the rest irregular and ragged and very impressive it was. We called at Aggy Fleming's she told us about her miserable house. She looked shockingly with her head tyed up. Her mother was there—the children looked healthy. We were very unsuccessful in our search after mosses.[3] Just when the evening was closing in Mr Clarkson came to the door. It was a fine frosty Evening. We played at cards.

Friday 11th. Baked pies and cakes. It was a stormy morning with hail showers. The Luffs dined with us—Mrs L. came with Mrs Olliff in the Gig. We sate lazily round the fire after dinner. Mr and Mrs Olliff drank tea and supped with us—a hard frost when they came.

Saturday 12th. A fine frosty morning—snow upon the

---

[1] D. W.'s spelling of Rowlandson. His cottage was on the site of the present 'Lancrigg'. (G. G. W.)

[2] Aggy lived at Gillside at the foot of Helm Crag.

[3] 'I began a letter to John' is erased.

ground. I made bread and pies. We walked with Mrs Luff to Rydale, and came home on the other side of the Lake. Met Townley with his dogs. All looked chearful and bright. Helm Crag rose very bold and craggy, a being by itself, and behind it was the large Ridge of mountain smooth as marble and snow white. All the mountains looked like solid stone on our left going from Grasmere, i.e. White Moss and Nab scar. The snow hid all the grass and all signs of vegetation and the Rocks shewed themselves boldly everywhere and seemed more stony than Rock or stone. The Birches on the crags beautiful, Red brown and glittering—the ashes glittering spears with their upright stems—the hips very beautiful, and so good!! and dear Coleridge—I ate twenty for thee when I was by myself. I came home first—they walked too slow for me. William went to look at Langdale Pikes. We had a sweet invigorating walk. Mr Clarkson came in before tea. We played at cards—sate up late. The moon shone upon the water below Silver-how, and above it hung, combining with Silver how on one side, a Bowl-shaped moon the curve downwards—the white fields, glittering Roof of Thomas Ashburner's house, the dark yew tree, the white fields—gay and beautiful. William lay with his curtains open that he might see it.

Sunday 13th. Mr Clarkson left us leading his horse. Went to Brathay and Luffs. We drank tea at Betty Dixon's. Very cold and frosty—a pleasant walk home. William had been very unwell but we found him better. The Boy brought letters from Coleridge and from Sara. Sara in bad spirits about C.

Monday 14th December. Wm and Mary walked to Ambleside in the morning to buy mouse-traps. Mary fell and hurt her wrist. I accompanied them to the top of the hill—clear and frosty. I wrote to Coleridge, a very long letter while they were absent. Sate by the fire in the evening reading.

Tuesday 15th. Wm and I walked to Rydale for letters—found one from Joanna. We had a pleasant walk but coldish—it thawed a little.

Wednesday 16th. A very keen frost, extremely slippery. After dinner Wm and I walked twice up to the Swan and back again—met Miss Simpson. She came with us to Olliffs and we went back with her. Very cold.

Thursday 17th. Snow in the night and still snowing. We went to Mr Luff's to dine—met Mrs King. Hard frost and as light as day—we had a delightful walk and reached home a little after twelve. Mrs Luff ill. Ambleside looked excessively beautiful as we came out—like a village in another country; and the light chearful mountains were seen in the long long distance as bright and as clear as at midday with the blue sky above them. We heard waterfowl calling out by the lake side. Jupiter was very glorious above the Ambleside hills and one large star hung over the Coombe of the hills on the opposite side of Rydale water.

Friday 18th December 1801. Mary and Wm walked round the two lakes. I stayed at home to make bread, cakes and pies. I went afterwards to meet them, and I met Wm near Benson's. Mary had gone to look at Langdale pikes. It was a chearful glorious day. The Birches and all trees beautiful—hips bright red—mosses green. I wrote to Coleridge for money.[1]

Saturday 19th. I was not quite well and did not rise to breakfast. We walked by Brathay to Ambleside—called at the Lloyds —they were at Kendal. Dined with the Luffs—and came home in the evening—the evening cloudy and promising snow. The day very beautiful—Brathay vale scattered and very chearful and interesting.

Sunday 20th December. It snowed all day. In the evening we went to tea at Thomas Ashburner's. It was a very deep snow. The Brooms were very beautiful, arched feathers with wiry stalks pointed to the end, smaller and smaller. They waved gently with the weight of the snow. We stayed at Thomas A.'s till after 9 o'clock. Peggy better—the Lasses neat and clean and rosy.

Monday 21st, being the shortest day. Mary walked to Ambleside for letters, it was a wearisome walk for the snow lay deep upon the Roads and it was beginning to thaw. I stayed at home and clapped[2] the small linen. Wm sate beside me and read the Pedlar, he was in good spirits, and full of hope of what he should do with it. He went to meet Mary and they brought 4 letters, 2 from Coleridge, one from Sara and one from

---

[1] W. W. had asked C. for £10. See *E.Y.*, p. 342, W. W. to Daniel Stuart, 21 December 1801. C. was working for Stuart, but he left London for Nether Stowey on 26 December. The money was probably needed for their journey to Eusemere, via Keswick. See below, 28 December ff.

[2] i.e. ironed.

France.[1] Coleridge's were very melancholy letters, he had been very ill in his bowels. We were made very unhappy. Wm wrote to him and directed the letter into Somersetshire. I finished it after tea. In the afternoon Mary and I ironed—afterwards she packed her clothes up and I mended Wm's stockings while he was reading the Pedlar. I then packed up for Mr Clarkson's —we carried the Boxes cross the Road to Fletcher's peat house,[2] after Mary had written to Sara and Joanna.

Tuesday 22nd. Still thaw. I washed my head. Wm and I went to Rydale for letters. The road was covered with dirty snow, rough and rather slippery. We had a melancholy letter from C., for he had been very ill, though he was better when he wrote. We walked home almost without speaking. Wm composed a few lines of the Pedlar. We talked about Lamb's Tragedy[3] as we went down the White Moss. We stopped a long time in going to watch a little bird with a salmon coloured breast—a white cross or T upon its wings, and a brownish back with faint stripes.[4] It was pecking the scattered Dung upon the road. It began to peck at the distance of 4 yards from us and advanced nearer and nearer till it came within the length of Wm's stick without any apparent fear of us. As we came up the White Moss we met an old man, who I saw was a beggar by his two bags hanging over his shoulder, but from a half laziness, half indifference and a wanting to *try* him if he would speak I let him pass. He said nothing, and my heart smote me. I turned back and said You are begging? 'Ay', says he. I gave him a halfpenny. William, judging from his appearance joined in I suppose you were a sailor? 'Ay', he replied, 'I have been 57 years at sea, 12 of them on board a man-of-war under Sir Hugh Palmer.' Why have you not a pension? 'I have no pension, but I could have got into Greenwich hospital but all my officers are dead.' He was 75 years of age, had a freshish colour in his cheeks, grey hair, a decent hat with a binding round the edge, the hat worn brown and glossy, his shoes were small thin shoes low in the quarters, pretty good. They had belonged to a gentleman. His coat was blue, frock shaped

---

[1] Probably from Annette Vallon.
[2] Fletcher, the Keswick carrier, kept his horses at Town End.
[3] *John Woodvill.*
[4] A most accurate description of a cock chaffinch.

coming over his thighs, it had been joined up at the seams behind with paler blue to let it out, and there were three Bell-shaped patches of darker blue behind where the Buttons had been. His breeches were either of fustian or grey cloth, with strings hanging down, whole and tight; he had a checked shirt on, and a small coloured handkerchief tyed round his neck. His bags were hung over each shoulder and lay on each side of him, below his breast. One was brownish and of coarse stuff, the other was white with meal on the outside, and his blue waist-coat was whitened with meal. In the coarse bag I guessed he put his scraps of meat etc. He walked with a slender stick decently stout, but his legs bowed outwards. We over-took old Fleming[1] at Rydale, leading his little Dutchman-like grandchild along the slippery road. The same pace seemed to be natural to them both, the old man and the little child, and they went hand in hand, the grandfather cautious, yet looking proud of his charge. He had two patches of new cloth at the shoulder blades of his faded claret coloured coat, like eyes at each shoulder, not worn elsewhere. I found Mary at home in her riding-habit all her clothes being put up. We were very sad about Coleridge. Wm walked further. When he came home he cleared a path to the necessary—called me out to see it but before we got there a whole housetop full of snow had fallen from the roof upon the path and it echoed in the ground beneath like a dull beating upon it. We talked of going to Ambleside after dinner to borrow money of Luff, but we thought we would defer our visit to Eusemere a day.—Half the seaman's nose was reddish as if he had been in his youth some-what used to drinking, though he was not injured by it.—We stopped to look at the Stone seat at the top of the Hill. There was a white cushion upon it round at the edge like a cushion and the Rock behind looked soft as velvet, of a vivid green and so tempting! The snow too looked as soft as a down cushion. A young Foxglove, like a star in the Centre. There were a few green lichens about it and a few withered Brackens of Fern here and there and upon the ground near. All else was a thick snow—no foot mark to it, not the foot of a sheep.—When we were at Thomas Ashburner's on Sunday Peggy talked about the Queen of Patterdale. She had been brought to drinking by her hus-

[1] Thomas Fleming kept the old Hare and Hounds Inn at Rydale. (G. G. W.)

band's unkindness and avarice. She was formerly a very nice tidy
woman. She had taken to drinking but that was better than if
she had taken to something worse (by this I suppose she meant
killing herself). She said that her husband used to be out all
night with other women and she used to *hear* him come in in
the morning for they never slept together—'Many a poor
Body a wife like me, has had a working heart for her, as much
stuff as she had'. We sate snugly round the fire. I read to them
the Tale of Custance and the Syrian monarch, also some of the
Prologues. It is the Man of Lawe's Tale. We went to bed early.
It snowed and thawed.

Wednesday 23rd. A downright thaw but the snow not gone
off the ground except on the steep hillsides—it was a thick black
heavy air. I baked pies and bread. Mary wrote out the Tales
from Chaucer for Coleridge. William worked at The Ruined
Cottage and made himself very ill. I went to bed without dinner, he went to the other bed—we both slept and Mary lay on
the Rug before the Fire. A broken soldier came to beg in the
morning. Afterwards a tall woman, dressed somewhat in a
tawdry style with a long checked muslin apron a beaver hat,
and throughout what are called good clothes. Her Daughter
had gone before with a soldier and his wife. She had buried
her husband at Whitehaven and was going back into
Cheshire.

Thursday 24th. Still a thaw. We walked to Rydale, Wm Mary
and I—left the patterns at Thomas Fleming's for Mrs King.
The Roads uncomfortable and slippery. We sate comfortably
round the fire in the Evening and read Chaucer. Thoughts of
last year. I took out my old Journal.

Friday 25th. Christmas day.[1] A very bad day. We drank tea
at John Fisher's—we were unable to walk. I went to bed after
dinner. The roads very slippery. We received a letter from
Coleridge while we were at John Fisher's. A terrible night—
little John brought the letter. Coleridge poorly but better—his
letter made us uneasy about him. I was glad I was not by myself when I received it.

Saturday 26th. My head ached and I lay long in bed and took
my breakfast there. Soon after I had breakfasted we went to
call at Mr Olliff's. They were not at home. It came on very wet.

[1] D. W.'s birthday. She was thirty.

Mary went in to the house, and Wm and I went up to Tom Dawson's to speak about his Grandchild. The rain went off and we walked to Rydale. It was very pleasant—Grasmere Lake a beautiful image of stillness, clear as glass, reflecting all things. The wind was up and the waters sounding. The lake of a rich purple, the fields a soft yellow, the Island yellowish-green, the copses Red Brown the mountains purple. The Church and buildings, how quiet they were! Poor Coleridge, Sara, and dear little Derwent here last year at this time. After tea we sate by the fire comfortably. I read aloud—The Miller's Tale. Wrote to Coleridge. The Olliffs passed in chaise and gig. Wm wrote part of the poem to Coleridge.[1]

Sunday 27th. A fine soft beautiful, mild day with gleams of sunshine. I lay in bed till 12 o'clock, Mr Clarkson's man came. We wrote to him.[2] We walked up within view of Rydale. William went to take in his Boat. I sate in John's Grove a little while. Mary came home. Mary wrote some lines of the 3d part of Wm's poem[3] which he brought to read to us when we came home. Mr Simpson came in at dinner time and stayed tea. They fetched in the Boat. I lay down upon the Bed in the mean time. A sweet evening.

Monday 28th December. William, Mary and I set off on foot to Keswick. We carried some cold mutton in our pockets, and dined at John Stanley's where they were making Christmas pies. The sun shone but it was coldish. We parted from Wm upon the Rays. He joined us opposite Sara's rock.[4] He was busy in composition and sate down upon the Wall. We did not see him again till we arrived at John Stanley's. There we roasted apples in the oven. After we had left John Stanley's Wm discovered that he had lost his gloves. He turned back but they were gone. We were tired and had bad head aches. We rested often. Once Wm left his Spenser and Mary turned back for it and found it upon the Bank where we had last rested. We reached Greta Hall at about $\frac{1}{2}$ past 5 o'clock. The Children

---

[1] *The Prelude.*

[2] i.e. to Mr. Clarkson to say when they were coming.

[3] i.e. *The Prelude*, Book III.

[4] Usually referred to in the W. family as the Rock of Names, on which were carved the initials W. W., M. H., D. W., S. T. C., J. W., S. H.; it was on the road, now submerged, along Thirlmere, midway between Grasmere and Keswick. See W.'s note to *The Waggoner*. (G. G. W.) (See also under 4 May 1802.)

and Mrs C. well. After Tea message came from Wilkinson[1] who had passed us on the road inviting Wm to sup at the Oak. He went. Met a young man (a predestined Marquis) called Johnston. He spoke to him familiarly of the LB. He had seen a copy presented by the Queen to Mrs Harcourt. Said he saw them everywhere and wondered they did not sell. We all went weary to bed. My Bowels very bad.

Tuesday 29th. A fine morning. A thin fog upon the hills which soon disappeared. The sun shone. Wilkinson went with us to the top of the hill.[2] We turned out of the road at the 2nd mile stone and passed a pretty cluster of houses at the foot of St John's Vale. The houses were among tall trees partly of Scotch fir, and some naked forest trees. We crossed a Bridge just below these houses and the river winded sweetly along the meadows. Our road soon led us along the sides of dreary bare hills, but we had a glorious prospect to the left of Saddleback, half way covered with snow and underneath the comfortable white houses and the village of Threlkeld. These houses and the village want trees about them. Skiddaw was behind us and dear Coleridge's desert home——As we ascended the hills it grew very cold and slippery. Luckily the wind was at our backs and helped us on. A sharp hail shower gathered at the head of Matterdale and the view upwards was very grand—the wild cottages seen through the hurrying hail shower. The wind drove and eddied about and about and the hills looked large and swelling through the storm. We thought of Coleridge. O the bonny nooks and windings and curlings of the Beck down at the bottom of the steep green mossy Banks. We dined at the publick house on porridge, with a second course of Christmas pies. We were well received by the Landlady, and her little Jewish daughters were glad to see us again. The husband a very handsome man. While we were eating our dinners a traveller came in. He had walked over Kirkstone that morning. We were much amused by the curiosity of the Landlord and Landlady to learn who he was, and by his mysterious manner of letting out a little bit of his errand and yet telling nothing. He had

[1] Joshua Lucock Wilkinson, formerly of Cockermouth, now a solicitor in London, and friend of R. W. See *E.Y.*, p. 344.

[2] i.e. the hill out of Keswick on the Penrith road. They were now on their way to the Clarksons at Eusemere.

business further up in the vale. He left them with this piece of information to work upon and I doubt not they discovered who he was and all his business before the next day at that hour. The woman told us of the Riches of a Mr Walker formerly of Grasmere. We said What does he do nothing for his relations? He has a sickly sister at Grasmere. 'Why' said the man 'I daresay if they had any sons to put forward he would do it for them, but he has children of his own.' N.B.—His fortune is above 60,000£ and he has two children!! The Landlord went about 1 mile and a ½ with us to put us in the right way. The road was often very slippery, the wind high, and it was nearly dark before we got into the right Road. I was often obliged to crawl upon all fours, and Mary fell many a time. A stout young man whom we met on the hills and who knew Mr Clarkson very kindly set us into the right road and we inquired again near some houses and were directed by a miserable poverty struck looking woman, who had been fetching water, to go down a nasty miry lane. We soon got into the main Road and reached Mr Clarkson's at Tea time. Mary H. spent the next day with us and we walked in Dunmallet[1] before dinner but it snowed a little. The day following being New Year's Eve we accompanied Mary to Stainton Bridge—met Mr Clarkson with a calf's head in a basket—we turned with him and parted from Mary.[2]

New Year's Day [*1802*]. We walked Wm and I towards Martindale.[3]

2nd January [*Saturday*]. It snowed all day. We walked near to Dalemain in the snow.

3rd January Sunday. Mary brought us letters from Sara and Coleridge and we went with her homewards to Sockbridge.[4] Parted at the style on the Poolley side. Thomas Wilkinson[5] dined with us, and stayed supper.

I do not recollect how the rest of our time was spent exactly.

---

[1] The round hill, now wooded, at the foot of Ullswater.

[2] M. H. went on to Penrith to her aunt, but returned to Eusemere on the 17th.

[3] A valley opening from the eastern shore of Ullswater.

[4] Sockbridge, in the parish of Barton: here Richard Wordsworth, William's grandfather, had a property, which now (1801) belonged to William's eldest brother Richard.

[5] The Quaker farmer of Yanwath near Penrith. See W. W.'s poem 'To the Spade of a Friend', *P.W.*, vol. IV, p. 75.

We had a very sharp frost which broke on Friday the 15th January, or rather on the morning of Saturday 16th.— — On Sunday the 17th we went to meet Mary—it was a mild gentle Thaw. She stayed with us till Friday 22nd January—she was to have left us on Thursday 23rd [21st] but it was too stormy. On Thursday we dined at Mr Myers's[1] and on Friday 24th [22nd], we parted from Mary. Before our parting we sate under a wall in the sun near a cottage above Stainton Bridge. The field in which we sate sloped downwards to a nearly level meadow round which the Emont flowed in a small half circle, as at Sockburn.[2] The opposite bank is woody, steep as a wall, but not high, and above that Bank the fields slope gently and irregularly down to it. These fields are surrounded by tall hedges with trees among them, and there are Clumps or grovelets of tall trees here and there. Sheep and cattle were in the fields. Dear Mary! there we parted from her. I daresay, as often as she passes that road she will turn in at the gate to look at this sweet prospect. There was a Barn and I think two or three cottages to be seen among the trees and slips of lawn and irregular fields. During our stay at Mr Clarkson's we walked every day, except that stormy Thursday and then Wm dined at Mr Myers's and I went after dinner on a double horse. Mrs Clarkson was poorly all the time we were there. We dined at Thomas Wilkinson's on Friday the 15th and walked to Penrith for Mary. The trees were covered with hoarfrost, grasses and trees and hedges beautiful—a glorious sunset frost keener than ever. Next day thaw. Mrs Clarkson amused us with many stories of her family and of persons whom she had known. I wish I had set them down as I heard them, when they were fresh in my memory. She had two old Aunts who lived at Norwich. The son of one of them (Mrs Barnard) had had a large fortune left him. The other sister rather piqued that her child had not got it says to her 'Well, we have one Squire in the family however'. Mrs Barnard replied with tears rushing out 'Sister Harmer Sister Harmer there you sit. My son's no more a Squire than yours. I take it very unkindly of you Sister Harmer.' She used to say 'Well I wish it may do him any

---

[1] See above, p. 41.

[2] The farmhouse on the Tees where Mary and Sara Hutchinson had lived with their brother Thomas. W. and D. W. had visited them there in 1799.

good'. When her son wished to send his carriage for her she said 'Nay I can walk to the Tabernacle and surely I may walk to see him.' She kept two maids yet she white-washed her kitchen herself—the two sisters lived together. She had a grand cleaning day twice a week and the sister had a fire made upstairs that all below might be thoroughly cleaned. She gave a great deal away in Charity, visited the sick and was very pious. Mrs Clarkson knew a clergyman and his wife who brought up ten children upon a Curacy, sent 2 sons to college, and he left 1000£ when he died. The wife was very generous gave to all poor people victuals and drink. She had a passion for feeding animals, she killed a pig with feeding it over much. When it was dead she said 'To be sure it's a great loss but I thank God it did not die *clemmed*' the Cheshire[1] word for starved. Her husband was very fond of playing Backgammon and used to play whenever he could get any Body to play with him. She had played much in her youth and was an excellent player but her husband knew nothing of this, till one day she said to him 'You're fond of Backgammon come play with me'. He was surprized. She told him that she had kept it to herself while she had a young family to attend to but that now she would play with him. So they began to play and played afterwards every night. Mr C. told us many pleasant stories. His journey from London to Wisbech on foot when a schoolboy, Irish murderer's knife and stick, Postboy, &c., the white horse sleeping at the turnpike gate, snoring of the turnpike man, clock ticking. The Burring story, the story of the mastiff, Bull-baitings by men at Wisbech. On Saturday January 23rd we left Eusemere at 10 o'clock in the morning, I behind Wm Mr C. on his Galloway.[2] The morning not very promising the wind cold. The mountains large and dark but only thinly streaked with snow—a strong wind. We dined in Grisdale on ham bread and milk. We parted from Mr C. at one o'clock—it rained all the way home. We struggled with the wind and often rested as we went along.— A hail-shower met us before we reached the Tarn[3] and the way often was difficult over the snow but at the Tarn the view closed in. We saw nothing but mists and snow and at first the

---

[1] D. W. wrote 'Suffolk' and erased it.
[2] A Galloway pony.
[3] Grisedale Tarn at the top of the pass between Patterdale and Grasmere.

ice on the Tarn below us, cracked and split yet without water, a dull grey white. We lost our path and could see the Tarn no longer. We made our way out with difficulty guided by a heap of stones which we well remembered. We were afraid of being bewildered in the mists till the Darkness should overtake us. We were long before we knew that we were in the right track but thanks to William's skill we knew it long before we could see our way before us. There was no footmark upon the snow either of man or beast. We saw 4 sheep before we had left the snow region. The Vale of Grasmere when the mists broke away looked soft and grave, of a yellow hue—it was dark before we reached home. We were not very much tired. My inside was sore with the cold. We had both of us been much heated upon the mountains but we caught no cold— —O how comfortable and happy we felt ourselves sitting by our own fire when we had got off our wet clothes and had dressed ourselves fresh and clean. We found 5£ from Montague and 20£ from Chris[tophe]r.[1] We talked about the Lake of Como, read in the descriptive Sketches, looked about us, and felt that we were happy. We indulged dear thoughts about home—poor Mary! we were sad to think of the contrast for her.[2]

Sunday 24th. We went into the orchard as soon as breakfast was over laid out the situation for our new room, and sauntered a while. We had Mr Clarkson's turkey for dinner, the night before we had broiled the gizzard and some mutton and made a nice piece of cookery for Wm's supper. Wm walked in the morning I wrote to Coleridge. After dinner I lay down till tea time. I rose fresher and better. Wm could not beat away sleep when I was gone. We went late to bed.

Monday 25th January. We did not rise so soon as we intended. I made bread and apple pies. We walked at dusk to Rydale— no letters! it rained all the way. I wrote to Chris[tophe]r and Mrs Clarkson and Mrs Coleridge, and sent off C.'s letter to Mary. William tired with composition.[3] We both went to bed at 10 o'clock.

Tuesday 26th. A dull morning. I have employed myself in

[1] This sum was the yearly allowance made by Christopher to his sister. John provided a similar sum and in June 1802 she asked R. W. to do the same so that she could live in financial independence when William married.

[2] M. H. was again staying at Penrith with her aunt.

[3] He was from now until March mainly occupied with *The Pedlar*.

writing this journal and reading newspapers till now ($\frac{1}{2}$ past 1 o'clock) we are going to walk, and I am ready and waiting by the kitchen fire for Wm. We set forward, intending to go into Easedale but the wind being rather loudish, and blowing down Easedale we turned under Silver How for a sheltered walk. We went a little beyond the Wyke then up to John's Grove, where the storm of Thursday has made sad ravages. Two of the finest trees are uprooted one lying with the turf about its root as if the whole together had been pared by a knife. The other is a larch. Several others are blown aside, one is snapped in two. We gathered together a faggot. William had tired himself with working—he resolved to do better. We received a letter from Mary by Fletcher with an account of C.'s arrival in London. I wrote to Mary before bed-time. We sate nicely together and talked by the fire[1] till we were both tired, for Wm wrote out part of his poem and endeavoured to alter it, and so made himself ill. I copied out the rest for him. We went late to bed. Wm wrote to Annette.

Wednesday 27th. A beautiful mild morning—the sun shone, the lake was still, and all the shores reflected in it. I finished my letter to Mary, Wm wrote to Stuart.[2] I copied out sonnets for him.[3] Mr Olliff called and asked us to tea tomorrow. We stayed in the house till the sun shone more dimly and we thought the afternoon was closing in but, though the calmness of the Lake was gone with the bright sunshine, yet it was delightfully pleasant. We found no letter from Coleridge. One from Sara which we sate upon the wall to read—a sweet long letter, with a most interesting account of Mr Patrick.[4] We had ate up the cold turkey before we walked so we cooked no dinner. Sate a while by the fire and then drank tea at Frank Baty's. As we went past the Nab, I was surprized to see the youngest child

[1] The words 'nicely together and talked by the fire', following 'sate', are erased in the MS.; cf. end of next day's entry, where they are almost repeated and where clearly they more properly belong. 'Went to bed' is erased as well.

[2] On 2 February, three poems by W. appeared in the *Morning Post*—'O Moon if e'er I joyed', 'Calm is all Nature as a resting wheel', and 'Dear Child of Nature, let them rail'.

[3] The words 'We walked to Rydale' have been erased.

[4] James Patrick of Kendal, 'the intellectual Pedlar', married a cousin of the Hutchinsons' mother. S. H. lived with them in Kendal as a child and said that 'the best part of her education was gathered from the stores of that good man's mind'. The portrait of The Wanderer in *The Excursion* owes much to her account of Patrick.

amongst the rest of them running about by itself with a canny round fat face, and rosy cheeks. I called in. They gave me some nuts—everybody surprised that we should come over Grisdale. Paid 1–3–3 for letters come since December 1st. Paid also about 8 shillings at Penrith. The Bees were humming about the hive. William raked a few stones off the garden, his first garden labour this year. I cut the shrubs. When we returned from Frank's William wasted his mind in the Magazines. I wrote to Coleridge and Mrs C., closed the letters up to [? Samson]. Then we sate by the fire and were happy only our tender thoughts became painful. Went to bed at ½ past 11.

Thursday 28th. A downright rain. A wet night. Wm slept better—better this morning—he had [written an] epitaph and altered one that he wrote when he was a Boy.[1] It cleared up after dinner. We were both in miserable spirits, and very doubtful about keeping our engagement to the Olliffs. We walked first within view of Rydale, then to Lewthwaite's, then we went to Mr Olliff's. We talked a while. William was tired. We then played at cards. Came home in the rain. Very dark. Came with a lantern. William out of spirits and tired. After we went to bed I heard him continually, he called at ¼ past 3 to know the hour.

Friday 29th January. William was very unwell. Worn out with his bad night's rest—he went to bed—I read to him to endeavour to make him sleep. Then I came into the other room, and read the 1st Book of Paradise Lost. After dinner we walked to Ambleside. Found Lloyds at Luff's—we stayed and drank tea by ourselves. A heart-rending letter from Coleridge— we were sad as we could be. Wm wrote to him. We talked about Wm's going to London. It was a mild afternoon—there was an unusual softness in the prospects as we went, a rich yellow upon the fields, and a soft grave purple on the waters. When we returned, many stars were out, the clouds were moveless, in the sky soft purple, the Lake of Rydale calm, Jupiter behind, Jupiter at least *we* call him, but William says we always call the largest star Jupiter. When we came home we both wrote to C. I was stupefied.

Saturday January 30th. A cold dark morning. William chopped wood—I brought it in in a basket. A cold wind. Wm slept better but he thinks he looks ill—he is shaving now. He asks

---

[1] It has not been possible to identify these epitaphs.

me to set down the story of Barbara Wilkinson's Turtle Dove. Barbara is an old maid. She had 2 turtle Doves. One of them died the first year I think. The other bird continued to live alone in its cage for 9 years, but for one whole year[1] it had a companion and daily visitor, a little mouse that used to come and feed with it, and the Dove would caress it, and cower over it with its wings, and make a loving noise to it. The mouse though it did not testify equal delight in the Dove's company yet it was at perfect ease. The poor mouse disappeared and the Dove was left solitary till its death. It died of a short sickness and was buried under a tree with funeral ceremony by Barbara and her maiden, and one or two others.

On *Saturday 30th*, William worked at the Pedlar all the morning. He kept the dinner waiting till 4 o'clock—he was much tired. We were preparing to walk when a heavy rain came on.

Sunday 31st. William had slept very ill—he was tired and had a bad headache. We walked round the two lakes. Grasmere was very soft and Rydale was extremely beautiful from the pasture side. Nab Scar was just topped by a cloud which cutting it off as high as it could be cut off made the mountain look uncommonly lofty. We sate down a long time in different places. I always love to walk that way because it is the way I first came to Rydale and Grasmere,[2] and because our dear Coleridge did also. When I came with Wm 6½ years ago[3] it was just at sunset. There was a rich yellow light on the waters and the Islands were reflected there. Today it was grave and soft but not perfectly calm. William says it was much such a day as when Coleridge came with him.[4] The sun shone out before we reached Grasmere. We sate by the roadside at the foot of the Lake close to Mary's dear name which she had cut herself upon the stone. William employed[5] cut at it with his knife to make it plainer. We amused ourselves for a long time in watching the Breezes some as if they came from the bottom of the lake spread in a circle,

[1] 'There was one year during which', erased.
[2] D. W. first wrote: 'because I first saw Rydale and Grasmere from that side of the water.'
[3] It was in April 1794, and therefore nearly eight years before.
[4] i.e. on 4 November 1799.
[5] The words 'employed himself in making' originally followed 'William'. D. W. has erased 'himself in making' but forgot to erase 'employed'.

brushing along the surface of the water, and growing more delicate, as it were thinner and of a *paler* colour till they died away.
Others spread out like a peacock's tail, and some went right
forward this way and that in all directions. The lake was still
where these breezes were not, but they made it all alive. I
found a strawberry blossom in a rock. The little slender flower
had more courage than the green leaves, for *they* were but half
expanded and half grown, but the blossom was spread full out.
I uprooted it rashly, and I felt as if I had been committing an
outrage, so I planted it again. It will have but a stormy life of
it, but let it live if it can. We found Calvert[1] here. I brought a
handkerchief full of mosses which I placed on the chimneypiece
when C. was gone. He dined with us and carried away the
Encyclopaedias. After they were gone I spent some time in
trying to reconcile myself to the change, and in rummaging
out and arranging some other books in their places. One good
thing is this—there is a nice Elbow place for William, and he
may sit for the picture of John Bunyan any day. Mr Simpson
drank tea with us. We payed our rent to Benson. William's head
bad after Mr S. was gone. I petted him on the carpet and began
a letter to Sara.

Monday February 1st. Wm slept badly. I baked pies and bread.
William worked hard at the Pedlar and tired himself. He
walked up with me towards Mr Simpson's. There was a purplish
light upon Mr Olliff's house which made me look to the other
side of the vale when I saw a strange stormy mist coming down
the side of Silver How of a reddish purple colour. It soon came
on a heavy rain. We parted presently. Wm went to Rydale—
I drank tea with Mrs S. The two Mr Simpsons both tipsy. I
came home with Jenny as far as the Swan—a cold night, dry
and windy—Jupiter above the Forest side. Wm pretty well but
he worked a little. In the morning a Box of clothes with Books
came from London.[2] I sate by his bedside, and read in the
Pleasures of Hope[3] to him, which came in the Box. He could
not fall asleep, but I found in the morning that he had slept
better than he expected. No letters.

[1] William Calvert, brother of Raisley Calvert, to whose legacy W. owed his
independence.

[2] The box was sent by their brother Richard and contained some 'cast-off clothes'
of Montagu's for W.'s use. See *E.T.*, p. 342.

[3] By Thomas Campbell, first published 1799.

Tuesday 2nd February. A fine clear morning but sharp and cold. William went into the orchard after breakfast to chop wood. I walked backwards and forwards on the platform. Molly called me down to Charles Lloyd, he brought me flower seeds from his Brother. William not quite well. We walked into Easedale—were turned back in the open field by the sight of a cow. Every horned cow puts me in terror. We walked as far as we could having crossed the foot-bridge, but it was dirty, and we turned back—walked backwards and forwards between Goody Bridge and Butterlip How. William wished to break off composition, and was unable, and so did himself harm. The sun shone but it was cold. After dinner Wm worked at The Pedlar. After tea I read aloud the 11th Book of Paradise Lost. We were much impressed and also melted into tears. The papers came in soon after I had laid aside the Book—a good thing for my William. I worked a little today at putting the Linen into repair that came in the Box. Molly washing.

Wednesday 3rd. A rainy morning. We walked to Rydal for letters, found one from Mrs Cookson and Mary H. It snowed upon the hills. We sate down on the wall at the foot of White Moss. Sate by the fire in the evening. William tired and did not compose. He went to bed soon and could not sleep. I wrote to Mary H., sent off the letter by Fletcher.[1] Wrote also to Coleridge—read Wm to sleep after dinner, and read to him in bed till ½ past one.

Thursday 4th. I was very sick, bad headach and unwell—I lay in bed till 3 o'clock that is I lay down as soon as breakfast was over. It was a terribly wet day. William sate in the house all day. Fletcher's Boy did not come home. I worked at Montagu's shirts. Wm thought a little about the Pedlar. I slept in the sitting room. Read Smollet's life.

Friday 5th. A cold snowy morning. Snow and hail showers. We did not walk. William cut wood a little. I read the story of Snell in Wanly Penson.[2] Sara's parcel came with waistcoat. The Chaucer not only misbound but a leaf or two wanting. I wrote about it to Mary and wrote to Soulby. We received the

---

[1] Fletcher the carrier, who often took their letters to post.

[2] *Wanly Penson, or The Melancholy Man*, a novel, published in 1792, in 3 vols. There were two stories, 'Old Snell' in vol. II and 'Young Snell' in vol. III. The latter is probably the story she read, or perhaps re-read. See *Notes and Queries*, January 1964, p. 16.

waistcoats, shoes and gloves from Sara by the Waggon. William
not well. Sate up late at the pedlar.

Saturday 6th February. William had slept badly. It snowed in
the night, and was, on Saturday, as Molly expressed it, a Cauld
Clash. William went to Rydale for letters, he came home with
two very affecting letters from Coleridge—resolved to try another Climate. I was stopped in my writing, and made ill by the
letters. William a bad headach; he made up a bed on the floor,
but could not sleep—I went to his bed and slept not—better
when I rose. Wrote again after tea and translated 2 or 3 of
Lessing's Fables.

Sunday 7th. A fine clear frosty morning. The Eaves drop with
the heat of the sun all day long. The ground thinly covered
with snow. The Road Black, rocks bluish. Before night the
Island was quite green, the sun had melted all the snow upon
it. Mr Simpson called before William had done shaving—
William had had a bad night and was working at his poem.
We sate by the fire and did not walk, but read the pedlar
thinking it done but lo, though Wm could find fault with no one
part of it—it was uninteresting and must be altered. Poor William.

Monday Morning 8th February 1802. It was very windy and
rained very hard all the morning.[1] William worked at his poem
and I read a little in Lessing and the Grammar. A chaise came
past to fetch Ellis the Carrier who had hurt his head. After
dinner (i.e. we set off at about $\frac{1}{2}$ past 4) we went towards Rydale
for letters. It was a cold '*Cauld Clash*'. The Rain had been so
cold that it hardly melted the snow. We stopped at Park's to get
some straw in William's shoes. The young mother was sitting
by a bright wood fire with her youngest child upon her lap
and the other two sate on each side of the chimney. The light
of the fire made them a beautiful sight, with their innocent
countenances, their rosy cheeks and glossy curling hair. We
sate and talked about poor Ellis, and our journey over the
Hawes.[2] It had been reported that we came over in the night.
Willy told us of 3 men who were once lost in crossing that way
in the night, they had carried a lantern with them—the lantern

---

[1] The words (repeated below) 'but it was so cold that the snow hardly
melted', are erased.

[2] i.e. the Grisedale Pass. She is referring to their adventurous walk on 23
January from Patterdale.

went out at the Tarn and they all perished. Willy had seen their cloaks drying at the public house in Patterdale the day before their funeral. We walked on very wet through the clashy cold roads in bad spirits at the idea of having to go as far as Rydale, but before we had come again to the shore of the Lake, we met our patient, bow-bent Friend with his little wooden box at his Back. 'Where are you going?' said he. 'To Rydale for letters.' 'I have two for you in my Box.' We lifted up the lid and there they lay. Poor Fellow, he straddled and pushed on with all his might but we soon outstripped him far away when we had turned back with our letters. We were very thankful that we had not to go on, for we should have been sadly tired. In thinking of this I could not help comparing lots with him! He goes at that slow pace every morning, and after having wrought a hard day's work returns at night, however weary he may be, takes it all quietly,[1] and though perhaps he neither feels thankfulness, nor pleasure when he eats his supper, and has no luxury to look forward to but falling asleep in bed, yet I daresay he neither murmurs nor thinks it hard. He seems mechanized to labour. We broke the seal of Coleridge's letter, and I had light enough just to see that he was not ill. I put it in my pocket but at the top of the White Moss I took it to my bosom, a safer place for it. The night was wild. There was a strange Mountain lightness when we were at the top of the White Moss. I have often observed it there in the evenings, being between the two valleys. There is more of the sky there than any other place. It has a strange effect sometimes along with the obscurity of evening or night. It seems almost like a peculiar *sort* of light. There was not much wind till we came to John's Grove, then it roared right out of the grove, all the trees were tossing about. C.'s letter somewhat damped us, it spoke with less confidence about France.[2] William wrote to him. The other letter was from Montagu with 8£. William was very unwell, tired when he had written he went to bed, and left me to write to M. H., Montagu and Calvert, and Mrs Coleridge. I had written in his letter to Coleridge. We wrote to Calvert to beg him not to fetch us on Sunday. Wm left me with a *little* peat fire—it grew less.

[1] 'As a thing of course', erased.
[2] Coleridge had suggested a plan for their all going to live in France. See Griggs, vol. II, p. 788.

I wrote on and was starved.[1] At 2 o'clock I went to put my letters under Fletcher's door. I never felt such a cold night. There was a strong wind and it froze very hard. I collected together all the clothes I could find (for I durst not go into the pantry for fear of waking William). At first when I went to bed I seemed to be warm, I suppose because the cold air, which I had just left, no longer touched my body, but I soon found that I was mistaken. I could not sleep from sheer cold. I had baked pies and bread in the morning. Coleridge's letter contained prescriptions. N.B. The moon came out suddenly when we were at John's Grove, and 'a star or two beside'.[2]

Tuesday [*9th*]. William had slept better. He fell to work, and made himself unwell. We did not walk. A funeral came by of a poor woman who had drowned herself, some say because she was hardly treated by her husband, others that he was a very decent respectable man and *she* but an indifferent wife. However this was she had only been married to him last Whitsuntide and had had very indifferent health ever since. She had got up in the night and drowned herself in the pond. She had requested to be buried beside her mother and so she was brought in a hearse. She was followed by several decent-looking men on horseback, her Sister, Thomas Fleming's wife, in a Chaise, and some others with her, and a cart full of women. Molly says folks thinks o' their mothers. Poor Body *she* has been little thought of by any body else. We did a little of Lessing. I attempted a fable, but my head ached my bones were sore with the cold of the day before and I was downright stupid. We went to bed but not till William had tired himself.

Wednesday 10th. A very snowy morning. It cleared up a little however for a while but we did not walk. We sent for our letters by Fletcher and for some writing paper etc. He brought us word there were none. This was strange for I depended upon Mary. While I was writing out the Poem as we hope for a final writing, a letter was brought me by John Dawson's Daughter, the letter written at Eusemere.—I paid Wm Jackson's Bill by John Fisher. Sent off a letter to Montagu by Fletcher. After

[1] North Country dialect for cold.
[2] From *The Ancient Mariner*, l. 265:

> Softly she was going up,
> And a star or two beside—

Molly went we read the first part of the poem and were delighted with it, but Wm afterwards got to some ugly places and went to bed tired out. A wild, moonlight night.

Thursday 11th. A very fine clear sunny frost the ground white with snow—William rose before Molly was ready for him, I rose at a little after nine. William sadly tired and working still at the Pedlar. Miss Simpson called when he was worn out—he escaped and sate in his own room till she went. She was very faint and ill, had had a tooth drawn and had suffered greatly. I walked up with her past Goan's.[1] The sun was very warm till we got past Lewthwaite's—then it had little power, and had not melted the roads. As I came back again I felt the vale like a different Climate. The vale was bright and beautiful. Molly had linen hung out. We had pork to dinner sent us by Mrs Simpson. William still poorly. We made up a good fire after dinner, and William brought his Mattrass out, and lay down on the floor. I read to him the life of Ben Johnson and some short Poems of his which were too *interesting* for him, and would not let him go to sleep. I had begun with Fletcher, but he was too *dull* for me. Fuller says in his life of Johnson, (speaking of his plays) 'If his latter be not so spriteful and vigorous as his first pieces all that are old, and all who desire to be old, should excuse him therein'. He says he '*beheld*' wit combats between Shakespeare and Johnson, and compares Shakespeare to an English man of war, Jonson to a Spanish great Galleon. There is one affecting line in Jonson's epitaph on his first Daughter

> Here lies to each her Parents ruth,
> *Mary the Daughter of their youth*
> At six months end she parted hence
> In safety of her Innocence.

I have been writing this journal while Wm has had a nice little sleep. Once he was waked by Charles Lloyd who had come to see about Lodgings for his children in the hooping cough. It is now 7 o'clock—I have a nice coal fire—Wm is still on his bed. 2 beggars today. I continued to read to him. We were much delighted with the Poem of Penshurst. William rose better. I was chearful and happy but he got to work again and went to bed unwell.

[1] Gawain Mackereth, who lived near the Swan Inn.

Friday 12th. A very fine bright, clear, hard frost. William working again. I recopied the Pedlar, but poor William all the time at work. Molly tells me 'What! little Sally's gone to visit at Mr Simpson's. They say she's very smart she's got on a new bed-gown that her Cousin gave her. It's a very bonny one they tell me, but I've not seen it. Sally and me's in Luck.' In the afternoon a poor woman came, *she said* to beg some rags for her husband's leg which had been wounded by a slate from the Roof in the great wind—but she has been used to go a-begging, for she has often come here. Her father lived to the age of 105. She is a woman of strong bones with a complexion that has been beautiful, and remained very fresh last year, but now she looks broken, and her little Boy, a pretty little fellow, and whom I have loved for the sake of Basil,[1] looks thin and pale. I observed this to her. Aye says she we have all been ill. Our house was unroofed in the storm nearly and *so* we lived in it for more than a week. The Child wears a ragged drab coat and a fur cap, poor little fellow, I think he seems scarcely at all grown since the first time I saw him. William was with me—we met him in a lane going to Skelwith Bridge. He looked very pretty. He was walking lazily in the deep narrow lane, overshadowed with the hedge-rows, his meal poke hung over his shoulder. He said he was going 'a laiting'.[2] He now wears the same coat he had on at that time. Poor creatures! When the woman was gone, I could not help thinking that we are not half thankful enough that we are placed in that condition of life in which we are. We do not so often bless god for this as we wish for this 50£ that 100£ etc. etc. We have not, however to reproach our-selves with ever breathing a murmur. This woman's was but a *common* case.—The snow still lies upon the ground. Just at the closing in of the Day I heard a cart pass the door, and at the same time the dismal sound of a crying Infant. I went to the window and had light enough to see that a man was driving a cart which seemed not to be very full, and that a woman with an infant in her arms was following close behind and a dog close to her. It was a wild and melancholy sight.—William rubbed his Table after candles were lighted, and we sate a long time with the windows unclosed. I almost finished writing The Pedlar,

---

[1] Basil Montagu, son of W.'s friend; see p. 24.
[2] i.e. seeking food. See under 16 June 1800.

but poor William wore himself and me out with labour. We had an affecting conversation. Went to bed at 12 o'clock.

Saturday 13th. It snowed a little this morning—still at work at the Pedlar, altering and refitting. We did not walk though it was a very fine day. We received a present of Eggs and milk from Janet Dockeray, and just before she went the little Boy from the Hill brought us a letter from Sara H., and one from the Frenchman[1] in London. I wrote to Sara after tea and Wm took out his old newspapers, and the new ones came in soon after. We sate, after I had finished the letter, talking and William read parts of his Recluse aloud to me. We did not drink tea till ½ past 7.

Sunday 14th February. A fine morning. The sun shines but it has been a hard frost in the night. There are some little snowdrops that are afraid to pop their white heads quite out, and a few blossoms of Hepatica that are half starved. William left me at work altering some passages of the Pedlar, and went into the orchard. The fine day pushed him on to resolve and as soon as I had read a letter to him which I had just received from Mrs Clarkson he said he would go to Penrith,[2] so Molly was dispatched for the horse. I worked hard, got the backs pasted the writing finished, and all quite trim. I wrote to Mrs Clarkson and put up some letters for Mary H., and off he went in his blue Spenser and a pair of *new* pantaloons fresh from London. He turned back when he had got as far as Frank's to ask if he had his letters safe, then for some apples—then fairly off. We had money to borrow for him.—It was a pleasant afternoon. I ate a little bit of cold mutton without laying cloth and then sate over the fire reading Ben Jonson's Penshurst, and other things. Before sunset I put on my shawl and walked out. The snow-covered mountains were spotted with rich sunlight, a palish buffish colour. The roads were very dirty, for though it was a keen frost the sun had melted the snow and water upon them. I stood at Sara's gate[3] and when I came in view of Rydale I cast a long look upon the mountains beyond. They were very white but I concluded that Wm would have a very safe passage over Kirkstone, and I was quite easy about him.

---

[1] Possibly a connection of Annette Vallon's.
[2] i.e. to see M. H.
[3] The Wishing Gate. See above p. 59.

III. *14 February 1802 to 2 May 1802*[1]

Sunday 14th February 1802. See the morning former book. After dinner a little before sunset I walked out.[2] About 20 yards above glowworm Rock I met a Carman, a Highlander I suppose, with 4 carts, the first 3 belonging to himself, the last evidently to a man and his family who had joined company with him and who I guessed to be Potters. The carman was cheering his horses and talking to a little lass about 10 years of age who seemed to make him her companion. She ran to the Wall and took up a large stone to support the wheel of one of his carts and ran on before with it in her arms to be ready for him. She was a beautiful creature and there was something uncommonly impressive in the lightness and joyousness of her manner. Her business seemed to be all pleasure—pleasure in her own motions—and the man looked at her as if he too was pleased and spoke to her in the same tone in which he[2] spoke to his horses. There was a wildness in her whole figure, not the wildness of a Mountain lass but a Road lass, a traveller from her Birth, who had wanted neither food nor clothes. Her Mother followed the last cart with a lovely child, perhaps about a year old, at her Back and a good-looking girl about 15 years old walked beside her. All the children were like the mother. She had a very fresh complexion, but she was blown with fagging up the hill with the steepness of the hill and the Bairn that she carried. Her husband was helping the horse to drag the cart up by pushing it with his Shoulder. I got tea when I reached home and read German till about 9 o'clock. Then Molly went away and I wrote to Coleridge. Went to bed at about 12 o'clock. I slept in Wm's bed, and I slept badly, for my thoughts were full of William.

Monday 15th February 1802. I was starching small linen all the morning. It snowed a good deal and was terribly cold. After dinner it was fair, but I was obliged to run all the way to

[1] The third volume of D. W.'s journal is bound in cloth with a brown paper cover. It also contains the rest of the 1798 Hamburgh Journal. C. W. noted on the flyleaf: 'This is continuation of book marked 1798.'

[2] D. W. had not had room in the former volume to finish the entry for 14 February, or the description of the child. She had written from 'About 20 yards...' to 'tone in which he' in the second notebook, but crossed it out and started again in the new book.

the foot of the White Moss to get the least bit of warmth into me. I found a letter from C.—he was much better—this was very satisfactory but his letter was not an answer to William's which I expected. A letter from Annette. I got tea when I reached home and then set on to reading German. I wrote part of a letter to Coleridge, went late to bed and slept badly.

Tuesday 16th. A fine morning but I had persuaded myself not to expect William, I believe because I was afraid of being disappointed. I ironed all day. He came in just at Tea time, had only seen Mary H. for a couple of hours between Emont Bridge and Hartshorn tree. Mrs C.[1] better. He had had a difficult journey over Kirkstone, and came home by Threlkeld —his mouth and breath were very cold when he kissed me. We spent a sweet evening. He was better—had altered the pedlar. We went to bed pretty soon and we slept better than we expected and had no bad dreams. Mr Graham[2] said he wished Wm had been with him the other day—he was riding in a post chaise and he heard a strange cry that he could not understand, the sound continued and he called to the chaise driver to stop. It was a little girl that was crying as if her heart would burst. She had got up behind the chaise and her cloak had been caught by the wheel and was jammed in and it hung there. She was crying after it. Poor thing. Mr Graham took her into the chaise and the cloak was released from the wheel but the child's misery did not cease for her cloak was torn to rags; it had been a miserable cloak before, but she had no other and it was the greatest sorrow that could befal her. Her name was Alice Fell.[3] She had no parents, and belonged to the next Town. At the next Town Mr G. left money with some respectable people in the town to buy her a new cloak.

Wednesday 17th. A miserable clashy snowy morning.[4] We did not walk. But the old man from the Hill brought us a short letter from Mary H. I copied the 2nd part of Peter Bell. William pretty well.

---

[1] i.e. Mrs. Clarkson.

[2] Robert Graham of Glasgow, a solicitor; his brother James Graham, a poet, author of *The Sabbath* and *Birds of Scotland*, visited Grasmere in 1806.

[3] W. W.'s poem 'Alice Fell' was written in celebration of this incident. See p. 190, and also p. 145.

[4] Erased: 'We walked to Rydale after dinner when it cleared up a little.' (Repeated under Saturday 20th.)

Thursday 18th. A foggy morning but it cleared up in the afternoon and Wm went to Mrs Simpson's to Tea. I went with him to Goan Mackereth's. Roads very dirty. I copied third part of Peter Bell in his absence and began a letter to Coleridge. Wm came in with a letter from Coleridge that came by Keswick. We talked together till 11 o'clock. Then Wm got to work and was the worse for it. Hard frost.

Friday 19th. Hard frost this morning—but it soon snowed, then thawed. A miserable afternoon. Williamson came and cut William's hair—I wrote to C. He carried the letter to Ambleside. Afterwards I wrote to Mary and Sara, tired and went early to bed.

Saturday 20th. A very rainy morning, but it cleared up a little. We walked to Rydale. There were no letters. The Roads were very dirty. We met little Dawson on horseback and desired him to bring us paper from Mrs Jameson's. After Tea I wrote the first part of Peter Bell. William better.

Sunday 21st. A very wet morning. I wrote the 2nd prologue to Peter Bell, then went to Mrs Olliff's. After dinner I wrote the 1st Prologue. William walked to the Tailor's[1] while I was at Mrs O.'s it rained all the time. Snowdrops quite out, but cold and winterly—yet for all this a thrush that lives in our orchard has shouted and sung its merriest all day long.[2] In the evening I wrote to Mrs Clarkson, and my Br Richard. Wm went to bed exhausted.

Monday 22nd. A wet morning. I lay down as soon as breakfast was over very unwell. I slept. Wm brought me 4 letters to bed—from Annette and Caroline, Mary and Sara, and Coleridge.[3] C. had had another attack in his Bowels—otherwise mending—M. and S. both well. M. reached Middleham[4] the Monday night before at 12 o'clock. Tom there.—In the evening we walked to the top of the hill, then to the bridge, we hung over the wall, and looked at the deep stream below; it came

[1] Lenty Fleming, the tailor, lived in the house under Loughrigg now known as The Stepping Stones. (G. G. W.)

[2] In the fold of a manuscript of *Peter Bell* D. W. has written: 'Grasmere Sunday, ½ past five o'clock by the gold watch now hanging above the fire—a rainy coldish day—snow on the ground—but there is a thrush singing. February 21st, 1802.'

[3] See note under 24 February.

[4] i.e. Bishop Middleham, Co. Durham, where M. H.'s brother George was farming.

with a full steady yet very rapid flow down to the lake. The sykes made a sweet sound everywhere, and looked very interesting in the twilight. That little one above Mr Olliff's house was very impressive—a ghostly white serpent line—it made a sound most distinctly heard of itself. The mountains were black and steep—the tops of some of them having yet snow visible, but it rained so hard last night that much of it has been washed away. After tea I was just going to write to Coleridge when Mr Simpson came in. Wm began to read Peter Bell to him so I carried my writing to the kitchen fire. Wm called me up stairs to read the 3rd part. Mr S. had brought his first engraving to let us see—he supped with us. William was tired with reading and talking and went to bed in bad spirits.

Tuesday 23rd. A misty rainy morning—the lake calm. I baked bread and pies. Before dinner worked a little at Wm's waistcoat—after dinner read German Grammar. Before tea we walked into Easedale. We turned aside in the Parson's field, a pretty field with 3 pretty prospects. Then we went to the first large field, but such a cold wind met us that we turn'd again. The wind seemed warm when we came out of our own door. That dear thrush was singing upon the topmost of the smooth branches of the Ash tree at the top of the orchard. How long it had been perched on that same tree I cannot tell but we had heard its dear voice in the orchard the day through, along with a chearful undersong[1] made by our winter friends the Robins. We came home by Goan's. I picked up a few mosses by the Roadside, which I left at home. We then went to John's Grove. There we sate a little while looking at the fading landscape. The lake, though the objects on the shore were fading, seemed brighter than when it is perfect day, and the Island pushed itself upwards, distinct and large—all the shores marked. There was a sweet sea-like sound in the trees above our heads. We walked backwards and forwards some time for dear John's sake, then walked to look at Rydale. Darkish when we reached home and we got tea immediately with candles. William now reading in Bishop Hall—I going to read German. We have a nice singing fire, with one piece of wood. Fletcher's carts are arrived but no papers from Mrs Coleridge.

[1] Cf. the last line of 'Personal Talk', 1: 'Or kettle whispering its faint undersong.'

Wednesday 24th.[1] A rainy day. We were busy all day unripping William's Coats for the tailor. William wrote to
Annette, to Coleridge and the Frenchman—I received a letter
from Mrs. Clarkson, a very kind affecting letter which I
answered telling her I would go to Eusemere when William
went to Keswick—I wrote a little bit to Coleridge. We sent
off these letters by Fletcher. It was a tremendous night of wind
and rain. Poor Coleridge! A sad night for a traveller such as
he.[2] God be praised he was in safe quarters. Wm went out and
put the letters under the door—he never felt a colder night.

Thursday 25th.—A fine mild grey beautiful morning. The
tailor here. I worked at unripping. William wrote to Montagu
in the morning. After dinnèr he went to Lloyd's—I accompanied him to the gate in the corner or turning of the vale
close to the river side beyond Lenty Fleming's Cottage. It was
coldish and like for frost—a clear evening. I reached home just
before dark, brought some mosses and ivy, then got tea, and
fell to work at German. I read a good deal of Lessing's Essay.
William came home between nine and 10 o'clock. We sate
nicely together by the fire till bedtime. William not very much
tired. I was bad in my Bowels.[3]

Friday 26th. A grey morning till 10 o'clock. Then the sun
shone beautifully. Mrs Lloyd's children and Mrs Luff came in a
chaise, were here at 11 o'clock then went to Mrs Olliff. Wm
and I accompanied them to the gate. I prepared dinner, sought
out Peter Bell, gave Wm some cold meat, and then we went to
walk. We walked first to Butterlip How, where we sate and
overlooked the vale, no sign of spring but the Red tints of the
upper twigs of the woods and single trees. Sate in the sun. Met
Charles Lloyd near the Bridge. Got dinner. I lay down unwell
—got up to tea. Mr and Mrs Luff walked home. The Lloyds

---

[1] D. W. here repeated, and then crossed out, the first sentences of the entry of
Monday 22 February. The crossed-out version reads: 'A rainy morning. I had slept
badly and was unwell in the morning—I went to bed directly after breakfast and
lay till William returned from Rydale very wet with letters he brought a short one
from C. a very long one from Mary.' She then started again, 'A rainy day'.

[2] Coleridge was in London, apparently not intending to return northwards for
a fortnight. See his letters to his wife and Thomas Poole, Griggs, vol. II, pp. 785,
786, dated 19 February 1802. In fact he arrived at Gallow Hill on 2 March, and
stayed there with the Hutchinsons until 13 March, arriving at Keswick 15 March.
He evidently did not inform the Wordsworths of this excursion.

[3] Erased.

stayed till 8 o'clock. We always get on better with conversation at home than elsewhere—discussion about Mrs King and
Mrs Olliff.—The Chaise driver brought us a letter from M. H.—
a short one from C. We were perplexed about Sara's coming. I
wrote to Mary. Wm closed his letter to Montagu, and wrote to
Calvert and to Mrs Coleridge.[1] Birds sang divinely today.
Bowels and head bad. William better.

Saturday 27th.[2] We walked in the afternoon towards Rydale
returning to tea. Mr Barth Simpson called after supper a little
tipsy. Fletcher said he had had no papers. Wm was not very
well. I sate in the orchard after dinner—we walked in the
evening towards Rydale.

Sunday 28th February. Wm very ill, employed with the pedlar.
We got papers in the morning. William shaved himself. I was
obliged to go to bed after dinner—rose better—Wrote to Sara
H. and Mrs Clarkson—no walk. Disaster pedlar.[3]

Monday [1st March]. A fine pleasant day. We walked to
Rydale. I went on before for the letters, brought 2 from M.
and S. H. We climbed over the wall and read them under the
shelter of a mossy rock. We met Mrs Lloyd in going—Mrs
Olliff's child ill. The catkins are beautiful in the hedges. The
ivy is very green. Robert Newton's Paddock is greenish—that
is all we see of spring. Finished and sent off the Letter to Sara
and wrote to Mary. Wrote again to Sara, and William wrote
to Coleridge. Mrs Lloyd called when I was in bed.

Tuesday [2nd]. A fine grey morning. I was baking bread and
pies. After dinner I read german and a little before dinner. Wm
also read. We walked on Butterlip How under the wind. It
rained all the while but we had a pleasant walk. The mountains
of Easedale, black or covered with snow at the tops, gave a
peculiar softness to the valley. The clouds hid the tops of
some of them. The valley was populous and enlivened with
streams. Mrs Lloyd drove past without calling.

Wednesday [3rd]. I was so unlucky as to propose to rewrite

---

[1] He wrote to Calvert for the loan of a horse and to Mrs. Coleridge to warn her
that he was coming. See entries for 4 March below.

[2] After '27th' a few words are erased: 'I was again obliged to go to bed in the
afternoon. We did not walk today.' They really belong to the next day, 28th.

[3] The character of the disaster is not known, but possibly some of the MSS. on
which W. was working had become almost illegible with his corrections. See
under 3 March.

The Pedlar. Wm got to work and was worn to death. We did not walk. I wrote in the afternoon.

Thursday [*4th*]. Before we had quite finished Breakfast Calvert's man brought the horses for Wm.[1] We had a deal to do to shave—pens to make—poems to put in order for writing, to settle the dress pack up etc. The man came .before the pens were made and he was obliged to leave me with only two. Since he has left me (at ½ past 11) it is now 2 I have been putting the Drawers into order, laid by his clothes which we had thrown here and there and everywhere, filed two months' newspapers and got my dinner 2 boiled eggs and 2 apple tarts.[2] I have set Molly on to clear the garden a little, and I myself have helped. I transplanted some snowdrops—The Bees are busy—Wm has a nice bright day. It was hard frost in the night. The Robins are singing sweetly. Now for my walk. I *will* be busy, I *will* look well and be well when he comes back to me. O the Darling! Here is one of his bitten apples! I can hardly find in my heart to throw it into the fire. I must wash myself, then off—I walked round the two Lakes crossed the stepping stones at Rydale Foot. Sate down where we always sit. I was full of thoughts about my darling. Blessings on him. I came home at the foot of our own hill under Loughrigg. They are making sad ravages in the woods. Benson's Wood is going and the wood above the River. The wind has blown down a [?small] fir tree on the Rock that terminates John's path—I suppose the wind of Wednesday night. I read German after my return till tea time. After tea I worked and read the LB, enchanted with the Idiot Boy. Wrote to Wm then went to Bed. It snowed when I went to Bed.

Friday [*5th*]. First walked in the garden and orchard. A frosty sunny morning. After dinner I gathered mosses in Easedale. I saw before me sitting in the open field upon his Sack of Rags the old Ragman that I know. His coat is of scarlet in a thousand patches. His Breeches knees were untied—the breeches have been given him by some one. He has a round hat pretty good, small crowned but large rimmed. When I came

[1] This expedition was to Keswick (see under 8 March). Coleridge was not yet at Keswick (see above under 24 February), but Wordsworth clearly expected he would be there.

[2] Here about six words are erased. They appear to be arrangements about 'next washing day'.

to him he said Is there a brigg yonder that'll carry me ow'r t'watter? He seemed half stupid. When I came home Molly had shook the carpet and cleaned every thing upstairs. When I see her so happy in her work and exulting in her own importance I often think of that affecting expression which she made use of to me one evening lately. Talking of her good luck in being in this house, 'Aye Mistress them 'at's Low laid would have been a proud creature could they but have [seen] where I is now fra what they thought mud be my Doom.'—I was tired when I reached home. I sent Molly Ashburner to Rydale. No letters! I was sadly mortified. I expected one fully from Coleridge. Wrote to William. Read the L B, got into sad thoughts, tried at German but could not go on—Read LB.—Blessings on that Brother of mine! Beautiful new moon over Silver How.

Saturday Morning [*6th*]. I awoke with a bad head ache and partly on that account partly for ease I lay in bed till one o'clock. At one I pulled off my nightcap—$\frac{1}{2}$ past one sate down to breakfast. A very cold sunshiny frost. I wrote the Pedlar, and finished it before I went to Mr Simpson's to drink tea. Miss S. at Keswick but she came home. Mrs Jameson came in. I stayed supper. Fletcher's carts went past and I let them go with William's letter. Mr B. S. came nearly home with me. I found letters from Wm, Mary and Coleridge. I wrote to C. Sate up late and could not fall asleep when I went to bed.

Sunday Morning [*7th*]. A very fine clear frost. I stitched up the Pedlar—wrote out Ruth—read it with the alterations. Then wrote Mary H. Read a little German—got my dinner. Mrs Lloyd called at the door; and in came William. I did not expect him till tomorrow. How glad I was. After we had talked about an hour I gave him his dinner a Beef Steak, we sate talking and happy. Mr and Miss Simpson came in at Tea time. William came home very well—he had been a little fatigued with reading his poems. He brought two new stanzas of Ruth.[1] We went to bed pretty soon and slept well. A mild grey evening.

Monday Morning [*8th*]. A soft Rain and mist. We walked to Rydale for letters. The Vale looked very beautiful, in excessive simplicity yet at the same time in uncommon obscurity. The Church stood alone no mountains behind. The meadows looked

---

[1] These were ll. 163–8 and 175–80; see *P.W.*, vol. II, p. 232.

calm and rich bordering on the still lake; nothing else to be seen but Lake and Island—Found a very affecting letter from Montague also one from Mary—We read Montagu's in walking on. Sate down to read Mary's. I came home with a bad head-ach and lay down. I slept but rose little better. I have got tea and am now much relieved. On friday evening the moon hung over the Northern side of the highest point of Silver How, like a gold ring snapped in two and shaven off at the ends it was so narrow. Within this Ring lay the circle of the round moon, as *distinctly* to be seen as ever the enlightened moon is. William had observed the same appearance at Keswick perhaps at the very same moment hanging over the Newlands fells.[1] Sent off a letter to Mary H. also to Coleridge and Sara, and rewrote in the Evening the alterations of Ruth which we sent off at the same time.[2]

Tuesday Morning [9th]. William was reading in Ben Jonson— he read me a beautiful poem on Love. We then walked. The first part of our walk was melancholy—We went within view of Rydale then we sate in Sara's seat. We walked afterwards into Easedale. It was cold when we returned. We met Sally Newton and her Water Dog. We sate by the fire in the evening and read the Pedlar over. William worked a little and altered it in a few places. I was not very well. Mended stockings.

Wednesday [10th]. A fine mildish morning that is, not frost. Wm read in Ben Jonson in the morning. I read a little German altered [? Sara's] waistcoats. We then walked to Rydale— No letters! They are slashing away in Benson's wood—We walked round by the Church, through Olliff's field when we returned, then home and went up into the orchard. We sate on the Seat, talked a little by the fire, and then got our tea. William has since Tea been talking about publishing the Yorkshire Wolds poem[3] with the Pedlar.

Thursday [11th]. A fine morning. William worked at the poem of the Singing Bird.[4] Just as we were sitting down to dinner we heard Mr Clarkson's voice—I ran down. William followed. He

[1] Here D. W. first wrote and then erased: 'Tuesday a fine pleasant morning. We sate reading' before completing the entry for Monday.

[2] Probably to the printer, for inclusion in the second edition of *Lyrical Ballads* which appeared in the summer. See entry below for 22 June.

[3] *Peter Bell.*

[4] Published as 'The Sailor's Mother'. See p. 192.

was so finely mounted that William was more intent upon the
Horse than the Rider an offence easily forgiven for Mr Clarkson was as proud of it himself as he well could be. We ate our
dinner after Mr Clarkson came. We walked with him round
by the White Bridge after dinner. The vale in mist, rather the
mountains, big with the rain soft and beautiful. Mr C. was
sleepy and went soon to bed.

Friday [12th]. A very fine morning. We went to see Mr
Clarkson off. Then we went up towards Easedale but a shower
drove us back. The sun shone while it rained, and the stones of
the walls and the pebbles on the road glittered like silver.
When William was at Keswick I saw Jane Ashburner driving
the cow along the high road from the well where she had been
watering it. She had a stick in her hand and came tripping
along in the Jig step, as if she were dancing—Her presence was
bold and graceful, her cheeks flushed with health and her
countenance was free and gay. William finished his poem of
the singing bird. In the meantime I read the remainder of
Lessing. In the Evening after tea William wrote Alice Fell[1]—
he went to bed tired with a wakeful mind and a weary Body.
A very sharp clear night.

Saturday Morning [13th]. It was as cold as ever it has been all
winter very hard frost. I baked pies Bread, and seed-cake for
Mr Simpson. William finished Alice Fell, and then he wrote the
Poem of the Beggar woman[2] taken from a Woman whom I
had seen in May—(now nearly 2 years ago) when John and
he were at Gallow Hill. I sate with him at Intervals all the
morning, took down his stanzas etc. After dinner we walked to
Rydale, for letters—it was terribly cold we had 2 or 3 brisk
hail showers. The hail stones looked clean and pretty upon the
dry clean Road. Little Peggy Simpson[3] was standing at the
door catching the Hail-stones in her hand. She grows very like
her Mother. When she is sixteen years old I daresay, that to her
Grandmother's eye she will seem as like to what her Mother
was as any rose in her garden is like the Rose that grew there
years before.[4] No letters at Rydale. We drank tea as soon as

[1] See p. 190.
[2] See p. 176, and the entry for 10 June 1800 above. The poem was ultimately
named 'Beggars'.
[3] This child became in 1817 the wife of De Quincey.
[4] Two lines are erased here; they cannot be read.

we reached home. After tea I read to William that account of the little Boys belonging to the tall woman[1] and an unlucky thing it was for he could not escape from those very words, and so he could not write the poem. He left it unfinished and went tired to Bed. In our walk from Rydale he had got warmed with the subject and had half cast the Poem.

Sunday Morning [*14th*]. William had slept badly—he got up at 9 o'clock, but before he rose he had finished the Beggar Boys—and while we were at Breakfast that is (for I had breakfasted) he, with his Basin of Broth before him untouched and a little plate of Bread and butter he wrote the Poem to a Butterfly![2] He ate not a morsel, nor put on his stockings but sate with his shirt neck unbuttoned, and his waistcoat open while he did it. The thought first came upon him as we were talking about the pleasure we both always feel at the sight of a Butterfly. I told him that I used to chase them a little but that I was afraid of brushing the dust off their wings, and did not catch them— He told me how they used to kill all the white ones when he went to school because they were frenchmen. Mr Simpson came in just as he was finishing the Poem. After he was gone I wrote it down and the other poems and I read them all over to him. We then called at Mr Olliff's. Mr O. walked with us to within sight of Rydale—the sun shone very pleasantly, yet it was extremely cold. We dined and then Wm went to bed. I lay upon the fur gown before the fire but I could not sleep—I lay there a long time—it is now half past 5 I am going to write letters. I began to write to Mrs Rawson—William rose without having slept we sate comfortably by the fire till he began to try to alter the butterfly, and tired himself—he went to bed tired.

Monday Morning [*15th*]. We sate reading the poems and I read a little German. Mr Luff came in at one o'clock. He had a long talk with William—he went to Mr Olliff's after dinner and returned to us to tea. During his absence a sailor who was travelling from Liverpool to Whitehaven called he was faint and pale when he knocked at the door, a young Man very well dressed. We sate by the kitchen fire talking with him for 2 hours—he told us [? most] interesting stories of his life. His

---

[1] i.e. the beggar boys of the 10 June 1800 entry.
[2] See p. 193.

name was Isaac Chapel—he had been at sea since he was 15 years old. He was by trade a sail-maker. His last voyage was to the Coast of Guinea. He had been on board a slave ship the Captain's name Maxwell where one man had been killed a Boy put to lodge with the pigs and was half eaten, one Boy set to watch in the hot sun till he dropped down dead. He had been cast away in North America and had travelled 30 days among the Indians where he had been well treated—He had twice swum from a King's ship in the night and escaped, he said he would rather be in hell than be pressed. He was now going to wait in England to appear against Captain Maxwell. 'O he's a Rascal, Sir, he ought to be put in the papers!' The poor man had not been in bed since[1] Friday Night. He left Liverpool at 2 o'clock on Saturday morning. He had called at a farm house to beg victuals and had been refused. The woman said she would give him nothing. 'Won't you? Then I can't help it.' He was excessively like my Brother John. A letter was brought us at tea time by John Dawson from M. H. I wrote to her, to Sara about Mr Olliff's gig, and to Longman and Rees[2]—I wrote to Mrs Clarkson by Mr Luff.

Tuesday [*16th*]. A very fine morning. Mrs Luff called. William went up into the orchard while she was here and wrote a part of The Emigrant Mother. After dinner I read him to sleep—I read Spenser while he leaned upon my shoulder. We walked to look at Rydale. Then we walked towards Goan's. The moon was a good height above the mountains. She seemed far and distant in the sky there were two stars beside her, that twinkled in and out, and seemed almost like butterflies[3] in motion and lightness. They looked to be far nearer to us than the Moon.

Wednesday [*17th*]. William went up into the orchard and finished the Poem. Mrs Luff and Mrs Olliff called I went with Mrs O. to the top of the White Moss—Mr O. met us and I went to their house he offered me manure for the garden. I went and sate with W. and walked backwards and forwards in the orchard till dinner time—he read me his poem. I broiled Beefsteaks. After dinner we made a pillow of my shoulder, I

---

[1] Here the words '12 o'clock' are erased.
[2] Publishers of *Lyrical Ballads*.
[3] Two words erased: 'or skylarks'.

read to him and my Beloved slept—I afterwards got him the pillows and he was lying with his head on the table when Miss Simpson came in. She stayed tea. I went with her to Rydale. No letters! A sweet Evening as it had been a sweet day, a grey evening, and I walked quietly along the side of Rydale Lake with quiet thoughts—the hills and the lake were still—the Owls had not begun to hoot, and the little Birds had given over singing. I looked before me and I saw a red light upon Silver How as if coming out of the vale below,

> 'There was a light of most strange birth
> A Light that came out of the earth
> And spread along the dark hill-side.' [1]

Thus I was going on when I saw the shape of my Beloved in the Road at a little distance—we turned back to see the light but it was fading—almost gone. The owls hooted when we sate on the Wall at the foot of White Moss. The sky broke more and more and we saw the moon now and then. John Green passed us with his cart—we sate on. When we came in sight of our own dear Grasmere, the Vale looked fair and quiet in the moonshine, [2] the Church was there and all the cottages. There were high slow-travelling clouds in the sky that threw large masses of Shade upon some of the Mountains. We walked backwards and forwards between home and Oliffs till I was tired. William kindled and began to write the poem. [3] We carried cloaks into the orchard and sate a while there, I left him and he nearly finished the poem. I was tired to death and went to bed before him—he came down to me and read the Poem to me in bed.—A sailor begged here today going to Glasgow he spoke chearfully in a sweet tone.

Thursday [*18th*]. A very fine morning. The sun shone but it was far colder than yesterday. I felt myself weak, and William charged me not to go to Mrs Lloyd's. I seemed indeed, to myself unfit for it but when he was gone [4] I thought I would get

---

[1] Might these be lost lines from *Peter Bell*, which D. W. was copying about this time? (H. D.)

[2] D. W. wrote first, 'quiet and fair in the moonlight', then erased it.

[3] D. W. does not say what poem this was, but it was probably 'The Emigrant Mother'. (See p. 193.) The first sentence of the day's entry seems to fit better here.

[4] To Keswick to see Coleridge who had just arrived there and came to Grasmere next day, with W. See under 19 March.

the visit over if I could—So I ate a Beef-steak thinking it would strengthen me so it did, and I went off. I had a very pleasant walk. Rydale vale was full of life and motion. The wind blew briskly and the lake was covered all over with Bright silver waves that were there each the twinkling of an eye, then others rose up and took their place as fast as they went away.[1] The Rocks glittered in the sunshine, the crows and the ravens were busy, and the thrushes and little Birds sang. I went through the fields, and sate ½ an hour afraid to pass a Cow. The Cow looked at me and I looked at the Cow and whenever I stirred the Cow gave over eating. I was not very much tired when I reached Lloyds, I walked in the garden. Charles is all for agriculture. Mrs L. in her kindest way. A parcel came in from Birmingham, with Lamb's play for us and for C. They came with me as far as Rydale. As we came along Ambleside vale in the twilight— it was a grave evening—there was something in the air that compelled me to serious thought. The hills were large, closed in by the sky. It was nearly dark when I parted from the Lloyds that is, night was come on and the moon was overcast. But as I climbed Moss[2] the moon came out from behind a mountain mass of Black clouds—O the unutterable darkness of the sky and the earth below the moon! and the glorious bright-ness of the moon itself! There was a vivid sparkling streak of light at this end of Rydale water but the rest was very dark and Loughrigg fell and Silver How were white and bright as if they were covered with hoar frost. The moon retired again and appeared and disappeared several times before I reached home. Once there was no moonlight to be seen but upon the Island house and the promontory of the Island where it stands, 'That needs must be a holy place'[3] etc. etc. I had many very exquisite feelings and when I saw this lowly Building in the waters among the Dark and lofty hills, with that bright soft light upon it, it made me more than half a poet. I was tired when I reached home. I could not sit down to reading and tried to write verses but alas! I gave up expecting William and went soon to bed. Fletcher's carts came home late.

Friday [19th]. A very rainy morning. I went up into the lane

---

[1] D. W. first wrote, 'as the former disappeared'.
[2] i.e. White Moss Common.
[3] This line is untraced. It could perhaps be from an early version of *Kubla Khan*.

to collect a few green mosses to make the chimney gay against my darling's return. Poor C! I did not wish for, or expect him it rained so. Mr Luff came in before my dinner. We had a long talk. He left me before 4 o'clock, and about ½ an hour after Coleridge came in. His eyes were a little swollen with the wind. I was much affected with the sight of him—he seemed half stupefied. William came in soon after. Coleridge went to bed late, and Wm and I sate up till 4 o'clock. A letter from Sara sent by Mary. They disputed about Ben Jonson. My spirits were agitated very much.[1]

Saturday [*20th*]. A tolerably fine morning after 11 o'clock but when I awoke the whole vale was covered with snow. William and Coleridge walked to Borwick's. I followed but did not find them—came home and they were here—We had a little talk about going abroad. We sate pleasantly enough. After tea Wm read the Pedlar. After supper we talked about various things—christening the children etc. etc. Went to bed at 12 o'clock.

Sunday [*21st*]. A showery day. Coleridge and William lay long in bed. We sent up to G. Mackareth's for the horse to go to Keswick but we could not have it. Went with C. to Borwick's where he left us. William was very unwell this evening. We had a sweet and tender conversation. I wrote to Mary and Sara.

Monday [*22nd*]. A rainy day. William very poorly. Mr Luff came in after dinner and brought us 2 letters from Sara H. and one from poor Annette. I read Sara's letters while he was here. I finished my letters to M. and S. and wrote to my Br Richard. We talked a good deal about C. and other interesting things. We resolved to see Annette, and that Wm should go to Mary.[2] We wrote to Coleridge not to expect us till Thursday or Friday.

Tuesday [*23rd*]. A mild morning. William worked at the Cuckow poem.[3] I sewed beside him. After dinner he slept I

---

[1] D. W.'s agitation was probably due to the sad state of Coleridge's domestic affairs and also perhaps to the realization that he was taking opium. This may be the meaning of 'he seemed half stupefied'.

[2] The visit to Calais to see Annette took place in August. W. went to see M. H. at Bishop Middleham on 7 April, doubtless to consult her about this visit. See below, p. 108.

[3] 'To the Cuckoo', p. 196.

read German, and at the closing in of day went to sit in the orchard. He came to me, and walked backwards and forwards. We talked about C. Wm repeated the poem to me. I left him there and in 20 minutes he came in, rather tired with attempting to write. He is now reading Ben Jonson I am going to read German it is about 10 o'clock, a quiet night. The fire flutters and the watch ticks I hear nothing else save the Breathing of my Beloved and he now and then pushes his book forward and turns over a leaf. Fletcher is not come home. No letter from C.

Wednesday [*24th*]. We walked to Rydale for letters. It was a beautiful spring morning—warm and quiet with mists. We found a letter from M. H. I made a vow that we would not leave this country for G. Hill[1] Sara and Tom not being going to the Wolds. I wrote to Mary in the evening. I went to bed after dinner. William walked out and wrote Peggy Ashburner.[2] I rose better. Wm altered the Butterfly as we came from Rydale.

Thursday [*25th*]. We did not walk though it was a fine day. Mr Simpson drank tea with us. No letter from Coleridge.

Friday [*26th*]. A beautiful morning. William wrote to Annette then worked at the Cuckow. I was ill and in bad spirits—after dinner I sate 2 hours in the orchard. William and I walked together after tea first to the top of White Moss, then to Mr Olliff's. I left Wm and while he was absent wrote out poems. I grew alarmed and went to seek him—I met him at Mr Olliff's. He had been trying without success to alter a passage in Silver How poem[3]—he had written a conclusion just before he went out. While I was getting into bed he wrote the Rainbow.[4]

Saturday [*27th*]. A divine morning. At Breakfast Wm wrote part of an ode.[5] Mr Olliff sent the dung and Wm went to work in the garden. We sate all day in the orchard.

Sunday [*28th*]. We went to Keswick. Arrived wet to skin—a

---

[1] Gallow Hill.

[2] At present away from Grasmere.

[3] The 'Silver How poem' may be identical with 'The Firgrove' ('When to the attractions of the busy world'), mentioned by D. W. on 1 September 1800. Silver How is mentioned in it, though it is not its main subject.

[4] i.e. 'My heart leaps up.' See p. 198.

[5] i.e. 'Ode: Intimations of Immortality', probably the first four stanzas. See p.198.

letter from Mary—C. was not tired with walking to meet us. I lay down after dinner with a bad head ach.

Monday [29th]. A cold day. I went down to Miss Crosthwaite's to unpack the Box. Wm and C. went to Armathwaite—a letter from S. H.—had head ach and lay till after tea. Conversation with Mrs Coleridge.

Tuesday 30th March. We went to Calverts. I was somewhat better though not well.

Wednesday 31st March 1802.[1] Very unwell. We walked to Portinscale lay upon the turf and saw into the Vale of Newlands. Up to Borrowdale and down to Keswick a soft venetian view. I returned better. Calvert and Wilkinsons[2] dined with us. I walked with Mrs W. [to] the Quakers' meeting met Wm and we walked in the field together.

Thursday 1st April.[3] Mrs C., Wm, C. and I went to the How—a pleasant morning. We came home by Portinscale—sate for some time on the hill.

Friday [2nd]. Wm and I sate all the morning in the field I nursed Derwent. Drank tea with the Miss Cockins.

Saturday 3rd. Wm went on to Skiddaw with C. We dined at Calverts, fine day.

Sunday 4th. We drove in the gig to Water End. I walked down to Coleridge's. Mrs C.[4] came to Greta Bank to Tea. Wm walked down with Mrs C. I repeated his verses to them. We sate pleasantly enough after supper.

Monday 5th. We came to Eusemere. Coleridge walked with us to Threlkeld. Reached Eusemere to tea. The schoolmistress at Dacre and her scholars. Mrs C.[5] at work in the garden. She met us.

Tuesday 6th. Mrs C., Wm. and I walked to Water side. Wm and I walked together in the evening towards Dalemain. The moon and stars.

---

[1] D. W. wrote '1st April', then '30th', altering the date finally to '31st March'.

[2] Of Ormathwaite, Keswick. He was the Revd. Joseph Wilkinson, and later became rector of West Wretham, Norfolk. In 1809–10 W. wrote the letter-press for Wilkinson's drawings of the Lake District, and in 1820 published it as *A Description of the Scenery of the Lakes in the North of England*, later known as his 'Guide to the Lakes'. See *E.Y.*, pp. 363, 472.

[3] On the entries from 1st to 4th April, D. W. wrote the dates 2nd to 5th and then corrected them. See *CNB*, vol. III, p. 3304.

[4] i.e. Mrs. Coleridge. Greta Bank was the home of the Calverts.

[5] Mrs. Clarkson.

Wednesday 7th. Wm's birthday. Wm went to Middleham.[1]
I walked 6 miles with him. It rained a little but a fine day.
Broth to supper and went soon to bed.

Thursday 8th. Mrs C. and I walked to Woodside. We slept
after dinner on the sofa—sate up till ½ past 10. Mrs C. tired. I
wrote to M. H. in the morning to Sara in the evening.

Friday 9th. Mrs C. planting. Sent off letters. A windy morning
—rough lake—sun shines very cold—a windy night. Walked
in Dunmallet marked our names on a tree.

Saturday 10th April. Very cold—a stormy night, wrote to
C. A letter from Wm and S. H.

Sunday 11th. Very stormy and cold. I did not walk.

Monday 12th. Had the mantua-maker. The ground covered
with snow. Walked to T. Wilkinson's[2] and sent for letters. The
Woman brought me one from Wm and Mary. It was a sharp
windy night. Thomas Wilkinson came with me to Barton, and
questioned me like a catechizer all the way. Every question was
like the snapping of a little thread about my heart I was so full
of thoughts of my half-read letter and other things. I was
glad when he left me. Then I had time to look at the moon
while I was thinking over my own thoughts. The moon
travelled through the clouds tinging them yellow as she passed
along, with two stars near her, one larger than the other. These
stars grew or diminished as they passed from or went into the
clouds. At this time William as I found the next day was riding
by himself between Middleham and Barnard Castle having
parted from Mary. I read over my letter when I got to the
house. Mr and Mrs C. were playing at cards.

Tuesday 13th April. I had slept ill and was not well and
obliged to go to bed in the afternoon—Mrs C. waked me from
sleep with a letter from Coleridge. After tea I went down to see
the Bank and walked along the Lake side to the field where Mr
Smith thought of building his house. The air was become still
the lake was of a bright slate colour, the hills darkening. The
Bays shot into the low fading shores. Sheep resting all things
quiet. When I returned Jane met me—*William* was come. The
surprize shot through me. He looked well but he was tired and
went soon to bed after a dish of Tea.

[1] Bishop Middleham, Co. Durham, to see M. H. See entry for 22 March.
[2] i.e. at Yanwath, close to Eamont Bridge, about four miles from Eusemere.

Wednesday 14th. William did not rise till dinner time. I walked with Mrs C. I was ill out of spirits—disheartened. Wm and I took a long walk in the Rain.

Thursday 15th. It was a threatening misty morning—but mild. We set off after dinner from Eusemere. Mrs Clarkson went a short way with us but turned back. The wind was furious and we thought we must have returned. We first rested in the large Boat-house, then under a furze Bush opposite Mr Clarkson's. Saw the plough going in the field. The wind seized our breath the Lake was rough. There was a Boat by itself floating in the middle of the Bay below Water Millock. We rested again in the Water Millock Lane. The hawthorns are black and green, the birches here and there greenish but there is yet more of purple to be seen on the Twigs. We got over into a field to avoid some cows—people working, a few primroses by the roadside, wood-sorrel flower, the anemone, scentless violets, strawberries, and that starry yellow flower which Mrs C. calls pile wort.[1] When we were in the woods beyond Gowbarrow park we saw a few daffodils[2] close to the water side. We fancied that the lake had floated the seeds ashore and that the little colony had so sprung up. But as we went along there were more and yet more and at last under the boughs of the trees, we saw that there was a long belt of them[3] along the shore, about the breadth of a country turnpike road. I never saw daffodils so beautiful they grew among the mossy stones about and about them, some rested their heads upon these stones as on a pillow for weariness and the rest tossed and reeled and danced and seemed as if they verily laughed with the wind that blew upon them over the lake, they looked so gay ever glancing ever changing. This wind blew directly over the lake to them. There was here and there a little knot and a few stragglers a few yards higher up but they were so few as not to disturb the simplicity and unity and life of that one busy highway. We rested again and again. The Bays were stormy, and we heard the waves at different distances and in the middle of the water like the sea.

---

[1] The lesser celandine. See p. 204, and entry for 30 April.
[2] See p. 206. The poem was not written until 1804.
[3] Six words are erased here: 'the end we did not see.' In spite of the erasure, the sentence has an interest, for in 'I wandered lonely as a cloud' occurs the line, 'They stretched in never-ending line.'

Rain came on—we were wet when we reached Luffs[1] but we called in. Luckily all was chearless and gloomy so we faced the storm—we *must* have been wet if we had waited—put on dry clothes at Dobson's. I was very kindly treated by a young woman, the Landlady looked sour but it is her way. She gave us a goodish supper. Excellent ham and potatoes. We paid 7/ when we came away. William was sitting by a bright fire when I came downstairs. He soon made his way to the Library piled up in a corner of the window. He brought out a volume of Enfield's Speaker, another miscellany, and an odd volume of Congreve's plays. We had a glass of warm rum and water. We enjoyed ourselves and wished for Mary. It rained and blew when we went to bed. N.B. Deer in Gowbarrow park like skeletons.

Friday 16th April (Good Friday). When I undrew my curtains in the morning, I was much affected by the beauty of the prospect and the change. The sun shone, the wind had passed away, the hills looked chearful, the river was very bright as it flowed into the lake. The Church[2] rises up behind a little knot of Rocks, the steeple not so high as an ordinary 3 story house. Bees, in a row in the garden under the wall. After Wm had shaved we set forward. The valley is at first broken by little rocky woody knolls that make retiring places, fairy valleys in the vale, the river winds along under these hills travelling not in a bustle but not slowly to the lake. We saw a fisherman in the flat meadow on the other side of the water. He came towards us and threw his line over the two arched Bridge. It is a Bridge of a heavy construction, almost bending inwards in the middle, but it is grey and there is a look of ancientry in the architecture of it that pleased me. As we go on the vale opens out more into one vale with somewhat of a cradle Bed. Cottages with groups of trees on the side of the hills. We passed a pair of twin Children 2 years old—Sate on the next bridge which we crossed a single arch. We rested again upon the Turf and looked at the same Bridge. We observed arches in the water occasioned by the large stones sending it down in two streams. A Sheep came plunging through the river, stumbled up the Bank and passed

---

[1] The Luffs had two houses, and must have been at the one in Ambleside. See p. 55 n.

[2] Four words erased here: 'and the yew tree'.

close to us, it had been frightened by an insignificant little Dog on the other side,[1] its fleece dropped a glittering shower under its belly. Primroses by the roadside, pile wort that shone like stars of gold in the Sun, violets, strawberries, retired and half buried among the grass. When we came to the foot of Brothers water I left William sitting on the Bridge and went along the path on the right side of the Lake through the wood. I was delighted with what I saw. The water under the boughs of the bare old trees, the simplicity of the mountains and the exquisite beauty of the path. There was one grey cottage. I repeated the Glowworm[2] as I walked along. I hung over the gate, and thought I could have stayed for ever. When I returned I found William writing a poem descriptive of the sights and sounds we saw and heard.[3] There was the gentle flowing of the stream, the glittering lively lake,[4] green fields without a living creature to be seen on them, behind us, a flat pasture with 42 cattle feeding to our left the road leading to the hamlet, no smoke there, the sun shone on the bare roofs. The people were at work ploughing, harrowing and sowing—lasses spreading dung, a dog's barking now and then, cocks crowing, birds twittering, the snow in patches at the top of the highest hills, yellow palms, purple and green twigs on the Birches, ashes with their glittering spikes quite bare. The hawthorn a bright green with black stems under the oak. The moss of the oak glossy. We then went on, passed two sisters at work, *they first passed us*, one with two pitch forks in her hand. The other had a spade. We had some talk with them. They laughed aloud after we were gone perhaps half in wantonness, half boldness. William finished his poem[5] before we got to the foot of Kirkstone. There were hundreds of cattle in the vale. There we ate our dinner. The walk up Kirkstone was very interesting. The Becks among the rocks were all alive. Wm showed me the little mossy streamlet which he had before loved when he saw its bright green track in the snow. The view above Ambleside, very beautiful. There we sate and looked down on the green vale. We watched the crows at a little distance from us become white as silver as

---

[1] The words 'poor thing' are here erased.
[2] i.e. 'Among all lovely things my Love had been', p. 207.
[3] 'The Cock is crowing', p. 208.
[4] The word 'soft' is erased here, before 'green'.
[5] 'The Cock is crowing.'

they flew in the sunshine, and when they went still further they looked like shapes of water passing over the green fields. The whitening of Ambleside Church is a great deduction from the beauty of it seen from this point. We called at the Luffs, the Boddingtons there did not go in and went round by the fields. I pulled off my stockings intending to wade the Beck but I was obliged to put them on and we climbed over the wall at the Bridge. The post passed us. No letters! Rydale Lake was in its own evening brightness, the Islands and points distinct. Jane Ashburner came up to us when we were sitting upon the wall. We rode in her cart to Tom Dawson's. All well. The garden looked pretty in the half moonlight-half daylight. As we went up the vale of Brothers Water more and more cattle feeding 100 of them.

Saturday 17th. A mild warm rain. We sate in the garden all the morning. William dug a little. I transplanted a honey suckle. The lake was still the sheep on the island reflected in the water, like the grey deer we saw in Gowbarrow park.[1] We walked after tea by moonlight. I had been in bed in the afternoon and William had slept in his chair. We walked towards Rydale first then backwards and forwards below Mr Olliff's. The village was beautiful in the moonlight. Helm Crag we observed very distinct. The dead hedge round Benson's field bound together at the top by an interlacing of ash sticks which made a chain of silver when we faced the moon. A letter from C., and also from S. H. I saw a robin chacing a scarlet Butterfly this morning.

Sunday 18th. I lay in bed late. Again a mild grey morning with rising vapours. We sate in the orchard. William wrote the poem on the Robin and the Butterfly.[2] I went to drink tea at Luff's but as we did not dine till 6 o'clock it was late. It was mist and small rain all the way but very pleasant. William met me at Rydale—Aggie accompanied me thither. We sate up late. He met me with the conclusion of the poem of the Robin. I read it to him in Bed. We left out some lines.

Monday 19th. A mild rain very warm. Wm worked in the

---

[1] The words 'A letter from Coleridge, not one from Sara. We walked by moonlight', are erased here. It seems that a letter from Sara came later; see last sentence but one of entry.

[2] 'The Redbreast and the Butterfly.' See p. 208.

garden. I made pies and bread. After dinner the mist cleared
away and sun shone. William walked to Luff's. I was not very
well and went to bed. Wm came home pale and tired. I could
not rest when I got to bed.

Tuesday 20th. A beautiful morning. The sun shone. William
wrote a conclusion to the poem of the Butterfly—'I've watch'd
you now a full half-hour'.[1] I was quite out of spirits and went
into the orchard. When I came in he had finished the poem.
We sate in the orchard after dinner, it was a beautiful afternoon. The sun shone upon the Level fields and they grew
greener beneath the eye—houses village all chearful—people at
work. We sate in the Orchard and repeated the Glowworm
and other poems. Just when William came to a well or a
Trough which there is in Lord Darlington's Park[2] he began to
write that poem of the glow-worm. Not being able to ride[3]
upon the long Trot. Interrupted in going through the Town of
Staindrop. Finished it about 2 miles and a half beyond Staindrop. He did not feel the jogging of the horse while he was
writing but when he had done he felt the effect of it and his
fingers were cold with his gloves. His horse fell with him on the
other side of St Helen's, Auckland.—So much for the glow-
worm. It was written coming from Middleham on Monday
April 12th 1802. On Tuesday 20th when we were sitting after
Tea Coleridge came to the door. I startled Wm with my voice.
C. came up palish but I afterwards found he looked well.
William was not well and I was in low spirits.

Wednesday 21st. William and I sauntered a little in the garden.
Coleridge came to us and repeated the verses he wrote to
Sara.[4] I was affected with them and was on the whole, not
being well, in miserable spirits. The sunshine—the green fields
and the fair sky made me sadder; even the little happy sporting
lambs seemed but sorrowful to me. The pile wort spread out
on the grass a thousand [glossy][5] shining stars. The primroses

[1] Published as 'To a Butterfly'. See p. 210.

[2] Raby Park, near Barnard Castle.

[3] For 'write'—a slip. W. W. could write while the horse was walking, but not
trotting.

[4] The poem written on 4 April and published in shortened form as 'Dejection: An
Ode' in the *Morning Post*, 4 October 1802. C. originally called it 'Letter to ——'. It
was not published in full until 1937, in *Wordsworthian and Other Studies*, by E. de
Selincourt.

[5] Erased.

were there and the remains of a few Daffodils. The well which we cleaned out last night is still but a little muddy pond,[1] though full of water. I went to bed after dinner, could not sleep, went to bed again. Read Ferguson's life[2] and a poem or two—fell asleep for 5 minutes and awoke better. We got tea. Sate comfortably in the Evening. I went to bed early.

Thursday 22nd. A fine mild morning. We walked into Ease-dale. The sun shone. Coleridge talked of his plan of sowing the Laburnum in the woods. The waters were high for there had been a great quantity of rain in the night. I was tired and sate under the shade of a holly Tree that grows upon a rock. I sate there and looked down the stream. I then went to the single holly behind that single Rock in the field and sate upon the grass till they came from the Waterfall. I saw them there and heard Wm flinging stones into the River whose roaring was loud even where I was. When they returned William was repeating the poem 'I have thoughts that are fed by the Sun'.[3] It had been called to his mind by the dying away of the stunning of the waterfall when he came behind a stone. When we had got into the vale a heavy rain came on. We saw a family of little children sheltering themselves under a wall before the rain came on. They sate in a Row making a canopy for each other of their clothes. The servant lass was planting potatoes near them. Coleridge changed his clothes. We were all wet. Wilkinson[4] came in while we were at dinner. Coleridge and I after dinner drank black currants and water.

Friday 23rd April 1802.[5] It being a beautiful morning we set off at 11 o'clock intending to stay out of doors all the morning. We went towards Rydale and before we got to Tom Dawson's we determined to go under Nab Scar. Thither we went. The sun shone and we were lazy. Coleridge pitched upon several places to sit down upon but we could not be all of one mind respecting sun and shade so we pushed on to the Foot of the Scar. It was very grand when we looked up very stony, here and there a budding tree. William observed that the umbrella

---

[1] An echo from 'The Thorn', written at Alfoxden, 1798. See p. 167.

[2] Robert Fergusson (1750–74), Scottish poet. His *Poetical Works* were published in 1800.

[3] See p. 210. This poem was never printed by W.

[4] Probably the Revd. Joseph Wilkinson of Ormathwaite, Keswick. See also entry for 25 April, and p. 107 n.   [5] See *CNB*, vol. III, p. 1164.

Yew tree that breasts the wind had lost its character as a tree
and had become something like to solid wood. Coleridge and I
pushed on before. We left William sitting on the stones feasting
with silence—and C. and I sate down upon a rocky seat—a
Couch it might be under the Bower of William's Eglantine,
Andrew's Broom.[1] He was below us and we could see him. He
came to us and repeated his poems while we sate beside him
upon the ground. He had made himself a seat in the crumbly
ground. After we had lingered long looking into the vales—
Ambleside vale with the copses the village under the hill and
the green fields—Rydale with a lake all alive and glittering
yet but little stirred by Breezes, and our own dear Grasmere
first making a little round lake of nature's own with never a
house never a green field but the copses and the bare hills
enclosing it and the river flowing out of it. Above rose the
Coniston Fells in their own shape and colour. Not Man's hills
but all for themselves the sky and the clouds and a few wild
creatures. C. went to search for something new. We saw him
climbing up towards a Rock. He called us and we found him
in a Bower, the sweetest that was ever seen. The Rock on one
side is very high and all covered with ivy which hung loosely
about and bore bunches of brown berries. On the other side it
was higher than my head. We looked down upon the Ambleside vale that seemed to wind away from us the village *lying*
under the hill. The Fir tree Island was reflected beautifully.
We now first saw that the trees are planted in rows. About this
bower there is mountain ash, common ash, yew tree, ivy,
holly, hawthorn mosses and flowers, and a carpet of moss.
Above at the top of the Rock there is another spot—it is
scarce a Bower, a little parlour on[ly] not *enclosed* by walls but
shaped out for a resting place by the rocks and the ground
rising about it. It had a sweet moss carpet. We resolved to go
and plant flowers in both these places tomorrow. We wished
for Mary and Sara. Dined late. After dinner Wm and I
worked in the garden. C. read. A letter from Sara.

Saturday 24th. A very wet day. William called me out to see a
waterfall behind the Barberry tree—We walked in the evening
to Rydale. Coleridge and I lingered behind. C. stopped up the

[1] 'The Waterfall and the Eglantine' and 'The Oak and the Broom', *P.W.*, vol.
II, pp. 128 and 130.

little runner by the Road side to make a lake. We all stood to look at Glowworm Rock—a primrose that grew there, and just looked out on the Road from its own sheltered bower.[1] The clouds moved as William observed in one regular body like a multitude in motion a sky all clouds over, not one cloud.[2] On our return it broke a little out and we saw here and there a star. One appeared but for a moment in a lake [of] pale blue sky.

Sunday 25th April. After breakfast we set off with Coleridge towards Keswick. Wilkinson overtook us near the Potters and interrupted our discourse. C. got into a gig with Mr Beck, and drove away from us. A shower came on but it was soon over. We spent the morning in the orchard. Read the Pro-thalamium of Spenser—walked backwards and forwards. Mr Simpson drank tea with us. I was not well before tea. Mr S. sent us some quills by Molly Ashburner and his brother's book.[3] The Luffs called at the door.

Monday 26th. I copied Wm's poems for Coleridge. Letters from Peggy [4] and Mary H.—wrote to Peggy and Coleridge. A terrible rain and wind all day. Went to bed at 12 o'clock.

Tuesday 27th. A fine morning. Mrs Luff called. I walked with her to the Boat-house. William met me at the top of the hill with his fishing-rod in his hand. I turned with him and we sate on the hill looking to Rydale. I left him intending to join him but he came home, and said his lines would not stand the pulling. He had had several bites. He sate in the orchard—I made bread. Miss Simpson called. I walked with her to Goan's. When I came back I found that he and John Fisher had cleaned out the well. John had sodded about the Bee-stand. In the evening Wm began to write the Tinker.[5] We had a Letter and verses from Coleridge.

Wednesday 28th April. A fine sunny but coldish morning. I copied the Prioress's tale. Wm was in the orchard. I went to him—he worked away at his poem—though he was ill and tired. I happened to say that when I was a child I would not have pulled a strawberry blossom. I left him and wrote out the

[1] See 'The Primrose of the Rock', written many years later. *P.W.*, vol. II, p. 303.
[2] See 'To the Clouds', written in 1808. *P.W.*, vol. II, p. 316.
[3] Mr. Simpson's son, another Revd. Joseph Simpson, published a book of poems, *The Beauties of Spring*; this may be the volume D. W. means.
[4] i.e. Peggy Ashburner.
[5] See p. 211. This poem was never published by Wordsworth.

Manciple's Tale. At dinner-time he came in with the poem of
'Children gathering flowers'[1]—but it was not quite finished
and it kept him long off his dinner. It is now done he is working
at the Tinker. He promised me he would get his tea and do no
more but I have got mine an hour and a quarter and he has
scarcely begun his. I am not quite well. We have let the bright
sun go down without walking. Now a heavy shower comes on
and I guess we shall not walk at all. I wrote a few lines to
Coleridge. Then we walked backwards and forwards between
our house and Olliffs. We talked about T. Hutchinson and
Bell Addison.[2] William left me sitting on a stone. When we
came in we corrected the Chaucers but I could not finish them
to-night. Went to bed.

Thursday 29th. A beautiful morning. The sun shone and all
was pleasant. We sent off our parcel to Coleridge by the
waggon. Mr Simpson heard the Cuckow today. Before we went
out after I had written down the Tinker (which William
finished this morning) Luff called. He was very lame, limped
into the kitchen—he came on a little Pony.[3] We then went to
John's Grove, sate a while at first. Afterwards William lay, and
I lay in the trench[4] under the fence—he with his eyes shut and
listening to the waterfalls and the Birds. There was no one
waterfall above another—it was a sound of waters in the air—
the voice of the air. William heard me breathing and rustling
now and then but we both lay still, and unseen by one another.
He thought that it would be as sweet thus to lie so in the
grave, to hear the *peaceful* sounds of the earth and just to know
that our dear friends were near. The Lake was still. There was
a Boat out. Silver How reflected with delicate purple and
yellowish hues as I have seen Spar. Lambs on the island and
running races together by the half dozen in the round field
near us. The copses green*ish*, hawthorn green.—Came home to
dinner then went to Mr Simpson. We rested a long time under
a wall. Sheep and lambs were in the field—cottages smoking.
As I lay down on the grass, I observed the glittering silver line

[1] Published in 1807 as 'Foresight'. See p. 213.
[2] Isabella Addison of Penrith, sister of Richard W.'s partner, Richard Addison.
She eventually married John Monkhouse, first cousin of M. H. and Tom, but died
in 1807.
[3] Two words erased; perhaps 'Better morning'.
[4] The word 'hollow' is erased.

on the ridges of the Backs of the sheep, owing to their situation respecting the Sun—which made them look beautiful but with something of strangeness, like animals of another kind—as if belonging to a more splendid world. Met old Mr S. at the door—Mrs S. poorly. I got mullens and pansies. I was sick and ill and obliged to come home soon. We went to bed immediately—I slept up stairs. The air coldish where it was felt somewhat frosty.

Friday April 30th. We came into the orchard directly after Breakfast, and sate there. The lake was calm—the sky cloudy. We saw two fishermen by the lake side. William began to write the poem of the Celandine. I wrote to Mary H. sitting on the fur gown. Walked backwards and forwards with William—he repeated his poem to me. Then he got to work again and could not give over—he had not finished his dinner till 5 o'clock. After dinner we took up the fur gown into The Hollins above. We found a sweet seat and thither we will often go. We spread the gown put on each a cloak and there we lay. William fell asleep—he had a bad head ache owing to his having been disturbed the night before with reading C.'s letter which Fletcher had brought to the door. I did not sleep but I lay with half shut eyes, looking at the prospect as in a vision almost I was so resigned[1] to it. Loughrigg Fell was the most distant hill, then came the Lake slipping in between the copses and above the copse the round swelling field, nearer to me a wild intermixture of rocks trees, and slacks[2] of grassy ground.—When we turned the corner of our little shelter we saw the Church and the whole vale. It is a blessed place. The Birds were about us on all sides—Skobbys Robins Bullfinches. Crows now and then flew over our heads as we were warned by the sound of the beating of the air above. We stayed till the light of day was going and the little Birds had begun to settle their singing. But there was a thrush not far off that seemed to sing louder and clearer than the thrushes had sung when it was quite day. We came in at 8 o'clock, got tea. Wrote to Coleridge, and I wrote to Mrs Clarkson part of a letter. We went to bed at 20 minutes past 11 with prayers that Wm might sleep well.

[1] 'Resigned' is curiously used in the Lake District. A woman there once told me that Mr. Ruskin was 'very much resigned to his own company'. (W. K.).

[2] Dialect for a small hollow.

Saturday May 1st. Rose not till ½ past 8. A heavenly morning. As soon as Breakfast was over we went into the garden and sowed the scarlet beans about the house. It was a clear sky a heavenly morning. I sowed the flowers William helped me. We then went and sate in the orchard till dinner time. It was very hot. William wrote the Celandine.[1] We planned a shed for the sun was too much for us. After dinner we went again to our old resting place in the Hollins under the Rock. We first lay under a holly where we saw nothing but the holly tree and a budding elm mossed with [?][2] and the sky above our heads. But that holly tree had a beauty about it more than its own, knowing as we did where we were. When the sun had got low enough we went to the Rock shade. Oh the overwhelming beauty of the vale below—greener than green. Two Ravens flew high high in the sky and the sun shone upon their bellys and their wings long after there was none of his light to be seen but a little space on the top of Loughrigg Fell. We went down to tea at 8 o'clock—had lost the poem and returned after tea. The Landscape was fading, sheep and lambs quiet among the Rocks. We walked towards Kings[3] and backwards and forwards. The sky was perfectly cloudless. N.B. Is it often so? 3 solitary stars in the middle of the blue vault one or two on the points of the high hills. Wm wrote the Celandine 2nd part tonight. Heard the cuckow today this first of May.[4]

Sunday 2nd May. Again a heavenly morning. Letter from Coleridge.

[1] 'To the Small Celandine'. See p. 204.
[2] D. W. has omitted a word here, perhaps 'green', or 'lichen'.
[3] i.e. The Hollins, until a month or two before this occupied by the Olliffs.
[4] This sentence is written in large letters across the page.

IV. *4 May 1802 to 16 January 1803*[1]

Tuesday 4th May. William had slept pretty well and though he went to bed nervous and jaded in the extreme he rose refreshed. I wrote the Leech Gatherer[2] for him which he had begun the night before and of which he wrote several stanzas in bed this Monday morning. It was very hot, we called at Mr Simpson's door as we passed but did not go in. We rested several times by the way, read and repeated the Leech Gatherer. We were almost melted before we were at the top of the hill. We saw Coleridge on the Wytheburn side of the water. He crossed the Beck to us. Mr Simpson was fishing there. William and I ate a Luncheon, then went on towards the waterfall. It is a glorious wild solitude under that lofty purple crag. It stood upright by itself. Its own self and its shadow below, one mass—all else was sunshine. We went on further. A Bird at the top of the crags was flying round and round and looked in thinness and transparency, shape and motion like a moth. We climbed the hill but looked in vain for a shade except at the foot of the great waterfall, and there we did not like to stay on account of the loose stones above our heads. We came down and rested upon a moss covered Rock, rising out of the bed of the River. There we lay ate our dinner and stayed there till about 4 o'clock or later. Wm and C. repeated and read verses. I drank a little Brandy and water and was in Heaven. The Stags horn is very beautiful and fresh springing upon the fells. Mountain ashes, green. We drank tea at a farm house. The woman had not a pleasant countenance, but was civil enough. She had a pretty Boy a year old whom she suckled. We parted from Coleridge at Sara's Crag after having looked at the Letters which C. carved in the morning. I kissed them all. Wm deepened the T with C.'s penknife. We sate afterwards on

[1] The fourth and last volume of D. W.'s Grasmere journal is written in a notebook already containing at the beginning drafts of 'Michael' and 'Ruth', and at the other end extracts from Descartes, in W. W.'s hand. The notebook is bound in leather and interleaved with thin blotting-paper.

[2] i.e. 'Resolution and Independence'. See above under 3 October 1800, and p. 183.

the wall, seeing the sun go down and the reflections in the still water. C. looked well and parted from us chearfully, hopping up upon the side stones. On the Rays we met a woman with 2 little girls one in her arms the other about 4 years old walking by her side, a pretty little thing, but half starved. She had on a pair of slippers that had belonged to some gentleman's child, down at the heels—it was not easy to keep them on but, poor thing! young as she was, she walked carefully with them. Alas too young for such cares and such travels. The Mother when we accosted her told us that her husband had left her and gone off with another woman and how she '*pursued*' them. Then her fury kindled and her eyes rolled about. She changed again to tears. She was a Cockermouth woman 30 years of age—a child at Cockermouth when I was. I was moved and gave her a shilling—I believe 6ᵈ more than I ought to have given. We had the crescent moon with the 'auld moon in her arms'.[1] We rested often always upon the Bridges. Reached home at about 10 o'clock. The Lloyds had been here in our absence. We went soon to bed. I repeated verses to William while he was in bed—he was soothed and I left him. 'This is the spot'[2] over and over again.

Wednesday 5th May 1802. A very fine morning rather cooler than yesterday. We planted ¾ths of the Bower. I made bread. We sate in the orchard. The Thrush sang all day as he always sings. I wrote to the Hutchinsons and to Coleridge—packed off Thelaba.[3] William had kept off work till near Bedtime when we returned from our walk—then he began again and went to bed very nervous. We walked in the twilight and walked till night came on. The moon had the old moon in her arms but not so plain to be seen as the night before. When we went to bed it was a Boat without the circle. I read The Lover's Complaint[4] to Wm in bed and left him composed.

6th May Thursday 1802. A sweet morning. We have put the finishing stroke to our Bower and here we are sitting in the orchard. It is one o'clock. We are sitting upon a seat under the wall which I found my Brother building up when I came to him with his apple—he had intended that it should have been

[1] From the *Ballad of Sir Patrick Spens*, quoted as heading to Coleridge's 'Dejection: An Ode'; see entry for 21 April above, and n.

[2] See p. 214. These lines were never published by Wordsworth.

[3] By Southey, published 1801.   [4] By Shakespeare.

done before I came. It is a nice cool shady spot. The small Birds are singing, Lambs bleating, Cuckow calling. The Thrush sings by Fits. Thomas Ashburner's axe is going quietly (without passion) in the orchard. Hens are cackling, Flies humming, the women talking together at their doors: Plumb and pear trees are in Blossom—apple trees greenish the opposite woods green, the crows are cawing. We have heard Ravens. The ash trees are in blossom, Birds flying all about us. The stitchwort is coming out, there is one budding Lychnis, the primroses are passing their prime. Celandine violets and wood sorrel for ever more little geraniums and pansies on the wall. We walked in the evening to Tail End to enquire about hurdles for the orchard shed and about Mr Luff's flower. The flower dead—no hurdles. I went to look at the falling wood—Wm also when he had been at Benson's went with me. They have left a good many small oak trees but we dare not hope that they are all to remain. The Ladies are come to Mr Gell's cottage. We saw them as we went and their light when we returned. When we came in we found a Magazine and Review and a letter from Coleridge with verses to Hartley and Sara H.[1] We read the Review,[2] etc. The moon was a perfect Boat a silver Boat when we were out in the evening. The Birch Tree is all over green in *small* leaf more light and elegant than when it is full out. It bent to the breezes as if for the love of its own delightful motions. Sloe-thorns and Hawthorns in the hedges.

Friday 7th May. William had slept uncommonly well so, feeling himself strong, he fell to work at the Leech gatherer. He wrote hard at it till dinner time, then he gave over tired to death—he had finished the poem. I was making Derwent's frocks. After dinner we sate in the orchard. It was a thick hazy dull air. The Thrush sang almost continually—the little Birds were more than usually busy with their voices. The sparrows are now full fledged. The nest is so full that they lie upon one another, they sit quietly in their nest with closed mouths. I walked to Rydale after tea which we drank by the kitchen Fire. The Evening very dull—a terrible kind of threatening

---

[1] Probably the 'verses to Hartley' are 'Answer to a Child's Question' (*Poetical Works*, p. 386). The 'verses to Sara H.' are perhaps 'The Day-Dream: From an Emigrant to his Absent Wife' (ibid.). It is unlikely that D. W. means the 'Dejection' verses.

[2] Perhaps the *Monthly Review*.

brightness at sunset above Easedale. The Sloe thorn beautiful in the hedges, and in the wild spots higher up among the hawthorns. No letters. William met me. He had been digging in my absence and cleaning the well. We walked up beyond Lewthwaites—a very dull sky, coolish. Crescent moon now and then. I had a letter brought me from Mrs Clarkson. While we were walking in the orchard I observed the sorrel leaves opening at about 9 o'clock. William went to bed tired with thinking about a poem.

Saturday Morning May 8th 1802. We sowed the Scarlet Beans in the orchard I read Henry 5th there—William lay on his back on the seat. 'Wept, For names, sounds paths delights and duties lost' taken from a poem upon Cowley's wish to retire to the Plantations—read in the Review I finished Derwent's frocks—after dinner William added a step to the orchard steps.

Sunday Morning May 9th 1802. The air considerably colder today but the sun shone all day. William worked at the Leech gatherer almost incessantly from morning till tea-time. I copied the Leech-gatherer and other poems for Coleridge. I was oppressed and sick at heart for he wearied himself to death. After tea he wrote 2 stanzas in the manner of Thomson's Castle of Indolence,[1] and was tired out. Bad news of Coleridge.

Monday May 10th. A fine clear morning but coldish. William is still at work though it is past 10 o'clock—he will be tired out I am sure. My heart fails in me. He worked a little at odd things, but after dinner he gave over. An affecting letter from Mary H. We sate in the Orchard before dinner. Old Joyce spent the day. I wrote to Mary H. Mrs Jameson and Miss Simpson called just when William was going to bed at 8 o'clock. I wrote to Coleridge sent off Reviews and poems, went to bed at 12 o'clock. William did not sleep till 3 o'clock.

Tuesday May 11th. A cool air. William finished the stanzas about C. and himself—he did not go out today. Miss Simpson came in to tea which was lucky enough for it interrupted his labours. I walked with her to Rydale—the evening cool—the moon only now and then to be seen—the Lake purple as we went—primroses still in abundance. William did not meet me. He completely finished his poems I finished Derwent's frocks.

[1] See p. 214. Probably it was this poem which he was 'thinking about' on 7 May.

We went to bed at 12 o'clock. Wm pretty well—he looked very well. He complains that he gets cold in his chest.

Wednesday 12th. A sunshiny but coldish morning. We walked into Easedale and returned by George Rownson's and the lane. We brought home heckberry blossom, crab blossom—the anemone nemorosa—Marsh Marigold—Speedwell, that beautiful blue one the colour of the blue-stone or glass used in jewellery, with its beautiful pearl-like chives. Anemones are in abundance and still the dear dear primroses violets in beds, pansies in abundance and the little celandine. I pulled a branch of the taller celandine. Butterflies of all colours—I often see some small ones of a pale purple lilac or Emperor's eye colour something of the colour of that large geranium which grows by the lake side. Wm observed the beauty of Geordy Green's house.[1] We see it from our orchard. Wm pulled ivy with beautiful berries—I put it over the chimney-piece. Sate in the orchard the hour before dinner—coldish. We have now dined. My head aches—William is sleeping in the window. In the Evening we were sitting at the table, writing, when we were rouzed by Coleridge's voice below—he had walked, looked palish but was not much tired. We sate up till one o'clock all together then William went to bed and I sate with C. in the sitting room (where he slept) till $\frac{1}{4}$ past 2 o'clock. Wrote to M. H.

13th May Thursday 1802. The day was very cold, with snow showers. Coleridge had intended going in the morning to Keswick but the cold and showers hindered him. We went with him after tea as far as the plantations by the Roadside descending to Wytheburn—he did not look very well when we parted from him.—We sate an hour at Mr Simpson's.

Friday May 14th 1802. A very cold morning—hail and snow showers all day. We went to Brothers wood,[2] intending to get plants and to go along the shore of the lake to the foot. We did go a part of the way, but there was no pleasure in stepping along that difficult sauntering Road in this ungenial weather. We turned again and walked backwards and forwards in Brothers' wood. William teased himself with seeking an

---

[1] Pavement End, the farm at the head of the lake.
[2] The wood along the shore of Grasmere lake, called so by them because in it W. had partly composed 'The Brothers'.

epithet for the Cuckow. I sate a while upon my last summer's seat the mossy stone—William's unemployed beside me, and the space between where Coleridge has so often lain. The oak trees are just putting forth yellow knots of leaves. The ashes with their flowers passing away and leaves coming out. The blue Hyacinth is not quite full blown—Gowans[1] are coming out—marsh marygolds in full glory—the little star plant a star without a flower.[2] We took home a great load of Gowans and planted them in the cold about the orchard. After dinner I worked bread then came and mended stockings beside William. He fell asleep. After tea I walked to Rydale for Letters. It was a strange night. The hills were covered over with a slight covering of hail or snow, just so as to give them a hoary winter look with the black Rocks [underneath].[3] The woods looked miserable, the coppices green as grass which looked quite unnatural and they seemed half shrivelled up as if they shrunk from the air. O thought I! what a beautiful thing God has made winter to be by stripping the trees and letting us see their shapes and forms. What a freedom does it seem to give to the storms! There were several new flowers out but I had no pleasure in looking at them. I walked as fast as I could back again with my letter from S. H. which I skimmed over at Tommy Fleming's. Met Wm at the top of White Moss. We walked a little beyond Olliffs. Near 10 when we came in. Wm and Molly had dug the ground and planted potatoes in my absence. We wrote to Coleridge—sent off a letter to Annette, bread and frocks to the C.'s—Went to bed at ½-past 11. William very nervous—after he was in bed haunted with altering the Rainbow.

Saturday Morning [15th]. It is now ¼ past 10 and he is not up. Miss Simpson called when I was in bed. I have been in the garden. It looks fresh and neat in spite of the frost. Molly tells me they had thick ice on a jug at their door last night.

Saturday 15th.[4] A very cold and cheerless morning. I sate mending stockings all the morning. I read in Shakespeare. William lay very late because he slept ill last night. It snowed

[1] Daisies.

[2] Probably butterwort, which has a star-shaped rosette of sticky pale green leaves. Not every plant produces a flower.

[3] Erased.

[4] D. W. here repeats 'Saturday' and adds '15th'.

this morning just like Christmas. We had a melancholy letter
from Coleridge just at Bed-time. It distressed me very much and
I resolved upon going to Keswick the next day.

[*The following is written on the blotting-paper opposite this date:*]

S. T. Coleridge
Dorothy Wordsworth   William Wordsworth
Mary Hutchinson   Sara Hutchinson
William   Coleridge   Mary
Dorothy   Sara
16th May
1802
John Wordsworth

Sunday 16th. William was at work all the morning. I did not
go to Keswick. A sunny cold frosty day. A snow-shower at
night. We were a good while in the orchard in the morning.

Monday 17th May. William was not well—he went with me to
Wytheburn water. He left me in a post chaise.[1] Hail showers
snow and cold attacked me. The people were graving peats
under Nadel Fell.—A lark and thrush singing near Coleridge's house. Bancrofts there. A letter from M. H.

Tuesday 18th May. Terribly cold. Coleridge not well. Froude[2]
called, Wilkinsons[3] called, I not well. C. and I walked in the
evening in the garden. Warmer in the evening. Wrote to M.
and S.

Wednesday 19th May 1802. A grey morning—not quite so
cold. C. and I set off at ½ past 9 o'clock. Met William, near the
6 mile stone. We sate down by the Road Side, and then went to
Wytheburn water. Longed to be at the Island. Sate in the sun,
Coleridge's Bowels bad, mine also. We drank tea at John
Stanley's—the evening cold and clear. A glorious light on
Skiddaw. I was tired—brought a cloak down from Mr Simpson's. Packed up Books for Coleridge then got supper and went
to bed.

[1] D. W. now went alone to Keswick. See entry for 15 May.
[2] The Revd. Robert Hurrell Froude of Devonshire married Margaret Spedding
of Mirehouse, Keswick. Their sons were Richard Hurrell Froude (1803–36) and
James Anthony Froude (1818–94), the historian.
[3] The Revd. and Mrs. Joseph Wilkinson of Ormathwaite, Keswick. See under
31 March. Mrs. Wilkinson's two sisters married the two brothers of W.'s friend
James Losh. See *E.T.*, p. 472.

Thursday 20th May. A frosty clear morning. I lay in bed late. William got to work. I was somewhat tired. We sate in the orchard sheltered all the morning. In the evening there was a fine rain. We received a letter from Coleridge, telling us that he wished us not to go to Keswick.[1]

Friday 21st May. A very warm gentle morning—a little rain. Wm wrote two sonnets on Buonaparte[2] after I had read Milton's sonnets to him. In the evening he went with Mr Simpson with Borwick's Boat to gather Ling in Bainriggs. I planted about the well—was much heated and I think I caught cold.

Saturday 22nd May. A very hot morning. A hot wind as if coming from a sand desert. We met Coleridge, he was sitting under Sara's Rock when we reached him. He turned with us. We sate a long time under the Wall of a sheep-fold. Had some interesting melancholy talk about his private affairs. We drank tea at a farm house. The woman was very kind. There was a woman with 3 children travelling from Workington to Manchester. The woman served them liberally. Afterwards she said that she never suffered any to go away without a trifle 'sec as we have'. The woman at whose house we drank tea the last time was rich and senseless—she said 'she never served any but their own poor'.—C. came home with us. We sate some time in the orchard. Then they came in to supper—mutton chops and potatoes. Letters from S. and M. H.

Sunday [23rd]. I sate with C. in the orchard all the morning. William was very nervous.[3] I was ill in the afternoon, took laudanum. We walked in Bainriggs after tea. Saw the juniper—umbrella shaped.—C. went to S. and M. Points,[4] joined us on White Moss.

Monday 24th May. A very hot morning. We were ready to go off with Coleridge, but foolishly sauntered and Miss Taylor and Miss Stanley called. William and Coleridge and I went afterwards to the top of the Rays. I was ill and left them, lay

---

[1] This letter must have been written immediately after D. W. left Keswick. There had been discussion of a plan for the Wordsworths to go and live at Keswick; D. W. was opposed to it and had evidently while at Keswick brought Coleridge round to her view.

[2] One of these sonnets seems not to have survived; the other is 'I grieved for Buonaparté', the first of W.'s political sonnets. See p. 216.

[3] Erased.

[4] Sara Point and Mary Point.

down at Mrs Simpson's.[1] I had sent off a letter to Mary by C. I wrote again and to C., then went to bed. William slept not till 5 o'clock.

Tuesday 25th. Very hot—I went to bed after dinner.—We walked in the evening. Papers and short note from C.—again no sleep for Wm.

Wednesday 26th. I was very unwell—went to bed again after dinner. We walked a long time backwards and forwards between John's Grove and the Lane upon the turf. A beautiful night, not cloudless. It has never been so since May day.

Thursday 27th. I was in bed all day—very ill. William wrote to Rd Cr and Cook.[2] Wm went after tea into the orchard. I slept in his bed—he slept downstairs. He slept better than before.[3]

Friday 28th. I was much better than yesterday, though poorly. William tired himself with hammering at a passage. I was out of spirits.[3] After dinner he was better and I [?greatly] better. We sate in the orchard. The sky cloudy the air sweet and cool. The young Bullfinches in their party coloured Raiment bustle about among the Blossoms and poize themselves like Wire-dancers or tumblers, shaking the twigs and dashing off the Blossoms. There is yet one primrose in the orchard. The stitchwort is fading. The wild columbines are coming into beauty. The vetches are in abundance, Blossoming and seeding. That pretty little waxy-looking Dial-like yellow flower,[4] the speedwell, and some others whose names I do not yet know. The wild columbines are coming into beauty—some of the gowans fading. In the garden we have lilies and many other flowers. The scarlet Beans are up in crowds. It is now between 8 and nine o'clock. It has rained sweetly for two hours and a half—the air is very mild. The heckberry blossoms are dropping off fast, almost gone—barberries are in beauty—snowballs coming forward—May roses blossoming.

---

[1] This sentence erased.

[2] i.e. Richard and Christopher Wordsworth and Richard Cooke, a friend of Montagu's and R. W.'s, concerned in the matter of Montagu's old debt to Wordsworth.

[3] This sentence erased.

[4] On the first fly-leaf of the Wordsworths' copy of Withering's *An Arrangement of British Plants*, vol. 1, is a note in D. W.'s hand: 'Lysimachia Nemorum, Yellow Pimpernell of the Woods Pimpernel Loosestrife May 30th 1802.' Thus she identified it two days later.

Saturday 29th. I was much better. I made bread and a wee Rhubarb Tart and batter pudding for William. We sate in the orchard after dinner. William finished his poem on Going for Mary.[1] I wrote it out. I wrote to Mary H., having received a letter from her in the evening. A sweet day. We nailed up the honeysuckles, and hoed the scarlet beans.

Sunday 30th May 1802. I wrote to Mrs Clarkson. It was a clear but cold day. The Simpsons called in the Evening. I had been obliged to go to bed before tea and was unwell all day. Gooseberries a present from Peggy Hodgson. I wrote to my Aunt Cookson.[2]

Monday 31st. I was much better. We sate out all the day. Mary Jameson dined. I wrote out the poem on 'Our Departure'[1] which he seemed to have finished. In the evening Miss Simpson brought us a letter from M. H. and a complimentary and critical letter to W. from John Wilson of Glasgow[3] Post Paid. I went a little way with Miss S. My tooth broke today. They will soon be gone.[4] Let that pass I shall be beloved—I want no more.

Tuesday [1st]. A very sweet day, but a sad want of rain. We went into the Orchard before dinner after I had written to M. H. Then on to Mr Olliff's Intakes. We found some torn Birds' nests. The Columbine was growing upon the Rocks, here and there a solitary plant—sheltered and shaded by the tufts and Bowers of trees. It is a graceful slender creature, a female seeking retirement and growing freest and most graceful where it is most alone. I observed that the more shaded plants were always the tallest. A short note and gooseberries from Coleridge.

Wednesday 2nd June 1802. In the morning we observed that the scarlet Beans were drooping in the leaves in great numbers owing, we guess, to an insect. We sate a while in the orchard—then we went to the old carpenter's about the hurdles. Yesterday an old man called, a grey-headed man, above 70 years of age. He said he had been a soldier, that his wife and children had died in Jamaica. He had a Beggar's wallet over his

[1] Published as 'A Farewell', 1807. See also under 17 June, and p. 217.

[2] Mrs. William Cookson, wife of D. W.'s uncle Canon Cookson, with whom she had lived in Norfolk from 1788 to 1795.

[3] Later known as 'Christopher North' and one of the chief contributors to *Blackwood's Magazine*.

[4] i.e. her teeth.

shoulders, a coat of shreds and patches altogether of a drab colour—he was tall and though his body was bent he had the look of one used to have been upright. I talked a while to him, and then gave him a piece of cold Bacon and a penny. Said he 'You're a fine woman!' I could not help smiling. I suppose he meant 'You're a kind woman'. Afterwards a woman called travelling to Glasgow. After dinner William was very unwell.[1] We went into Frank's field, crawled up the little glen and planned a seat then went to Mr Olliff's Hollins and sate there —found a beautiful shell-like purple fungus in Frank's field. After tea we walked to Butterlip How and backwards and for- wards there. All the young oak tree leaves are dry as powder. A cold south wind portending Rain.[2] After we came in we sate in deep silence at the window—I on a chair and William with his hand on my shoulder. We were deep in Silence and Love, a blessed hour. We drew to the fire before bed-time and ate some Broth for our suppers. I ought to have said that on Tuesday evening, namely June 1st, we walked upon the Turf near John's Grove. It was a lovely night. The clouds of the western sky reflected a saffron light upon the upper end of the lake. All was still. We went to look at Rydale. There was an alpine fire-like red upon the tops of the mountains. This was gone when we came in view of the lake. But we saw the Lake in a new and most beautiful point of view between two little rocks, and behind a small ridge that had concealed it from us.—This White Moss a place made for all kinds of beautiful works of art and nature, woods and valleys, fairy valleys and fairy Tairns,[3] miniature mountains, alps above alps. Little John Dawson came past us from the woods with a huge stick over his shoulder.

Thursday 3rd June 1802. A very fine rain. I lay in bed till 10 o'clock. William much better than yesterday. We walked into Easedale—sheltered in a Cow-house. Came home wet. The cuckow sang and we watched the little Birds as we sate at the door of the Cow-house. The oak copses are brown, as in

[1] These last four words erased.
[2] There is here an erasure which appears to be 'Mr B. [probably Batey] [?pass- ing] here and there in the Hollins'. But see under 3 June, 'On Tuesday evening' etc. This may be the reason for the erasure. The next three sentences, down to 'Broth for our suppers', are erased.
[3] A spelling of 'tarns' often used by Coleridge.

autumn with the late frosts—scattered over with green Trees, Birches or hazels. The ashes are coming into full leaf—some of them injured.[1] We came home quite wet. We have been reading the Life and some of the writings of poor Logan[2] since dinner. 'And everlasting longings for the lost.' It is an affecting line. There are many affecting lines and passages in his poems. William is now sleeping, with the window open lying on the window Seat. The thrush is singing. There are I do believe a thousand Buds on the honeysuckle tree all small and far from blowing, save one that is retired behind the twigs close to the wall and as snug as a Bird's nest. John's Rose tree is very beautiful blended with the honeysuckle.

On Tuesday Evening when we were among the rocks we saw in the woods what seemed to be a man, resting or looking about him[3]—he had a piece of wood near him. William was on before me when we returned, and as I was going up to him, I found that this supposed man was John Dawson. I spoke to him and I suppose he thought I asked him what my Brother had said to him before, for he replied: '*William* asks me how my head is.' Poor fellow!—he says it is worse and worse and he walks as if he were afraid of putting his Body in motion.

Yesterday morning William walked as far as the Swan with Aggy Fisher. She was going to attend upon Goan's dying Infant. She said 'There are many heavier crosses than the death of an Infant', and went on 'There was a woman in this vale who buried 4 grown-up children in one year, and I have heard her say when many years were gone by that she had more pleasure in thinking of those 4 than of her living Children, for as Children get up and have families of their own their duty to their parents "*wears out and weakens*". She could trip lightly by the graves of those who died when they were young, with a light step, as she went to Church on a Sunday.'

Thursday June 3rd. We walked while dinner was getting ready up into Mr King's Hollins. I was weak and made my way down alone, for Wm took a difficult way. After dinner we walked upon the Turf path—a showery afternoon. A very affecting letter came from M. H. while I was sitting in the

---

[1] i.e. by the frost. See entries for 16 and 17 May.
[2] John Logan (1747–88), Scottish poet, author of *The Braes of Yarrow*.
[3] See above p. 130, n. 2.

window reading Milton's Penseroso to William. I answered this letter before I went to bed.

Friday June 4th. It was a very sweet morning. There had been much rain in the night. William had slept miserably [? but knowing] this I lay abed late—he got some sleep but was much disordered, he shaved himself then we went into the orchard.[1] Dined late. In the evening we walked on our favourite path.[2] Then we came in and sate in the orchard. The evening was dark and warm—a tranquil night. I left William in the orchard. I read Mother Hubbard's tale[3] before I went to bed.

Saturday 5th. A fine showery morning. I made both pies and bread, but we first walked into Easedale, and sate under the oak trees upon the mossy stones. There were one or two slight showers. The Gowans were flourishing along the Banks of the stream. The strawberry flower (Geum) hanging over the Brook—all things soft and green.—In the afternoon William sate in the orchard. I went there, was tired and fell asleep. Mr Simpson drank tea, Mrs Smith called with her daughter. We walked late in the Evening upon our path. We began the letter to John Wilson.[4]

Sunday 6th June 1802. A showery morning. We were writing the letter to John Wilson when Ellen[5] came. Molly at Goan's child's funeral. After dinner I walked into John Fisher's Intake with Ellen. She brought us letters from Coleridge, Mrs Clarkson and Sara Hutchinson. William went out in the Evening and sate in the orchard. It was a showery day. In the evening there was one of the heaviest showers I ever remember.

Monday June 7th. I wrote to Mary H. this morning, sent the C. Indolence poem.[6] Copied the letter to John Wilson, and wrote to my Brother Richard and Mrs Coleridge. In the evening I walked with Ellen to Butterlip How and to George Mackareth's for the horse. It was a very sweet evening. There was the cuckow and the little Birds—the copses still injured,

---

[1] This sentence, from 'William had slept', erased.

[2] The path is still traceable. Starting from the Wishing Gate road immediately under Dry Close it skirts the east wall of John's Grove till the highest point of the latter is reached; then it bears away to the left and skirts the hillside till it joins the road opposite White Moss Tarn. (G. G. W.)

[3] By Spenser. Published 1591, as *Prosopopeia, or Mother Hubberd's Tale.*

[4] For the letter see *E.Y.*, p. 352.

[5] A servant of Mrs. Clarkson's at Eusemere.

[6] See above, under 9 May.

but the trees in general looked most soft and beautiful in tufts. William was walking when we came in—he had slept miserably for 2 nights past so we all went to bed soon. I went with Ellen in the morning to Rydale Falls. Letters from Annette, Mary H. and Cook.

Tuesday June 8th. Ellen and I rode to Windermere. We had a fine sunny day, neither hot nor cold. I mounted the horse at the quarry. We had no difficulties or delays but at the gates. I was enchanted with some of the views. From the High Ray the view is very delightful, rich and festive, water and wood houses groves hedgerows green fields and mountains, white Houses large and small.—We passed 2 or 3 nice looking states-men's houses. Mr Curwen's shrubberies looked pitiful enough under the native trees. We put up our horses, ate our dinner by the water-side and walked up to the Station.[1] Then we went to the Island, walked round it, and crossed the lake with our horse in the Ferry. The shrubs have been cut away in some parts of the island. I observed to the Boatman that I did not think it improved. He replied: 'We think it is for one could hardly see the house before.' It seems to me to be, however, no better than it was. They have made no natural glades, it is merely a lawn with a few miserable young trees standing as if they were half-starved. There are no sheep no cattle upon these lawns. It is neither one thing or another—neither *natural* nor wholly culti-vated and artificial which it was before. And that great house! Mercy upon us! If it *could* be concealed it *would* be well for all who are not pleased to see the pleasantest of earthly spots deformed by man. But it *cannot* be covered. Even the tallest of our old oak trees would not reach to the top of it. When we went into the boat there were two men standing at the landing place. One seemed to be about 60, a man with a jolly red face—he looked as if he might have lived many years in Mr Curwen's house. He wore a blue jacket and trowsers, as the people who live close by Windermere, particularly at the places of chief resort, in affectation, I suppose. He looked significantly at our Boatman just as we were rowing off and said, 'Thomas mind you take off the directions off that cask. You know what I mean. It will serve as a blind for them, *you* know. It was a blind business both for you and the coachman and me and all of us.

[1] A well-known view-point on the western side of Windermere above the ferry.

Mind you take off the directions. A wink's as good as a nod with some folks'—and then he turned round looking at his companion with such an air of self-satisfaction and deep insight into unknown things!—I could hardly help laughing outright at him. The Laburnums blossom freely at the Island and in the shrubbery on the shore—they are blighted everywhere else. Roses of various sorts were out. The Brooms were in full glory everywhere 'veins of gold'[1] among the copses. The hawthorns in the valley fading away—beautiful upon the hills. We reached home at 3 o'clock. After tea William went out and walked and wrote that poem,

'The sun has long been set' etc.[2]

He first went up to G. Mackareth's with the horse, afterwards he walked on our own path and wrote the lines—he called me into the orchard and there repeated them to me—he then stayed there till 11 o'clock.

Wednesday June 9th. Wm slept ill. A soaking all-day rain. We should have gone to Mr Simpson's to tea but we walked up after tea. Lloyds called. The hawthorns on the mountain sides like orchards in blossom. Brought Rhubarb down. It rained hard. Ambleside Fair. I wrote to Christ[ophe]r and M. H.

Thursday June 10th. I wrote to Mrs Clarkson and Luff—went with Ellen to Rydale. Coleridge came in with a sack-full of Books etc. and a Branch of mountain ash. He had been attacked by a cow. He came over by Grisdale. A furious wind. Mr Simpson drank tea. William very poorly—we went to bed latish. I slept in sitting room.

Friday June 11th. A wet day. William had slept very ill. Wm and C. walked out. I went to bed after dinner not well. I was tired with making beds cooking etc., Molly being very ill.

Saturday June 12th. A rainy morning. C. set off before Dinner. We went with him to the Rays but it rained so we went no further. Sheltered under a wall. He would be sadly wet for a furious shower came on just when we parted.—We got no dinner,

[1] She quotes from 'To Joanna':

> 'Twas that delightful season when the broom,
> Full-flowered, and visible on every steep,
> Along the copses runs in veins of gold.

[2] See p. 219. This poem was published in *Poems in Two Volumes,* 1807, but not again by W. until 1835, when it was placed among *Evening Voluntaries.*

but gooseberry pie to our tea. I baked both pies and bread, and walked with William first on our own path but it was too wet there, next over the rocks to the Road, and backward and forward, and last of all up to Mr King's. Miss Simpson and Robert had called. Letters from Sara and Annette.

Sunday June 13th. A fine morning. Sunshiny and bright, but with rainy clouds. William had slept better but not well—he has been altering the poem to Mary this morning, he is now washing his feet. I wrote out poems for our journey[1] and I wrote a letter to my Uncle Cookson. Mr Simpson came when we were in the orchard in the morning and brought us a beautiful drawing which he had done. In the evening we walked first on our own path—there we walked a good while. It was a silent night. The stars were out by ones and twos but no cuckow, no little Birds, the air was not warm, and we have observed that since Tuesday 8th when William wrote, 'The sun has long been set', that we have had no Birds singing after the Evening is fairly set in. We walked to our new view of Rydale, but it put on a sullen face. There was an owl hooting in Bainriggs. Its first halloo was so like a human shout that I was surprized when it made its second call, tremulous and lengthened out, to find that the shout had come from an owl. The full moon (not quite full) was among a company of steady island clouds, and the sky bluer about it than the natural sky blue. William observed that the full moon above a dark fir grove is a fine image of the descent of a superior being. There was a shower which drove us into John's grove before we had quitted our favourite path. We walked upon John's path before we went to view Rydale. We went to Bed immediately on our return home.

Monday June 14th. I was very unwell—went to bed before I drank my tea—was sick and afterwards almost asleep when Wm brought me a letter from Mary which he read to me sitting by the bed-side. Wm wrote to Mary and Sarah about the Leechgatherer.[2] I wrote to both of them in one and to Annette, to Coleridge also. I was better after tea.—I walked with Wm when

---

[1] i.e. to Gallow Hill, where W. W. was to marry M. H.; a journey which also included the visit to Calais to see Annette.

[2] This letter, and D. W.'s, went as one letter to the two sisters. For its text, see *E.Y.*, p. 361.

I had put up my parcel on our own path. We were driven away by the horses that go on the commons. Then we went to look at Rydale, walked a little in the fir grove, went again to the top of the hill and came home. A mild and sweet night. Wm stayed behind me. I threw him the cloak out of the window. The moon overcast. He sate a few minutes in the orchard, came in sleepy, and hurried to bed. I carried him his bread and butter.

Tuesday 15th. A sweet grey mild morning. The birds sing soft and low. William has not slept all night. It wants only 10 minutes of 10 and he is in bed yet. After William rose we went and sate in the orchard till dinner time.[1] We walked a long time in the Evening upon our favourite path. The owls hooted, the night hawk[2] sang to itself incessantly, but there were no little Birds, no thrushes. I left William writing a few lines about the night-hawk and other images of the evening, and went to seek for letters. None were come.—We walked backwards and forwards a little, after I returned to William, and then up as far as Mr King's. Came in. There was a Basket of Lettuces, a letter from M. H. about the delay of mine and telling of one she had sent by the other post, one from Wade[3] and one from Sara to C. William did not read them. M. H. growing fat.

Wednesday 16th. We walked towards Rydale for letters— met Frank Baty with the expected one from Mary. We went up into Rydale woods and read it there. We sate near an old wall which fenced a Hazel grove, which Wm said was exactly like the filbert grove at Middleham. It is a beautiful spot, a sloping or rather steep piece of ground, with hazels growing 'tall and erect'[4] in clumps at distances almost seeming regular as if they had been planted. We returned to Dinner. I wrote to Mary after dinner while Wm sate in the orchard. Old Mr Simpson drank tea with us. When Mr S. was gone I read my letter to William, speaking to Mary about having a cat. I spoke of the little Birds keeping us company—and William told me that that very morning a Bird had perched upon his leg. He had been lying very still and had watched this little

---

[1] Erased: 'Mr Simpson came and drank tea with us.' See under 16 June.

[2] i.e. the night-jar, also called the dor-hawk.

[3] Josiah Wade of Bristol, a friend of Coleridge's.

[4] She quotes from 'Nutting', first published in *Lyrical Ballads*, 1800, where the hazels are 'Tall and erect, with milk-white clusters hung'.

creature, it had come under the Bench where he was sitting and then flew up to his leg; he thoughtlessly stirred himself to look further at it and it flew onto the apple tree above him. It was a little young creature, that had just left its nest, equally un-acquainted with man and unaccustomed to struggle against storms and winds. While it was upon the apple tree the wind blew about the stiff boughs and the Bird seemed bemazed and not strong enough to strive with it. The swallows come to the sitting-room window as if wishing to build but I am afraid they will not have courage for it, but I believe they will build at my room window.[1] They twitter and make a bustle and a little chearful song hanging against the panes of glass, with their soft white bellies close to the glass, and their forked fish-like tails. They swim round and round and again they come.—It was a sweet evening. We first walked to the top of the hill to look at Rydale and then to Butterlip How. I do not now see the brownness that was in the coppices. The lower hawthorn blossoms passed away. Those on the hills are a faint white. The wild guelder rose is coming out, and the wild roses. I have seen no honeysuckles yet except our own one nestling and a tree of the yellow kind at Mrs Townley's the day I went with Ellen to Windermere. Foxgloves are now frequent, the first I saw was that day with Ellen, and the first ripe strawberries. A letter from Coleridge. I read the first Canto of the Fairy Queen to William.[2] William went to bed immediately.

Thursday 17th. William had slept well. I took castor oil and lay in bed till 12 o'clock. William injured himself with working a little.—When I got up we sate in the orchard, a sweet mild day. Miss Hudson called. I went with her to the top of the hill. When I came home I found William at work, attempting to alter a stanza in the poem on our going for Mary [3] which I convinced him did not need altering. We sate in the house after dinner. In the evening walked on our favourite path. A short letter from Coleridge. William added a little to the Ode he is writing.[4]

Friday June 18th. When we were sitting after Breakfast,

---

[1] D. W. was at present sleeping upstairs; they had changed bedrooms presumably to try whether a change would help W. to sleep better. See entry for 27 May, and *E.Y.*, p. 361.

[2] These two sentences erased.

[3] i.e. 'A Farewell'. See above, under 29 May.

[4] 'Ode: Intimations of Immortality'.

William about to shave Luff came in. It was a sweet morning. He had rode over the Fells. He brought news about Lord Lowther's intention to pay all debts [1] etc. and a letter from Mr Clarkson. He saw our garden was astonished at the Scarlet Beans etc. etc. When he was gone we wrote to Coleridge, M. H., and my B[rothe]r R[ichar]d about the affair. Wm determined to go to Eusemere on Monday.[2] In the afternoon we walked to Rydale with our letters—found no letters there. A sweet evening. I had a woful headache, and was ill in stomach from agitation of mind—went to bed at nine o'clock but did not sleep till late.

Saturday 19th. The Swallows were very busy under my window this morning. I slept pretty well, but William has got no sleep. It is after 11 and he is still in bed. A fine morning. Coleridge when he was last here, told us that for many years there being no Quaker meeting held at Keswick, a single old Quaker woman used to go regularly alone every Sunday, to attend the meeting-house and there used to sit and perform her worship, alone in that beautiful place among those fir-trees, in that spacious vale, under the great mountain Skiddaw!!! Poor old Willy[3]—we never pass by his grave close to the Churchyard gate without thinking of him and having his figure brought back to our minds. He formerly was an ostler at Hawkshead having spent a little estate. In his old age he was boarded or as they say *let* by the parish. A boy of the house that hired him was riding one morning pretty briskly beside John Fisher's—'Hallo! has aught particular happened', said John to the Boy. 'Nay naught at aw nobbut auld Willy's dead.' He was going to order the passing bell to be told.[4]—On Thursday morning Miss Hudson of Workington called. She said 'O! I love flowers! I sow flowers in the Parks several miles from home and my mother and I visit them and watch them

[1] William, Lord Lowther, was heir to James, Earl of Lonsdale, who had just died. The Earl had owed about £4,000 to the Wordsworths' father, his agent, who died in 1783; the money had been assigned to the Wordsworth children at the end of a long lawsuit but was never paid. Lord Lowther paid the debt, including the interest, in the course of the next two years. He became Earl of Lonsdale, by a second creation, in 1807.

[2] To consult with the Clarksons about the payment of the 'Lowther debt'. See under 21 June.

[3] Possibly 'the poor Pensioner' of *The Excursion*, v. 880–90.

[4] D. W.'s spelling of 'tolled'.

how they grow.' This may show that Botanists may be often deceived when they find rare flowers growing far from houses. This was a very ordinary young woman, such as in any town in the North of England one may find a score. I sate up a while after William—he then called me down to him. (I was writing to Mary H.) I read Churchill's Rosciad. Returned again to my writing and did not go to bed till he called to me. The shutters were closed, but I heard the Birds singing. There was our own Thrush shouting with an impatient shout—so it sounded to me. The morning was still, the twittering of the little Birds was very gloomy. The owls had hooted a ¼ of an hour before, now the cocks were crowing. It was near daylight, I put out my candle and went to bed. In a little time I thought I heard William snoring, so I composed myself to sleep—smiling at my sweet Brother. Charles Lloyd called.

Sunday 20th. He had slept better than I could have expected but he was far from well all day; we were in the orchard a great part of the morning. After tea we walked upon our own path for a long time. We talked sweetly together about the disposal of our riches. We lay upon the sloping Turf. Earth and sky were so lovely that they melted our very hearts. The sky to the north was of a chastened yet rich yellow fading into pale blue and streaked and scattered over with steady islands of purple melting away into shades of pink. It made my heart almost feel like a vision to me. We afterwards took our cloaks and sate in the orchard. Mr and Miss Simpson called. We told them of our expected good fortune. We were astonished and somewhat hurt to see how coldly Mr Simpson received it—Miss S. seemed very glad. We went into the house when they left us, and Wm went to bed. I sate up about an hour. He then called me to talk to him—he could not fall asleep. I wrote to Montagu.

Monday 21st. William was obliged to be in Bed late, he had slept so miserably. It was a very fine morning, but as we did not leave home till 12 o'clock, it was very hot. I parted from my Beloved[1] in the green lane above the Blacksmith's, then went to dinner at Mr Simpson's. We walked afterwards in the garden. Betty Towers and her son and daughter came to tea. The little Lad is 4 years old almost as little a thing as Hartley and as sharp too, they say, but I saw nothing of this, being a stranger,

[1] W. W. was going to Eusemere, over the Grisedale Pass.

except in his bonny eyes, which had such a sweet brightness in them when any thing was said to him that made him ashamed and draw his chin into his neck, while he sent his eyes upwards to look at you. His Mother is a delicate woman. She said she thought that both she and her husband were so tender in their health that they must be obliged to sell their land. Speaking of old Jim Jackson she said 'They might have looked up with the best in Grasmere if they had but been careful.' They began with a clear estate and had never had but one child, he to be sure is a half-wit. 'How did they get through with their money?' 'Why in eating and drinking.' The wife would make tea 4 or 5 times in a day and 'sec folks for sugar!' Then she would have nea Teapot but she would take the water out of a Brass pan on the fire and pour it on to the Tea in a quart pot. This all for herself, for she boiled the tea leaves always for her Husband and their son. I brought plants home, sunflowers, and planted them.

Tuesday Morning [*22nd*]. I had my breakfast in bed, being not quite well—I then walked to Rydale, I waited long for the post lying in the field and looking at the distant mountains,—looking and listening to the River. I met the post. Letters from Montagu and R[ichar]d. I hurried back, forwarded these to William and wrote to Montagu. When I came home I wrote to my B[rothe]r Christopher. I could settle to nothing. Molly washed and glazed the curtains. I read the 'Midsummer Night's dream' and began 'As You Like It'. Miss Simpson called—Tamar brought me some Berries. I resolved to go to William and for that purpose John Fisher promised to go over the Fells with me. Miss Simpson ate pie, and then left me reading Letters from Mary and Coleridge. The news came that a house was taken for Betsy.[1]

Aggy Fisher was talking with me on Monday morning 21st June about her son. She went on. Old Mary Watson was at Goan's there when the child died. I had never seen her before since her son was drowned last summer, 'We were all in trouble, and trouble opens folks' hearts'. She began to tell about her daughter that's married to Leonard Holmes, how now that sickness is come upon him they are breaking down and failing in the world. Debts are coming in every day and

[1] M. H.'s mentally defective sister.

he can do nothing, and they fret and jar together. One day he came riding over to Grasmere—I wondered what was the matter and I resolved to speak to him when he came back. He was as pale as a ghost and he did not suffer the horse to gang quicker than a snail could crawl. He had come over in a trick of passion to auld Mary to tell her she might take her own again, her Daughter and the Bairns. Mary replied 'nobly (said Aggy) that she would not part man and wife but that all should come together, and she would keep them while she had anything'. Old Mary went to see them at Ambleside afterwards and he begged her pardon. Aggy observed that they would never have known this sorrow if it had pleased God to take him off suddenly.[1]

I wrote to Mary H. and put up a parcel for Coleridge. The LB[2] arrived. I went to bed at ½ past 11.

Wednesday June 23rd. I slept till ½ past 3 o'clock—called Molly before 4 and had got myself dressed and breakfasted before 5, but it rained and I went to bed again. It is now 20 minutes past 10, a sunshiny morning. I walked to the top of the hill and sate under a wall near John's Grove facing the sun. I read a scene or two in As You Like It. I met Charles Lloyd and old Mr Lloyd was upstairs—Mrs Ll. had been to meet me. I wrote a line to Wm by the Lloyds. Coleridge and Leslie[3] came just as I had lain down after dinner. C. brought me Wm's letter. He had got well to Eusemere. C. and I accompanied Leslie to the Boat House. It was a sullen coldish Evening, no sunshine, but after we had parted from Leslie a light came out suddenly that repaid us for all. It fell only upon one hill, and the island, but it arrayed the grass and trees in gem-like brightness. I cooked C. his supper. We sate up till one o'clock.

Thursday June 24th. I went with C. half way up the Rays. It was a cool morning. I dined at Mr Simpson's and helped Aggy Fleming to quilt a petticoat. Miss Simpson came with me after tea round by the White Bridge. I ground paint when I reached home, and was tired. Wm came in just when Molly had left me. It was a mild rainy Evening—he was cool and fresh, rested[4]

---

[1] This paragraph on a page by itself, perhaps written some days later.

[2] The new edition of *Lyrical Ballads*, 1802.

[3] Sir John Leslie (1766–1832), a mathematician and friend of Tom Wedgwood.

[4] The word 'rested' has been erased.

and smelt sweetly—his clothes were wet. We sate together talking till the first dawning of Day—a happy time. He was well and not much tired. He thought I looked well too.

Friday June 25th. Wm had not fallen asleep till after 3 o'clock but he slept tolerably. Miss Simpson came to colour the rooms. I began with white-washing the ceiling. I worked with them (William was very busy) till dinner time but after dinner I went to bed and fell asleep. When I rose I went just before tea into the garden. I looked up at my Swallow's nest and it was gone. It had fallen down. Poor little creatures they could not themselves be more distressed than I was. I went upstairs to look at the Ruins. They lay in a large heap upon the window ledge; these Swallows had been ten days employed in building this nest, and it seemed to be almost finished. I had watched them early in the morning, in the day many and many a time and in the evenings when it was almost dark I had seen them sitting together side by side in their unfinished nest both morning and night. When they first came about the window they used to hang against the panes, with their white Bellies and their forked tails looking like fish, but then they fluttered and sang their own little twittering song. As soon as the nest was broad enough, a sort of ledge for them they sate both mornings and evenings, but they did not pass the night there. I watched them one morning, when William was at Eusemere, for more than an hour. Every now and then there was a feeling motion in their wings, a sort of tremulousness and they sang a low song to one another.

[*Tuesday 29th June.*] . . .[1] that they would not call here. I was going to tea. It is an uncertain day, sunshine showers and wind. It is now 8 o'clock I will go and see if my swallows are on their nest. Yes! there they are side by side both looking down into the garden. I have been out on purpose to see their faces. I knew by looking at the window that they were there. Young George Mackareth is come down from London. Molly says: 'I did not get him asked if he had got his laal green purse yet.' When he went away he went round to see aw't neighbours

[1] A page has been torn out here, with entries presumably for 26, 27, and 28 June. Probably they recorded another visit of W. W. to Keswick (see entry for 29 June). They also must have described the rebuilding by the swallows of their nest.

and some gave him 6^d, some a shilling, and I have heard his mother say 't laal green purse was never out of his hand. I wrote to M. H., my B[rothe]r Chris[tophe]r and Miss Griffith then went to bed in the sitting room. C. and Wm came in at about ½ past eleven. They talked till after 12.

Wednesday 30 June. William slept ill, his head terribly bad. We walked part of the way up the Rays with Coleridge, a threatening windy coldish day. We did not go with C. far up the Rays but sate down a few minutes together before we parted. I was not very well. I was inclined to go to bed when we reached home, but Wm persuaded me to have tea instead. We met an old man between the Potter's shed and Lewthwaite's. He wore a rusty but untorn hat, an excellent blue coat, waistcoat and Breeches and good mottled worsted stockings. His beard was very thick and grey of a fortnight's growth, we guessed, it was a regular beard like grey *plush*. His Bundle contained Sheffield ware. William said to him after he had asked him what his business was 'You are a very old man?' 'Aye, I am 83.' I joined in 'Have you any children' Children yes plenty. I have children and grand-children and great grand-children. 'I have a great grand-daughter, a fine Lass 13 years old.' I then said What, they take care of you—he replied half offended Thank God I can take care of myself. He said he had been a servant of the Marquis of Granby—'O he was a good Man he's in heaven—I hope he is.' He then told us how he shot himself at Bath, that he was with him in Germany and travelled with him everywhere. 'He was a famous Boxer, sir.' And then he told us a story of his fighting with his Farmer. He used always to call me Hard and Sharp. Then every now and then he broke out, 'He was a good Man! When we were travelling he never asked at the public-houses' as it might be there (pointing to the Swan) what we were to pay but he would put his hand into his pocket and give them what he liked and when he came out of the house he would say 'Now they would have charged me a shilling or 10^d God help them poor creatures!' I asked him again about his Children how many he had. Says he 'I cannot tell you' (I suppose he confounded Children and grand children together). 'I have one Daughter that keeps a boarding school at Skipton in Craven. She teaches flowering and marking, and another that

keeps a Boarding school at Ingleton. I brought up my family
under the Marquis.' He was familiar with all parts of Yorkshire.
He asked us where we lived. 'At Grasmere.' 'The bonniest Dale
in all England!' says the old man. I bought a pair of scissors of
him, and we sate together by the Road-side. When we parted I
tried to lift his bundle, and it was almost more than I could do.
We got tea and I was somewhat better. After tea I wrote to
Coleridge and closed up my letter to M. H. We went soon to
bed. A weight of Children a poor man's blessing. I [? resigned]
myself.[1]

Thursday July 1st. A very rainy day. We did not go out at all,
till evening. I lay down after dinner, but first we sate quietly
together by the fire. In the evening we took my cloak and
walked first to the top of White Moss, then round by the White
Bridge and up again beyond Mr Olliff's. We had a nice walk,
and afterwards sate by a nice snug fire and William read Spenser and I read 'As you like it'. The saddle bags came from
Keswick with a l[ette]r from M. H. and from C., and Wilkinson's drawings,[2] but no letter from Richard.

Friday July 2nd. A very rainy morning. There was a gleam
of fair weather and we thought of walking into Easedale. Molly
began to prepare the linen for putting out, but it rained worse
than ever. In the evening we walked up to the view of Rydale,
and afterwards towards Mr King's. I left William and wrote a
short letter to M.H. and to Coleridge and transcribed the alterations in the Leech gatherer.

Saturday July 3rd. I breakfasted in bed, being not very well.
Aggy Ashburner helped Molly with the Linen. I made veal and
gooseberry pies. It was very cold. Thomas Ashburner went for
coals for us. There was snow upon the mountain tops. Letters
from M. H. and Annette—A.'s letter sent from G. Hill[3]—
written at Blois 23rd.

Sunday July 4th. Cold and rain and very dark. I was sick and
ill had been made sleepless by letters. I lay in bed till 4 o'clock.
When I rose I was very far from well but I grew better after
tea. William walked out a little I did not. We sate at the win-

---

[1] The words 'A weight', etc., are added later at the end of the entry.

[2] Revd. Joseph Wilkinson. See above, under 31 March. It was for these drawings
that W. later wrote his *Description of the Scenery of the Lakes.*

[3] i.e. Gallow Hill.

dow together. It came on a terribly wet night. Wm finished the Leech gatherer today.

Monday 4 July.[1] A very sweet morning. William stayed some time in the orchard. I went to him there. It was a beautiful morning. I copied out the L[eech] G[atherer] for Coleridge and for us. Wrote to Annette Mrs Clarkson, M. H., and Coleridge. It came on a heavy rain and we could not go to Dove Nest as we had intended though we had sent Molly for the horse and it was come. The Roses in the garden are fretted and battered and quite spoiled the honey suckle though in its glory is sadly teazed. The peas are beaten down. The Scarlet Beans want sticking. The garden is overrun with weeds.

Tuesday 5th July. It was a very rainy day but in the afternoon it cleared up a little and we set off towards Rydale to go for letters. The Rain met us at the top of the White Moss and it came on very heavily afterwards. It drove past Nab Scar in a substantial shape, as if going Grasmere-wards as fast as it could go. We stopped at Willy Park's and borrowed a plaid. I rested a little while till the rain seemed passing away and then I went to meet William. I met him near Rydale with a letter from Christopher. We had a pleasant but very rainy walk home. A letter came from Mary in the morning and in the evening one from Coleridge by Fletcher. The swallows have completed their beautiful nest. I baked bread and pies.

Wednesday 6th. A very fine day. William had slept ill so he lay in bed till 11 o'clock. I wrote to John, ironed the linen, packed up. Lay in the orchard all the afternoon. In the morning Wm nailed up the trees while I was ironing. We lay sweetly in the orchard. The well is beautiful. The orchard full of Foxgloves the honeysuckle beautiful—plenty of roses but they are battered. Wrote to Molly Ritson and Coleridge. Walked on the White Moss. Glow-worms. Well for them children are in bed when they shine.

Thursday 7th. A rainy morning. I paid Thomas Ashburner, and Frank Baty. When I was coming home, a post chaise passed with a little girl behind in a patched ragged red cloak. The child and cloak—Alice Fell's own self.[2] We sate in tranquil-

[1] Actually 5 July. From here until the end of the Grasmere entries (9 July) D. W.'s dates are one day behind the correct ones.

[2] For Alice Fell, see above under 16 February 1802. These words, 'The child . . . self', have not been included in previous editions, although they are not erased.

lity together by the fire in the morning. In the afternoon after we had talked a little, Wm fell asleep, I read the Winter's Tale. Then I went to bed but did not sleep. The Swallows stole in and out of their nest, and sate there *whiles* quite still, *whiles* they sung low for 2 minutes or more at a time just like a muffled Robin. William was looking at the Pedlar when I got up. He arranged it, and after tea I wrote it out—280 lines. In the meantime the evening being fine he carried his coat to the Tailor's and went to George Mackareth's to engage the horse. He came in to me at about ½ past nine pressing me to go out; he had got letters which we were to read out of doors—I was rather unwilling, fearing I could not see to read the letters, but I saw well enough. One was from M. H., a very tender affecting letter, another from Sara to C., from C. to us, and from my B[rothe]r R[ichar]d. The moon was behind. William hurried me out in hopes that I should see her. We walked first to the top of the hill to see Rydale. It was dark and dull but our own vale was very solemn. The shape of Helm Crag was quite distinct, though black. We walked backwards and forwards on the White Moss path there was a sky-like white brightness on the lake. The Wyke Cottage Light at the foot of Silver How. Glow-worms out, but not so numerous as last night. O beautiful place! Dear Mary William. The horse is come Friday morning, so I must give over. William is eating his Broth. I must prepare to go. The Swallows I must leave them the well the garden the Roses, all. Dear creatures!! they sang last night after I was in bed—seemed to be singing to one another, just before they settled to rest for the night. Well, I must go. Fare-well.— — —

On Friday morning, July 9th William and I set forward to Keswick on our road to Gallow Hill. We had a pleasant ride though the day was showery. It rained heavily when Nelly Mackareth took the horse from us, at the Blacksmith's. Cole-ridge met us at Sara's Rock. He had inquired about us before of Nelly Mackareth, and we had been told by a handsome man, an inhabitant of Wytheburne with whom he had been talking (and who seemed by the Bye much pleased with his companion) that C. was waiting for us. We reached Keswick against tea-time. We called at Calverts on the Saturday Evening. On

Sunday I was poorly and the day was wet, so we could not move from Keswick, but on Monday 11th[1] July 1802 we went to Eusemere. Coleridge walked with us 6 or 7 miles. He was not well and we had a melancholy parting after having sate together in silence by the Road-side. We turned aside to explore the country near Hutton John, and had a new and delightful walk. The valley which is subject to the decaying Mansion that stands at its head seems to join its testimony to that of the house to the falling away of the family greatness.[2] The hedges are in bad condition, the Land wants draining and is over-run with Brackens, yet there is a something everywhere that tells of its former possessors. The trees are left scattered about as if intended to be like a park, and these are very interesting, standing as they do upon the sides of the steep hills, that slope down to the Bed of the River, a little stony bedded stream that spreads out to a considerable breadth at the village of Dacre. A little above Dacre we came into the right road to Mr Clarkson's after having walked through woods and fields never exactly knowing whether we were right or wrong. We learnt, however, that we had saved half a mile. We sate down by the River side to rest and saw some swallows flying about and about under the Bridge, and two little Schoolboys were loitering among the Scars seeking after their nests. We reached Mr Clarkson's at about 8 o'clock after a sauntering walk, having lingered and loitered and sate down together that we might be alone. Mr and Mrs C. were just come from Luff's.

We spent Tuesday the 12th[3] of July at Eusemere, and on Wednesday morning, the 13th,[4] we walked to Emont Bridge and mounted the coach between Bird's Nest[5] and Hartshorn tree. Mr Clarkson's Bitch followed us so far. A soldier and his young wife wanted to be taken up by the Coachman but there was no Room. We had a chearful ride though cold, till we got on to Stanemoor, and then a heavy shower came on, but we buttoned ourselves up, both together in the Guard's coat and we liked the hills and the Rain the better for bringing [us] so

[1] Actually 12th.

[2] Hutton John was the seat of the Hudlestons. The owner in 1802 was a somewhat eccentric barrister, and the air of neglect may have been due to him. But the 'family greatness' had not been reduced, nor was the house in fact 'decaying'.

[3] Corrected to '13th'. [4] Actually 14th.

[5] The old name for Brougham Hall.

close to one another—I never rode more snugly. At last, however, it grew so very rainy that I was obliged to go into the Coach at Bowes. Lough of Penrith was there, and very impertinent—I was right glad to get out again to my own dear Brother at Greta Bridge, the sun shone chearfully and a glorious ride we had over Gaterly Moor. Every Building was bathed in golden light. The trees were more bright than earthly trees, and we saw round us miles beyond miles—Darlington Spire, etc. etc. We reached Leming Lane[1] at about 9 o'clock, supped comfortably and enjoyed our fire. On Thursday morning, at a little before 7, being the 14th[2] July we got into a post chaise and went to Thirsk[3] to Breakfast. We were well treated but when the Landlady understood that we were going to *walk* off and leave our luggage behind she threw out some saucy words in our hearing. The day was very hot and we rested often and long before we reached the foot of the Ham[b]leton Hills, and while we were climbing them still oftener. We had a Sandwich in our pockets which we finished when we had climbed part of the hill, and we were almost overpowered with thirst when I heard the trickling of a little stream of water. I was before William and I stopped till he came up to me. We sate a long time by this water, and climbed the hill slowly. I was footsore, the Sun shone hot, the little Scotch cattle panted and tossed fretfully about. The view was hazy and we could see nothing from the top of the hill but an indistinct wide-spreading country, full of trees, but the Buildings, towns and houses were lost. We stopped to examine that curious stone, then walked along the flat common. It was now cooler, but I was still footsore, and could not walk quick so I left Wm sitting 2 or three times, and when he followed me he took a sheep for me, and then me for a sheep. I rested opposite the sign of the Sportsman and was questioned by the Landlady. Arrived very hungry at Ryvaux.[4] Nothing to eat at the Millers, as we expected but, at an exquisitely neat farmhouse we got some boiled milk and bread. This strengthened us, and I went down to look at the

[1] Leeming Lane, the local name for the section of the great trunk road between Boroughbridge and Piercebridge. (G. G. W.)

[2] Actually the 15th.

[3] Thirsk, 13 miles from Leeming Lane. The inn was The Three Tuns, in the market-place, still the principal inn. (G. G. W.)

[4] D. W.'s spelling of Rievaulx.

Ruins—thrushes were singing, cattle feeding among green grown hillocks about the Ruins. These hillocks were scattered over with *grovelets* of wild roses and other shrubs, and covered with wild flowers. I could have stayed in this solemn quiet spot till evening without a thought of moving but William was waiting for me, so in a quarter of an hour I went away. We walked upon Mr Duncombe's terrace and looked down upon the Abbey. It stands in a larger valley among a Brotherhood of valleys of different lengths and breadths all woody, and running up into the hills in all directions. We reached Helmsly just at Dusk. We had a beautiful view of the Castle from the top of the hill. Slept at a very nice Inn[1] and were well treated—bright bellows and floors as smooth as ice. On Friday morning the 15th July we walked to Kirby. Met people coming to Helmsly fair— were misdirected and walked a mile out of our way—met a double horse at Kirby. A beautiful view above Pickering[2]— Sinnington village very beautiful. Met Mary and Sara 7 miles from G. H. Sheltered from the Rain, beautiful glen, spoiled by the large house—sweet Church and Churchyard.[3] Arrived at Gallow Hill at 7 o'clock.

Friday Evening 15th July.[4] The weather bad, almost all the time. Sara Tom and I rode up Bedale. Wm Mary Sara and I went to Scarborough, and we walked in the Abbey pasture, and to Wykeham and on Monday the 26th we went off with Mary in a post chaise. We had an interesting Ride over the Wolds, though it rained all the way. Single thorn bushes were scattered about on the Turf, Sheep Sheds here and there, and now and then a little hut—swelling grounds, and sometimes a single tree or a clump of trees. Mary was very sick, and every time we stopped to open a gate, she felt the motion in her whole body, indeed I was sick too, and perhaps the smooth gliding of the Chaise over the Turf made us worse. We passed through one or two little villages, embosomed in tall trees. After we had parted from Mary there were gleams of sunshine, but with showers. We saw Beverly in a heavy rain and yet were much pleased with the beauty of the town. Saw the Minster a pretty clean

[1] The Old Manor House. See also below, under 4 October.

[2] The 'beautiful view' is from Wrelton Park, 3 miles to the west. (G. G. W.)

[3] The glen, church, and churchyard are those of Brompton, where William was to be married. (G. G. W.)

[4] Actually 16th.

Building but injured very much with Grecian architecture.
The country between Beverly and Hull very rich but miserably
flat—brick houses, windmills, houses again—dull and endless.
Hull a frightful, Dirty, *brick housey* tradesmanlike, rich, vulgar
place—yet the River though the shores are so low that they can
hardly be seen looked beautiful with the evening lights upon
it and Boats moving about. We walked a long time and returned
to our dull day Room, but quiet evening one, quiet and our own,
to supper.

Tuesday 26th.[1] Market day. Streets dirty, very rainy, did not
leave Hull till 4 o'clock, and left Barton at about 6—rained all
the way almost. A beautiful village at the foot of a hill with
trees—a gentleman's house converted into a Lady's Boarding
school. We had a woman in bad health in the coach, and took
in a Lady and her Daughter—supped at Lincoln. Duck and
peas, and cream cheese—paid 2/-. We left Lincoln on Wednesday morning 27th July[2] at six o'clock it rained heavily and we
could see nothing but the antientry of some of the Buildings
as we passed along. The night before, however, we had seen
enough to make us regret this. The minster stands at the edge
of a hill, overlooking an immense plain. The country very flat
as we went along—the Day mended. We went to see the outside
of the Minster while the passengers were dining at Peter-
borough—the West End very grand. The little girl who was a
great scholar, and plainly her Mother's favourite tho' she
had a large family at home had bought The Farmer's Boy.[3]
She said it was written by a man without education and was
very wonderful.

On Thursday morning, 29th, we arrived in London. Wm
left me at the Inn—I went to bed. Etc. etc. After various troubles
and disasters we left London on Saturday morning at ½ past
5 or 6, the 31st of July (I have forgot which). We mounted the
Dover Coach at Charing Cross. It was a beautiful morning.
The City, St Paul's, with the River and a multitude of little
Boats, made a most beautiful sight as we crossed Westminster
Bridge. The houses were not overhung by their cloud of smoke
and they were spread out endlessly, yet the sun shone so

[1] Actually 27th.
[2] Actually 28th.
[3] By Robert Bloomfield, first published in 1800.

brightly with such a pure light that there was even something like the purity of one of nature's own grand spectacles.[1]
We rode on chearfully now with the Paris Diligence before
us, now behind. We walked up the steep hills, beautiful prospects everywhere, till we even reached Dover. At first the rich
populous wide spreading woody country about London, then
the River Thames, ships sailing, chalk cliffs, trees, little villages.
Afterwards Canterbury, situated on a plain, rich and woody,
but the City and Cathedral disappointed me. Hop grounds on
each side of the road some miles from Canterbury, then we
came to a common, the race ground, an elevated plain, villages
among trees in the bed of a valley at our right, and rising above
this valley, green hills scattered over with wood—neat gentle-
men's houses. One white house almost hid with green trees
which we longed for and the parson's house as neat a place as
could be which would just have suited Coleridge. No doubt we
might have found one for Tom Hutchinson and Sara and a
good farm too. We halted at a halfway house—fruit carts
under the shade of trees, seats for guests, a tempting place to
the weary traveller. Still as we went along the country was
beautiful, hilly, with cottages lurking under the hills and their
little plots of hop ground like vineyards. It was a bad hop-
year. A woman on the top of the coach said to me 'It is a sad
thing for the poor people for the hop-gathering is the women's
harvest, there is employment about the hops both for women
and children'. We saw the Castle of Dover and the sea beyond
4 or 5 miles before we reached D. We looked at it through a
long vale, the castle being upon an eminence, as it seemed at
the end of this vale which opened to the Sea. The country now
became less fertile but near Dover it seemed more rich again.
Many buildings stand on the flat fields, sheltered with tall trees.
There is one old chapel that might have been there just in the
same state in which it now is, when this vale was as retired and
as little known to travellers, as our own Cumberland mountain
wilds 30 years ago. There was also a very old Building on the
other side of the road which had a strange effect among the
many new ones that are springing up everywhere.[2] It seemed

---

[1] See 'Sonnet Composed upon Westminster Bridge', p. 219. Here two lines are
heavily erased.
[2] 'About it', erased.

odd that it could have kept itself pure in its ancientry among so many upstarts. It was near dark when we reached Dover. We were told that the packet was about to sail, so we went down to the Custom-house in half an hour had our luggage examined etc. etc. and then we drank tea, with the honorable Mr Knox and his Tutor. We arrived at Calais at 4 o'clock on Sunday morning, the 31st of July.[1] We stayed in the vessel till ½-past 7, then Wm went for Letters, at about ½ past 8 or 9 we found out Annette and C. chez Madame Avril dans la Rue de la Tête d'or. We lodged opposite two Ladies[2] in tolerably decent-sized rooms but badly furnished, and with large store of bad smells and dirt in the yard, and all about. The weather was very hot. We walked by the sea-shore almost every evening with Annette and Caroline or Wm and I alone. I had a bad cold and could not bathe at first but William did. It was a pretty sight to see as we walked upon the sands when the tide was low perhaps a hundred people bathing about ¼ of a mile distant from us, and we had delightful walks after the heat of the day was passed away—seeing far off in the west the Coast of England like a cloud crested with Dover Castle, which was but like the summit of the cloud. The Evening star and the glory of the sky.[3] The Reflections in the water were more beautiful than the sky itself, purple waves brighter than precious stones for ever melting away upon the sands. The fort, a wooden Building, at the Entrance of the harbour at Calais, when the Evening twilight was coming on, and we could not see anything of the building but its shape which was far more distinct than in perfect daylight, seemed to be reared upon pillars of Ebony, between which pillars the sea was seen in the most beautiful colours that can be conceived. Nothing in Romance was ever half so beautiful.[4] Now came in view as the Evening star sank down and the colours of the west faded away the two lights of England, lighted up by the Englishmen in our Country, to warn vessels

[1] It was in fact 1 August.

[2] On a separate sheet, probably copied by D. W. to send to Mrs. Clarkson, is written: 'Two ladies lived in the house opposite us, and we, in our idle moods, often amused ourselves with observing their still more idle way of spending their time; they seemed neither to have work nor books, but were mostly at the window. Our rooms were rather large, but ill-furnished, etc.'

[3] See the sonnet 'Fair Star of Evening', p. 220.

[4] Three lines erased here, which cannot be read.

of rocks or sands. These we used to see from the Pier when we
could see no other distant objects but the Clouds the Sky and
the Sea itself. All was dark behind. The town of Calais seemed
deserted of the light of heaven, but there was always light, and
life, and joy upon the Sea.—One night, though, I shall never forget. The day had been very hot, and William and I walked
alone together [1] upon the pier. The sea was gloomy for there was
a blackness over all the sky except when it was overspread with
lightning which often revealed to us a distant vessel. Near us the
waves roared and broke against the pier, and as they broke and a
Ray travelled towards us, [2] and they were interfused with greenish fiery light. The more distant sea always black and gloomy. It
was also beautiful on the calm hot night to see the little Boats
row out of harbour with wings of fire and the sail boats with the
fiery track which they cut as they went along and which closed
up after them with a hundred thousand sparkles balls shootings,
and streams of glowworm light. [3] Caroline was delighted. [4]

On Sunday the 29th of August we left Calais at 12 o'clock
in the morning, and landed at Dover at 1 on Monday the
30th. I was sick all the way. It was very pleasant to me when
we were in harbour at Dover to breathe the fresh air, and to
look up and see the stars among the Ropes of the vessel. The
next day was very hot. We both bathed and sate upon the
Dover Cliffs and looked upon France with many a melancholy
and tender thought. We could see the shores almost as plain as
if it were but an English Lake.—We mounted the coach at ½ past
4 and arrived in London at 6 the 30th August. [5] It was misty
and we could see nothing. We stayed in London till Wednesday
the 22nd of September, [6] and arrived at Gallow Hill on Friday

---

[1] i.e. without Annette, but clearly with Caroline, as appears below.

[2] The words 'as they . . . towards us' are erased.

[3] See p. 220, 'It is a beauteous evening, calm and free.'

[4] An incomplete and much-torn copy of the Calais portion of the journal,
perhaps intended to be lent to members of the family, exists on some loose MS.
sheets. There are some variations in the text, and the words 'Caroline was
delighted' are omitted. See *Journals of D. W.* edited by E. de Selincourt (1952),
vol. 1, p. 174 n.

[5] The date is much erased. They arrived 31 August.

[6] During these three weeks in London they saw their brother John who was there
between two East Indian voyages. In fact they never saw him again, for he did not
come to the North during his next return (autumn 1804), and in February 1805
he perished in the wreck of his ship, the *Abergavenny*. See *The Letters of John Wordsworth*, ed. Carl H. Ketcham (1969).

24th September. Mary first met us in the avenue. She looked so fat and well that we were made very happy by the sight of her. Then came Sara, and last of all Joanna. Tom was forking corn standing upon the corn cart. We dressed ourselves immediately and got tea—the garden looked gay with asters and sweet peas. I looked at everything with tranquillity and happiness—was ill on Saturday and on Sunday and continued to be during most of the time of our stay.[1] Jack and George came on Friday Evening 1st October. On Saturday 2nd we rode to Hackness, William Jack George and Sara single, I behind Tom. On Sunday 3rd Mary and Sara were busy packing. On Monday 4th October 1802, my Brother William was married to Mary Hutchinson. I slept a good deal of the night and rose fresh and well in the morning. At a little after 8 o'clock I saw them go down the avenue towards the Church. William had parted from me upstairs. I gave him the wedding ring—with how deep a blessing! I took it from my forefinger where I had worn it the whole of the night before—he slipped it again onto my finger and blessed me fervently.[2] When they were absent my dear little Sara prepared the breakfast. I kept myself as quiet as I could, but when I saw the two men[3] running up the walk, coming to tell us it was over, I could stand it no longer and threw myself on the bed where I lay in stillness, neither hearing or seeing any thing, till Sara came upstairs to me and said 'They are coming'. This forced me from the bed where I lay and I moved I knew not how straight forward, faster than my strength could carry me till I met my beloved William and fell upon his bosom. He and John Hutchinson led me to the house and there I stayed to welcome my dear Mary. As soon as we had breakfasted we departed. It rained when we set off. Poor Mary was much agitated when she parted from her Brothers and Sisters and her home. Nothing particular occurred till we reached Kirby.[4] We had sunshine and showers, pleasant talk, love and chearfulness. We were obliged to stay two hours at K. while the horses were feeding. We wrote a few lines to Sara and then walked out, the sun shone and we went to the

[1] This sentence is erased in the MS.
[2] From 'I gave' to 'fervently' is erased in the MS.
[3] M. H.'s brothers, John and Tom Hutchinson, who had witnessed the marriage.
[4] i.e. Kirby Moorside.

Church-yard after we had put a Letter into the Post offic
York Herald.[1] We sauntered about and read the Grave-
There was one to the memory of 5 Children, who ha
died within 5 years, and the longest lived had only liv 4
years. There was another stone erected to the memory of an
unfortunate woman (as we supposed, by a stranger). The verses
engraved upon it expressed that she had been neglected by her
Relations and counselled the Readers of those words to look
within and recollect their own frailties. We left Kirby at about
½ past 2. There is not much variety of prospect from K. to
Helmesly but the country is very pleasant, being rich and
woody, and Helmesly itself stands very sweetly at the foot of
the rising grounds of Duncombe Park which is scattered over
with tall woods and, lifting itself above the common buildings
of the Town stands Helmesly Castle, now a Ruin, formerly
inhabited by the gay Duke of Buckingham. Every foot of the
Road was, of itself interesting to us, for we had travelled along
it on foot Wm and I when we went to fetch our dear Mary, and
had sate upon the Turf by the roadside more than once. Before
we reached Helmesly our Driver told us that he could not take
us any further, so we stopped at the same Inn where we had
slept before. My heart danced at the sight of its cleanly outside,
bright yellow walls, casements overshadowed with jasmine and
its low, double gavel-ended front. We were not shewn into the
same parlour where Wm and I were; it was a small room with
a drawing over the chimney piece which the woman told us
had been bought at a sale. Mary and I warmed ourselves at
the kitchen fire. We then walked into the garden, and looked
over a gate up to the old ruin which stands at the top of a
mount, and round about it the moats are grown up into soft
green cradles, hollows surrounded with green grassy hillocks
and these are overshadowed by old trees, chiefly ashes. I prevailed upon William to go up with me to the ruins. We left
Mary sitting by the kitchen fire. The sun shone, it was warm
and very pleasant. One part of the castle seems to be inhabited.
There was a man mowing nettles in the open space which had
most likely once been the Castle Court. There is one gateway

[1] A notice of the marriage appeared in the *York Herald* of 9 October and the
York Courant of 11 October. The latter runs: 'On Monday last was married at
Brompton Mr. Wordsworth of Grasmere to Miss Hutchinson of Gallow Hill near
Scarboro'.' (G. G. W.)

exceedingly beautiful. Children were playing upon the sloping ground. We came home by the Street. After about an hour's delay we set forward again, had an excellent Driver who opened the gates so dexterously that the horses never stopped. Mary was very much delighted with the view of the Castle from the point where we had seen it before. I was pleased to see again the little path which we had walked upon the gate I had climbed over, and the Road down which we had seen the two little Boys drag a log of wood, and a team of horses struggle under the weight of a great load of timber. We had felt compassion for the poor horses that were under the governance of oppressive and ill-judging drivers, and for the poor Boys who seemed of an age to have been able to have dragged the log of wood merely out of the love of their own activity, but from poverty and bad food they panted for weakness and were obliged to fetch their father from the town to help them. Duncombe House looks well from the Road—a large Building, though I believe only 2 thirds of the original design are completed. We rode down a very steep hill to Ryvaux valley, with woods all round us. We stopped upon the Bridge to look at the Abbey and again when we had crossed it. Dear Mary had never seen a ruined Abbey before except Whitby. We recognized the cottages, houses, and the little valleys as we went along. We walked up a long hill, the Road carrying us up the cleft or valley with woody hills on each side of us. When we *went* to G. H. I had walked down this valley alone. Wm followed me. It was not dark evening when we passed the little publick house, but before we had crossed the Hambledon hills and reached the point overlooking Yorkshire it was quite dark.[1] We had not wanted, however, fair prospects before us, as we drove along the flat plain of the high hill, far far off us, in the western sky, we saw shapes of Castles, Ruins among groves, a great, spreading wood, rocks, and single trees, a minster with its tower unusually distinct, minarets in another quarter, and a round Grecian Temple also—the colours of the sky of a bright grey and the forms of a sober grey, with a dome. As we descended the hill there was no distinct view, but of a great space,

[1] See the sonnet 'Dark and more dark the shades of evening fell', p. 221, composed, as Wordsworth tells us, 'after a journey over the Hambleton Hills, on a day memorable to me—the day of my marriage.'

only near us, we saw the wild and (as the people say) bottom-
less Tarn[1] in the hollow at the side of the hill. It seemed to be
made visible to us only by its own light, for all the hill about us
was dark. Before we reached Thirsk we saw a light before us
which we at first thought was the moon, then Lime kilns, but
when we drove into the market place it proved a large Bonfire
with Lads dancing round it, which is a sight I dearly love. The
Inn was like an illuminated house—every Room full. We asked
the cause, and were told by the girl that it was 'Mr John Bell's
Birthday,[2] that he had heired his Estate!' The Landlady was
very civil. She did not recognise the despised foot-travellers.
We rode nicely in the dark, and reached Leming Lane at 11
o'clock. I am always sorry to get out of a Chaise when it is
night. The people of the house were going to bed and we were
not very well treated though we got a hot supper. We breakfasted the next morning and set off at about ½ past 8 o'clock. It
was a chearful sunny morning. We soon turned out of Leming
Lane and passed a nice village[3] with a beautiful church. We
had a few showers, but when we came to the green fields of
Wensley, the sun shone upon them all, and the Eure in its many
windings glittered as it flowed along under the green slopes of
Middleham and Middleham Castle. Mary looked about for
her friend Mr Place, and thought she had him sure on the con-
trary side of the vale from that on which we afterwards found
that he lived. We went to a new built house at Leyburn, the
same village where Wm and I had dined with George Hutchinson on our road to Grasmere 2 years and ¾ ago, but not the
same house. The Landlady was very civil, giving us cake and
wine but the horses being out we were detained at least 2
hours and did not set off till 2 o'clock. We paid for 35 miles, i.e.
to Sedbergh, but the Landlady did not encourage us to hope
to get beyond Hawes. A shower came on just after we left the
Inn while the rain beat against the windows we ate our dinners
which M. and W. heartily enjoyed—I was not quite well. When
we passed thro' the village of Wensly my heart was melted

---

[1] Gormire, which from the top of Sutton Bank resembles the crater of an
extinct volcano. (G. G. W.)

[2] John Bell, of Thirsk, was born 3 October 1764. As his birthday fell in 1802 on
a Sunday, the celebration took place on the 4th. Tradition of his lavish hospitality
still lingers. (G. G. W.)

[3] Bedale.

away with dear recollections, the Bridge, the little water-
spout the steep hill the Church. They are among the most vivid
of my own inner visions, for they were the first objects that I
saw after we were left to ourselves,[1] and had turned our whole
hearts to Grasmere as a home in which we were to rest. The
Vale looked most beautiful each way. To the left the bright
silver stream inlaid the flat and very green meadows, winding
like a serpent. To the Right we did not see it so far, it was lost
among trees and little hills. I could not help observing as we
went along how much more *varied* the prospects of Wensly
Dale are in the summer time than I could have thought possible in the winter. This seemed to be in great measure owing
to the trees being in leaf, and forming groves, and screens,
and thence little openings upon recesses and concealed retreats
which in winter only made a part of the one great vale The
beauty of the summer time here as much excels that of the
winter as the variety, owing to the excessive greenness of the
fields, and the trees in leaf half concealing, and where they do
not conceal, softening the hard bareness of the limey white
Roofs. One of our horses seemed to grow a little restive as we
went through the first village, a long village on the side of a
hill.[2] It grew worse and worse, and at last we durst not go on
any longer. We walked a while, and then the Post-Boy was
obliged to take the horse out and go back for another. We
seated ourselves again snugly in the Post Chaise. The wind
struggled about us and rattled the window and gave a gentle
motion to the chaise, but we were warm and at our ease within.
Our station was at the Top of a hill, opposite Bolton Castle,
the Eure flowing beneath. William has since wrote a sonnet
on this our imprisonment—Hard was thy Durance Queen
compared with ours.[3] Poor Mary! Wm fell asleep, lying
upon my breast and I upon Mary. I lay motionless for a
long time, but I was at last obliged to move. I became very
sick and continued so for some time after the Boy brought
the horse to us. Mary had been a little sick but it soon went

---

[1] i.e. in December 1799, after George Hutchinson, M. W.'s youngest brother,
left them.
[2] West Witton.
[3] This sonnet has not survived. It concerned Mary, Queen of Scots, at one time
imprisoned in Bolton Castle.

off.—We had a sweet ride till we came to a public house on the side of a hill where we alighted and walked down to see the waterfalls.[1] The sun was not set, and the woods and fields were spread over with the yellow light of Evening, which made their greenness a thousand times more green. There was too much water in the River for the beauty of the falls, and even the Banks were less interesting than in winter. Nature had entirely got the better in her struggles against the giants who first cast the mould of these works; for indeed it is a place that did not in winter remind one of God, but one could not help feeling as if there had been the agency of some 'Mortal Instruments' which Nature had been struggling against without making a perfect conquest. There was something so wild and new in this feeling, knowing as we did in the inner man that God alone had laid his hand upon it that I could not help regretting the want of it, besides it is a pleasure to a real lover of Nature to give winter all the glory he can, for summer *will* make its own way, and speak its own praises. We saw the pathway which Wm and I took at the close of Evening, the path leading to the Rabbit Warren where we lost ourselves.[2] The farm with its holly hedges was lost among the green hills and hedgerows in general, but we found it out and were glad to look at it again. When William had left us to seek the waterfalls Mary and I were frightened by a Cow. At our return to the Inn we found new horses and a new Driver, and we went on nicely to Hawes where we arrived before it was quite dark. Mary and I got tea, and William had a partridge and mutton chops and tarts for his supper. Mary sate down with him. We had also a shilling's worth of negus and Mary made me some Broth for all which supper we were only charged 2/-. I could not sit up long. I vomited, and took the Broth and then slept sweetly. We rose at 6 o'clock—a rainy morning. We had a good Breakfast and then departed. There was a very pretty view about a mile from Hawes, where we crossed a Bridge, bare, and very green fields with cattle, a glittering stream cottages, a few ill-grown trees, and high hills. The sun shone now. Before we got upon the bare hills there was a hunting lodge on our right exactly like Greta

[1] At Aysgarth.
[2] D. W. is referring to her walk with W. from Leyburn to Kendal in December 1799. See *E.Y.*, pp. 277–80.

Hill, with fir plantations about it.[1] We were very fortunate in the day, gleams of sunshine passing clouds, that travelled with their shadows below them. Mary was much pleased with Garsdale. It was a dear place to William and me. We noted well the publick-house (Garsdale Hall) where we had baited and drunk our pint of ale, and afterwards the mountain which had been adorned by Jupiter in his glory when we were here before.[2] It was mid-day when we reached Sedbergh, and *market* day. We were in the same Room where we had spent the Evening together in our road to Grasmere. We had a pleasant Ride to Kendal, where we arrived at about 2 o'clock. The day favored us. M. and I went to see the house where dear Sara had lived,[3] then we went to seek Mr Bousfield's shop but we found him not—he had sold all his goods the Day before. We then went to the Pot woman's and bought 2 jugs and a Dish, and some paper at Pennington's.[4] When we came to the Inn William was almost ready for us. The afternoon was not chearful but it did not rain till we came near Windermere. I am always glad to see Stavely it is a place I dearly love to think of—the first mountain village that I came to with Wm when we first began our pilgrimage together.[5] Here we drank a Bason of milk at a publick house, and here I washed my feet in the Brook and put on a pair of silk stockings by Wm's advice.—Nothing particular occurred till we reached Ing's chapel. The door was open and we went in. It is a neat little place, with a marble floor and marble communion Table with a painting over it of the last supper, and Moses and Aaron on each side. The woman told us that 'they had painted them as near as they could by the dresses as they are described in the Bible', and gay enough they are. The Marble had been sent by Richard Bateman[6] from Leghorn.

---

[1] Rigg House, two miles beyond Hawes. It is bow-fronted, which accounts for its resemblance to Greta Hall. (D. W. writes 'Hill'.) It is now partially pulled down.

[2] W. and D. W. had walked down Garsdale on their journey to Grasmere in 1799.

[3] i.e. that of the 'Pedlar', James Patrick. See under 27 January above.

[4] Pennington in 1809 printed the Prospectus to Coleridge's periodical *The Friend*.

[5] i.e. in April 1794, on their way to stay at Windy Brow (Calvert's house) at Keswick.

[6] For the story of Robert (*not* Richard, an error made by both W. and D. W.) Bateman, see 'Michael', ll. 258–70.

The woman told us that a Man had been at her house a few days before who told her he had helped to bring it down the Red Sea and she had believed him gladly. It rained very hard when we reached Windermere. We sate in the rain at Wilcock's to change horses, and arrived at Grasmere at about 6 o'clock on Wednesday Evening, the 6th of October 1802. Molly was overjoyed to see us, for my part I cannot describe what I felt, and our dear Mary's feelings would I dare say not be easy to speak of. We went by candle light into the garden and were astonished at the growth of the Brooms, Portugal Laurels, etc. etc. etc. The next day, Thursday, we unpacked the Boxes. On Friday 8th we baked Bread, and Mary and I walked, first upon the Hill side, and then in John's Grove, then in view of Rydale, the first walk that I had taken with my Sister.

Saturday 9th. William and I walked to Mr Simpson's.

Sunday 10th. Rain all day.

Monday 11th. A beautiful day. We walked to the Easedale hills to hunt waterfalls.[1] Wm and Mary left me sitting on a stone on the solitary mountains and went to Easedale Tairn. I grew chilly and followed them. This approach to the Tairn is very beautiful. We expected to have found C. at home but he did not come till after dinner. He was well but did not look so.

Tuesday 12th October 1802. We walked with C. to Rydale.

Wednesday 13th. Set forwards with him towards Keswick and he prevailed us to go on. We consented, Mrs C. not being at home. The day was delightful. We drank tea at John Stanley's. Wrote to Annette.

Thursday 14th. We went in the evening to Calverts. Moonlight. Stayed supper.

Friday 15th. Walked to L[or]d Wm Gordon's.

Saturday 16th. Came home Mary and I, William returned to Coleridge before we reached Nadel Fell. Mary and I had a pleasant walk, the day was very bright, the people busy getting in their corn—reached home at about 5 o'clock. I was not quite well but better after tea. We made Cakes etc.

[1] Two lines in 'Louisa', written before February 1802, run:

> When up she winds along the brook
> To hunt the waterfalls.

Sunday 17th. We had 13 of our neighbours to Tea. Wm came in just as we began tea.

Monday 18th. I was not very well. I walked up in the morning to the Simpsons.

Tuesday 19th. The Simpsons drank tea and supped. William was much oppressed.

Wednesday 20th. We all walked on Butterlip How—it rained.

Thursday 21st. I walked with Wm to Rydale.

Friday 22nd.

Saturday 23rd. Mary was baking. I walked with Wm to see Langdale Rydale and the Foot of Grasmere. We had a heavenly walk, but I came home in the toothache and have since that day been confined upstairs, till now namely Saturday 30th of October 1802. William is gone to Keswick. Mary went with him to the Top of the Rays. She is returned and is now sitting near me by the fire. It is a breathless grey day that leaves the golden woods of autumn quiet in their own tranquillity, stately and beautiful in their decaying, the lake is a perfect mirror.

Saturday 30th October. Wm met Stoddart at the Bridge at the foot of Legberthwaite dale. He returned with him and they surprized us by their arrival at 4 o'clock in the afternoon. Stoddart and W. dined. I went to bed, and after tea S. read in Chaucer to us.

Monday[1] 31st October. John Monkhouse[2] called. Wm and S. went to K[eswick]. Mary and I walked to the top of the hill and looked at Rydale. I was much affected when I stood upon the 2nd bar of Sara's Gate. The lake was perfectly still, the Sun shone on Hill and vale, the distant Birch trees looked like large golden Flowers. Nothing else in colour was distinct and separate but all the beautiful colours seemed to be melted into one another, and joined together in one mass so that there were no differences though an endless variety when one tried to find it out. The Fields were of one sober yellow brown. After dinner we both lay on the floor. Mary slept. I *could* not for I was thinking of so many things. We sate nicely together after Tea looking over old Letters. Molly was gone up to Mr Simpson's to see Mrs S. who was very ill.

Monday November 1st. I wrote to Miss Lamb. After dinner Mary

[1] Actually Sunday.

[2] See p. 117, n. 2.

walked to Mr Simpson's. Letters from Cook Wrangham[1] Mrs C.

Tuesday 2nd November. William returned from K.—he was not well. Baking Day. Mr B. S.[2] came in at tea time. Molly sate up with Mrs S. William was not well this evening.

Wednesday 3rd. Mr Luff came in to tea.

Thursday 4th. I scalded my foot with coffee after having been in bed in the afternoon—I was near fainting, and then bad in my bowels. Mary waited upon me till 2 o'clock, then we went to bed and with applications of vinegar I was lulled to sleep about 4.

Friday 5th. I was laid up all day. I wrote to Montagu and Cooke and sent off letters to Miss Lamb and Coleridge.

Saturday 6th.

Sunday 7th. Fine weather. Letters from Coleridge that he was gone to London. Sara at Penrith. I wrote to Mrs Clarkson. Wm began to translate Ariosto.[3]

Monday 8th. A beautiful day. William got to work again at Ariosto, and so continued all the morning, though the day was so delightful that it made my very heart linger to be out of doors, and see and feel the beauty of the Autumn in freedom. The trees on the opposite side of the Lake are of a yellow brown, but there are one or two trees opposite our windows, (an ash tree for instance) quite green, as in spring. The fields are of their winter colour, but the Island is as green as ever it was. Mary has been baking to-day, she is now sitting in the parlour. Wm is writing out his stanzas from Ariosto. We have a nice fire. The evening is quiet. Poor Coleridge! Sara is at Keswick I hope.—William has been ill in his stomach but he is better tonight. I have read one Canto of Ariosto today.

24th December 1802, Christmas Eve. William is now sitting by me at ½ past 10 o'clock. I have been beside him ever since tea running the heel of a stocking, repeating some of his sonnets to him, listening to his own repeating, reading some of Milton's and the Allegro and Penseroso. It is a quiet keen frost. Mary is in the parlour below attending to the baking of cakes and Jenny Fletcher's pies. Sara is in bed in the toothache, and so we are

---

[1] Francis Wrangham (1769–1842), an early friend of W.'s, was rector of Hunmanby in East Yorkshire and later Archdeacon of Cleveland. He was an energetic and scholarly man, of liberal views, particularly interested in national education.

[2] i.e. Mr. Bartholomew Simpson.

[3] A few stanzas of *Orlando Furioso* are printed in the *Poetical Works*, vol. IV, Appendix B. These are all that survive.

—beloved William is turning over the leaves of Charlotte Smith's sonnets, but he keeps his hand to his poor chest pushing aside his breastplate. Mary is well and I am well, and Molly is as blithe as last year at this time. Coleridge came this morning with Wedgwood.[1] We all turned out of Wm's bedroom one by one to meet him. He looked well. We had to tell him of the Birth of his little Girl, born yesterday morning at 6 o'clock.[2] W. went with them to Wytheburn in the Chaise, and M. and I met Wm on the Rays. It was not an unpleasant morning to the feelings—far from it. The sun shone now and then, and there was no wind, but all things looked chearless and distinct, no meltings of sky into mountains—the mountains like stone-work wrought up with huge hammers.—Last Sunday was as mild a day as I ever remember. We all set off together to walk. I went to Rydale and Wm returned with me. M. and S. went round the Lakes. There were flowers of various kinds the topmost bell of a fox-glove, geraniums, daisies—a buttercup in the water (but this I saw two or three days before) small yellow flowers (I do not know their name) in the turf a large bunch of strawberry blossoms. Wm sate a while with me, then went to meet M. and S.—Last Saturday I dined at Mr Simpson's also a beautiful mild day. Monday was a frosty day, and it has been frost ever since. On Saturday I dined with Mrs Simpson. It is today Christmas-day Saturday 25th December 1802. I am 31 years of age.—It is a dull frosty day.

Again I have neglected to write my Journal—New Year's Day is passed Old Christmas day and I have recorded nothing. —It is today January 11th Tuesday.—On Christmas Day I dressed myself ready to go to Keswick in a returned chaise, but did not go. On Thursday 30th December I went to K. Wm rode before me[3] to the foot of the hill nearest Keswick. There we parted close to a little water course, which was then noisy with water, but on my return a dry channel. We ate some potted Beef on Horseback, and sweet cake. We stopped our horse close to the hedge opposite a tuft of primroses three flowers in full blossom and a Bud, they reared themselves up among the green moss.

[1] Tom Wedgwood, brother of Josiah and John Wedgwood. See the Alfoxden Journal, 26 March 1798.
[2] Sara Coleridge (1802–52), afterwards the wife of S. T. C.'s nephew, Henry Nelson Coleridge.
[3] i.e. in front of her on the horse.

We debated long whether we should pluck [them] and at last left them to live out their day, which I was right glad of at my return the Sunday following for there they remained uninjured either by cold or wet. I stayed at K. over New Year's Day, and returned on Sunday the 2nd January. Wm Mackareth fetched me. (M. and S. walked as far as John Stanley's.) Wm was alarmed at my long delay and came to within 3 miles of Keswick. He mounted before me. It had been a sweet mild day and was a pleasant Evening. C. stayed with us till Tuesday January 4th. W. and I walked up to George M.'s to endeavour to get the horse, then walked with him to Ambleside. We parted with him at the turning of the Lane, he going on horseback to the top of Kirkstone. On Thursday 6th, C. returned, and on Friday the 7th he and Sara went to Keswick. W. accompanied them to the foot of Wytheburn—I to Mrs Simpson's and dined and called on Aggy Fleming sick in bed. It was a gentle day, and when Wm and I returned home just before sunset, it was a heavenly evening. A soft sky was among the hills, and a summer sunshine above, and blending with this sky, for it was more like sky than clouds. The turf looked warm and soft.

Saturday January 9th[1]. Wm and I walked to Rydale—no letters. Still as mild as Spring, a beautiful moonlight evening and a quiet night but before morning the wind rose and it became dreadfully cold. We were not well on Sunday Mary and I.

Sunday January 9th. Mary lay long in bed, and did not walk. Wm and I walked in Brothers Wood. I was *astonished* with the beauty of the place, for I had never been there since my return home—never since before I went away in June!! Wrote to Miss Lamb.

Monday January 10th. I lay in bed to have a Drench of sleep till one o'clock. Worked all Day petticoats—Mrs C.'s wrists. Ran Wm's woollen stockings for he put them on today for the first time. We walked to Rydale, and brought letters from Sara, Annette and Maggy[2]—furiously cold.

Tuesday January 11th. A very cold day. Wm promised me he would rise as soon as I had carried him his Breakfast but he lay in bed till between 12 and one. We talked of walking, but the blackness of the Cold made us slow to put forward and we did

[1] Actually the 8th.
[2] i.e. Peggy Ashburner.

not walk at all. Mary read the Prologue to Chaucer's tales to me, in the morning William was working at his poem to C. Letter from Keswick and from Taylor[1] on Wm's marriage. C. poorly, in bad spirits. Canaries.[2] Before tea I sate 2 hours in the parlour. Read part of The Knight's Tale with exquisite delight. Since Tea Mary has been down stairs copying out Italian poems for Stuart.[3] Wm has been working beside me, and here ends this imperfect summary. I will take a nice Calais Book[4] and *will* for the future write regularly and, if I can legibly so much for this my resolution on Tuesday night, January 11th 1803. Now I am going to take Tapioca for my supper; and Mary an Egg. William some cold mutton—his poor chest is tired.

Wednesday 12th. Very cold, and cold all the week.

Sunday the 16th. Intensely cold. Wm had a fancy for some ginger bread I put on Molly's Cloak and my Spenser, and we walked towards Matthew Newton's. I went into the house. The blind Man and his Wife and Sister were sitting by the fire, all dressed very clean in their Sunday's Clothes, the sister reading. They took their little stock of gingerbread out of the cubboard and I bought 6 pennyworth. They were so grateful when I paid them for it that I could not find it in my heart to tell them we were going to make Gingerbread ourselves. I had asked them if they had no thick 'No' answered Matthew 'there was none on Friday but we'll *endeavour* to get some.' The next Day the woman came just when we were baking and we bought 2 pennyworth.

Monda[*y*][5]

<hr>

[1] William Taylor of Norwich, translator of German poetry and plays.

[2] Coleridge thinks of a voyage to the Canaries.

[3] It is not clear what these poems were. W. is not known to have translated any Italian poems at this time, other than some of *Orlando Furioso*.

[4] Presumably a notebook bought in Calais.

[5] Here the journal ends, the notebook in which it was entered being full. It is improbable that D. W. continued it in spite of the 'resolution' of 11 January.

APPENDIX I

*Shorter poems of Wordsworth
referred to in the Journals*

THE THORN[1]
(p. 10)

I

'There is a Thorn—it looks so old,
In truth, you'd find it hard to say
How it could ever have been young,
It looks so old and grey.
Not higher than a two years' child
It stands erect, this aged Thorn;
No leaves it has, no prickly points;
It is a mass of knotted joints,
A wretched thing forlorn.
It stands erect, and like a stone
With lichens is it overgrown.

II

'Like rock or stone, it is o'ergrown,
With lichens to the very top,
And hung with heavy tufts of moss,
A melancholy crop:
Up from the earth these mosses creep,
And this poor Thorn they clasp it round
So close, you'd say that they are bent
With plain and manifest intent
To drag it to the ground;

[1] Composed at Alfoxden in 1798: 'It arose,' says W. W. in the Fenwick note to this poem, 'out of my observing, on the ridge of Quantock Hill, on a stormy day, a thorn which I had often passed in calm and bright weather without noticing it. I said to myself: "Cannot I, by some invention, do as much to make this thorn permanently an impressive object as the storm has made it to my eyes at this moment?" I began the poem accordingly, and composed it with great rapidity.'

And all have joined in one endeavour
To bury this poor Thorn for ever.

III

'High on a mountain's highest ridge,
Where oft the stormy winter gale
Cuts like a scythe, while through the clouds
It sweeps from vale to vale;
Not five yards from the mountain path,
This Thorn you on your left espy;
And to the left, three yards beyond,
You see a little muddy pond
Of water—never dry,
Though but of compass small, and bare
To thirsty suns and parching air.

IV

'And, close beside this aged Thorn,
There is a fresh and lovely sight,
A beauteous heap, a hill of moss,
Just half a foot in height.
All lovely colours there you see,
All colours that were ever seen;
And mossy network too is there,
As if by hand of lady fair
The work had woven been;
And cups, the darlings of the eye,
So deep is their vermilion dye.

V

'Ah me! what lovely tints are there
Of olive green and scarlet bright,
In spikes, in branches, and in stars,
Green, red, and pearly white!
This heap of earth o'ergrown with moss,
Which close beside the Thorn you see,
So fresh in all its beauteous dyes,
Is like an infant's grave in size,
As like as like can be:
But never, never any where,
An infant's grave was half so fair.

VI

'Now would you see this aged Thorn,
This pond, and beauteous hill of moss,
You must take care and choose your time
The mountain when to cross.
For oft there sits between the heap,
So like an infant's grave in size,
And that same pond of which I spoke,
A Woman in a scarlet cloak,
And to herself she cries,
"Oh misery! oh misery!
Oh woe is me! oh misery!"

VII

'At all times of the day and night
This wretched Woman thither goes;
And she is known to every star,
And every wind that blows;
And there, beside the Thorn, she sits
When the blue daylight's in the skies,
And when the whirlwind's on the hill,
Or frosty air is keen and still,
And to herself she cries,
"Oh misery! oh misery!
Oh woe is me! oh misery!" '

VIII

'Now wherefore, thus, by day and night,
In rain, in tempest, and in snow,
Thus to the dreary mountain-top
Does this poor Woman go?
And why sits she beside the Thorn
When the blue daylight's in the sky
Or when the whirlwind's on the hill,
Or frosty air is keen and still,
And wherefore does she cry?—
O wherefore? wherefore? tell me why
Does she repeat that doleful cry?'

IX

'I cannot tell; I wish I could;
For the true reason no one knows:
But would you gladly view the spot,
The spot to which she goes;
The hillock like an infant's grave,
The pond—and Thorn, so old and grey;
Pass by her door—'tis seldom shut—
And if you see her in her hut—
Then to the spot away!
I never heard of such as dare
Approach the spot when she is there.'

X

'But wherefore to the mountain-top
Can this unhappy Woman go,
Whatever star is in the skies,
Whatever wind may blow?'
'Full twenty years are past and gone
Since she (her name is Martha Ray)
Gave with a maiden's true good-will
Her company to Stephen Hill;
And she was blithe and gay,
While friends and kindred all approved
Of him whom tenderly she loved.

XI

'And they had fixed the wedding day,
The morning that must wed them both;
But Stephen to another Maid
Had sworn another oath;
And, with this other Maid, to church
Unthinking Stephen went—
Poor Martha! on that woeful day
A pang of pitiless dismay
Into her soul was sent;
A fire was kindled in her breast,
Which might not burn itself to rest.

XII

'They say, full six months after this,
While yet the summer leaves were green,
She to the mountain-top would go,
And there was often seen.
What could she seek?—or wish to hide?
Her state to any eye was plain;
She was with child, and she was mad;
Yet often was she sober sad
From her exceeding pain.
O guilty Father—would that death
Had saved him from that breach of faith!

XIII

'Sad case for such a brain to hold
Communion with a stirring child!
Sad case, as you may think, for one
Who had a brain so wild!
Last Christmas-eve we talked of this,
And grey-haired Wilfred of the glen
Held that the unborn infant wrought
About its mother's heart, and brought
Her senses back again:
And, when at last her time drew near,
Her looks were calm, her senses clear.

XIV

'More know I not, I wish I did,
And it should all be told to you;
For what became of this poor child
No mortal ever knew;
Nay—if a child to her was born
No earthly tongue could ever tell;
And if 'twas born alive or dead,
Far less could this with proof be said;
But some remember well,
That Martha Ray about this time
Would up the mountain often climb.

XV

'And all that winter, when at night
The wind blew from the mountain-peak,
'Twas worth your while, though in the dark,
The churchyard path to seek:
For many a time and oft were heard
Cries coming from the mountain head:
Some plainly living voices were;
And others, I've heard many swear,
Were voices of the dead:
I cannot think, whate'er they say,
They had to do with Martha Ray.

XVI

'But that she goes to this old Thorn,
The Thorn which I described to you,
And there sits in a scarlet cloak,
I will be sworn is true.
For one day with my telescope,
To view the ocean wide and bright,
When to this country first I came,
Ere I had heard of Martha's name,
I climbed the mountain's height:—
A storm came on, and I could see
No object higher than my knee.

XVII

' 'Twas mist and rain, and storm and rain:
No screen, no fence could I discover;
And then the wind! in sooth, it was
A wind full ten times over.
I looked around, I thought I saw
A jutting crag,—and off I ran,
Head-foremost, through the driving rain,
The shelter of the crag to gain;
And, as I am a man,
Instead of jutting crag, I found
A Woman seated on the ground.

XVIII

'I did not speak—I saw her face;
Her face!—it was enough for me;
I turned about and heard her cry,
'Oh misery! oh misery!'
And there she sits, until the moon
Through half the clear blue sky will go;
And when the little breezes make
The waters of the pond to shake,
As all the country know,
She shudders, and you hear her cry,
"Oh misery! oh misery!" '

XIX

'But what's the Thorn? and what the pond?
And what the hill of moss to her?
And what the creeping breeze that comes
The little pond to stir?'
'I cannot tell; but some will say
She hanged her baby on the tree;
Some say she drowned it in the pond,
Which is a little step beyond:
But all and each agree,
The little Babe was buried there,
Beneath that hill of moss so fair.

XX

'I've heard, the moss is spotted red
With drops of that poor infant's blood;
But kill a new-born infant thus,
I do not think she could!
Some say, if to the pond you go,
And fix on it a steady view,
The shadow of a babe you trace,
A baby and a baby's face,
And that it looks at you;
Whene'er you look on it, 'tis plain
That baby looks at you again.

XXI

'And some had sworn an oath that she
Should be to public justice brought;
And for the little infant's bones
With spades they would have sought.
But instantly the hill of moss
Before their eyes began to stir!
And, for full fifty yards around,
The grass—it shook upon the ground!
Yet all do still aver
The little Babe lies buried there,
Beneath that hill of moss so fair.

XXII

'I cannot tell how this may be,
But plain it is the Thorn is bound
With heavy tufts of moss that strive
To drag it to the ground;
And this I know, full many a time,
When she was on the mountain high,
By day, and in the silent night,
When all the stars shone clear and bright,
That I have heard her cry,
"Oh misery! oh misery!
Oh woe is me! oh misery!"'

A NIGHT-PIECE
(p. 2)

————The sky is overcast
With a continuous cloud of texture close,
Heavy and wan, all whitened by the Moon,
Which through that veil is indistinctly seen,
A dull, contracted circle, yielding light
So feebly spread that not a shadow falls,
Chequering the ground—from rock, plant, tree, or tower.
At length a pleasant instantaneous gleam
Startles the pensive traveller while he treads
His lonesome path, with unobserving eye

Bent earthwards; he looks up—the clouds are split
Asunder,—and above his head he sees
The clear Moon, and the glory of the heavens.
There, in a black-blue vault she sails along,
Followed by multitudes of stars, that, small
And sharp, and bright, along the dark abyss
Drive as she drives: how fast they wheel away,
Yet vanish not!—the wind is in the tree,
But they are silent;—still they roll along
Immeasurably distant; and the vault,
Built round by those white clouds, enormous clouds,
Still deepens its unfathomable depth.
At length the Vision closes; and the mind,
Not undisturbed by the delight it feels,
Which slowly settles into peaceful calm,
Is left to muse upon the solemn scene.

A WHIRL-BLAST FROM BEHIND THE HILL
(p. 10)

A whirl-blast from behind the hill
Rushed o'er the wood with startling sound;
Then—all at once the air was still,
And showers of hailstones pattered round.
Where leafless oaks towered high above,
I sat within an undergrove
Of tallest hollies, tall and green;
A fairer bower was never seen.
From year to year the spacious floor
With withered leaves is covered o'er,
And all the year the bower is green.
But see! where'er the hailstones drop
The withered leaves all skip and hop;
There's not a breeze—no breath of air—
Yet here, and there, and every where
Along the floor, beneath the shade
By those embowering hollies made,
The leaves in myriads jump and spring,

As if with pipes and music rare
Some Robin Good-fellow were there,
And all those leaves, in festive glee,
Were dancing to the minstrelsy.

BEGGARS
(p. 100)

She had a tall man's height or more;
Her face from summer's noontide heat
No bonnet shaded, but she wore
A mantle, to her very feet
Descending with a graceful flow,
And on her head a cap as white as new-fallen snow.

Her skin was of Egyptian brown:
Haughty, as if her eye had seen
Its own light to a distance thrown,
She towered, fit person for a Queen
To lead those ancient Amazonian files;
Or ruling Bandit's wife among the Grecian isles.

Advancing, forth she stretched her hand
And begged an alms with doleful plea
That ceased not; on our English land
Such woes, I knew, could never be;
And yet a boon I gave her, for the creature
Was beautiful to see—a weed of glorious feature.

I left her, and pursued my way;
And soon before me did espy
A pair of little Boys at play,
Chasing a crimson butterfly;
The taller followed with his hat in hand,
Wreathed round with yellow flowers the gayest of the land.

The other wore a rimless crown
With leaves of laurel stuck about;
And while both followed up and down,

Each whooping with a merry shout,
In their fraternal features I could trace
Unquestionable lines of that wild Suppliant's face.

Yet *they*, so blithe of heart, seemed fit
For finest tasks of earth or air:
Wings let them have, and they might flit
Precursors to Aurora's car,
Scattering fresh flowers; though happier far, I ween,
To hunt their fluttering game o'er rock and level green.

They dart across my path—but lo,
Each ready with a plaintive whine!
Said I, 'not half an hour ago
Your Mother has had alms of mine.'
'That cannot be,' one answered—'she is dead:'—
I looked reproof—they saw—but neither hung his head.

'She has been dead, Sir, many a day,'—
'Hush, boys! you're telling me a lie;
It was your Mother, as I say!'
And, in the twinkling of an eye,
'Come! come!' cried one, and without more ado
Off to some other play the joyous Vagrants flew!

TO JOANNA[1]
(p. 35)

Amid the smoke of cities did you pass
The time of early youth; and there you learned,
From years of quiet industry, to love
The living Beings by your own fire-side,
With such a strong devotion, that your heart
Is slow to meet the sympathies of them
Who look upon the hills with tenderness,
And make dear friendships with the streams and groves.
Yet we, who are transgressors in this kind,

[1] The incident recorded in this poem is not historical. Joanna Hutchinson had not yet visited Grasmere.

Dwelling retired in our simplicity
Among the woods and fields, we love you well,
Joanna! and I guess, since you have been
So distant from us now for two long years,
That you will gladly listen to discourse,
However trivial, if you thence be taught
That they, with whom you once were happy, talk
Familiarly of you and of old times.

While I was seated, now some ten days past,
Beneath those lofty firs, that overtop
Their ancient neighbour, the old steeple-tower,
The Vicar from his gloomy house hard by
Came forth to greet me; and, when he had asked,
'How fares Joanna, that wild-hearted Maid!
And when will she return to us?' he paused;
And, after short exchange of village news,
He with grave looks demanded, for what cause,
Reviving obsolete idolatry,
I, like a Runic Priest, in characters
Of formidable size had chiselled out
Some uncouth name upon the native rock,
Above the Rotha, by the forest-side.
—Now, by those dear immunities of heart
Engendered between malice and true love,
I was not loth to be so catechised,
And this was my reply:—'As it befell,
One summer morning we had walked abroad
At break of day, Joanna and myself.
—'Twas that delightful season when the broom,
Full-flowered, and visible on every steep,
Along the copses runs in veins of gold.
Our pathway led us on to Rotha's banks;
And when we came in front of that tall rock
That eastward looks, I there stopped short—and stood
Tracing the lofty barrier with my eye
From base to summit; such delight I found
To note in shrub and tree, in stone and flower,
That intermixture of delicious hues,
Along so vast a surface, all at once,

In one impression, by connecting force
Of their own beauty, imaged in the heart.
—When I had gazed perhaps two minutes' space,
Joanna, looking in my eyes, beheld
That ravishment of mine, and laughed aloud.
The Rock, like something starting from a sleep,
Took up the Lady's voice, and laughed again;
That ancient Woman seated on Helm-crag
Was ready with her cavern; Hammar-scar,
And the tall Steep of Silver-how, sent forth
A noise of laughter; southern Loughrigg heard,
And Fairfield answered with a mountain tone;
Helvellyn far into the clear blue sky
Carried the Lady's voice,—old Skiddaw blew
His speaking-trumpet;—back out of the clouds
Of Glaramara southward came the voice;
And Kirkstone tossed it from his misty head.
—Now whether (said I to our cordial Friend,
Who in the hey-day of astonishment
Smiled in my face) this were in simple truth
A work accomplished by the brotherhood
Of ancient mountains, or my ear was touched
With dreams and visionary impulses
To me alone imparted, sure I am
That there was a loud uproar in the hills,
And, while we both were listening, to my side
The fair Joanna drew, as if she wished
To shelter from some object of her fear.
—And hence, long afterwards, when eighteen moons
Were wasted, as I chanced to walk alone
Beneath this rock, at sunrise, on a calm
And silent morning, I sat down, and there,
In memory of affections old and true,
I chiselled out in those rude characters
Joanna's name deep in the living stone:—
And I, and all who dwell by my fireside,
Have called the lovely rock, Joanna's Rock.'

THE FIR-GROVE[1]
(p. 36)

When, to the attractions of the busy world
Preferring studious leisure, I had chosen
A habitation in this peaceful Vale,
Sharp season followed of continual storm
In deepest winter; and, from week to week,
Pathway, and lane, and public road, were clogged
With frequent showers of snow. Upon a hill,
At a short distance from my cottage, stands
A stately Fir-grove, whither I was wont
To hasten, for I found, beneath the roof
Of that perennial shade, a cloistral place
Of refuge, with an unincumbered floor.
Here, in safe covert, on the shallow snow,
And, sometimes, on a speck of visible earth,
The redbreast near me hopped; nor was I loth
To sympathize with vulgar coppice birds
That, for protection from the nipping blast,
Hither repaired.—A single beech-tree grew
Within this grove of firs! and, on the fork
Of that one beech, appeared a thrush's nest;
A last year's nest, conspicuously built
At such small elevation from the ground
As gave sure sign that they, who in that house
Of nature and of love had made their home
Amid the fir-trees, all the summer long
Dwelt in a tranquil spot. And oftentimes
A few sheep, stragglers from some mountain-flock,
Would watch my motions with suspicious stare,
From the remotest outskirts of the grove,—
Some nook where they had made their final stand,
Huddling together from two fears—the fear
Of me and of the storm. Full many an hour
Here did I lose. But in this grove the trees
Had been so thickly planted, and had thriven
In such perplexed and intricate array,

[1] Probably also to be identified with the 'Silver How poem', p. 106.

That vainly did I seek, beneath their stems,
A length of open space, where to and fro
My feet might move without concern or care;
And, baffled thus, though earth from day to day
Was fettered, and the air by storm disturbed,
I ceased the shelter to frequent,—and prized,
Less than I wished to prize, that calm recess.

The snows dissolved, and genial Spring returned
To clothe the fields with verdure. Other haunts
Meanwhile were mine; till one bright April day,
By chance retiring from the glare of noon
To this forsaken covert, there I found
A hoary pathway traced between the trees,
And winding on with such an easy line
Along a natural opening, that I stood
Much wondering how I could have sought in vain
For what was now so obvious. To abide,
For an allotted interval of ease,
Under my cottage-roof, had gladly come
From the wild sea a cherished Visitant;
And with the sight of this same path—begun,
Begun and ended, in the shady grove,
Pleasant conviction flashed upon my mind
That, to this opportune recess allured,
He had surveyed it with a finer eye,
A heart more wakeful; and had worn the track
By pacing here, unwearied and alone,
In that habitual restlessness of foot
That haunts the Sailor measuring o'er and o'er
His short domain upon the vessel's deck,
While she pursues her course through the dreary sea.

When thou hadst quitted Esthwaite's pleasant shore,
And taken thy first leave of those green hills
And rocks that were the play-ground of thy youth,
Year followed year, my Brother! and we two,
Conversing not, knew little in what mould
Each other's mind was fashioned; and at length,
When once again we met in Grasmere Vale,

Between us there was little other bond
Than common feelings of fraternal love.
But thou, a School-boy, to the sea hadst carried
Undying recollections; Nature there
Was with thee; she, who loved us both, she still
Was with thee; and even so didst thou become
A *silent* Poet; from the solitude
Of the vast sea didst bring a watchful heart
Still couchant, an inevitable ear,
And an eye practised like a blind man's touch.
—Back to the joyless Ocean thou art gone;
Nor from this vestige of thy musing hours
Could I withhold thy honoured name,—and now
I love the fir-grove with a perfect love.
Thither do I withdraw when cloudless suns
Shine hot, or wind blows troublesome and strong;
And there I sit at evening, when the steep
Of Silver-how, and Grasmere's peaceful lake,
And one green island, gleam between the stems
Of the dark firs, a visionary scene!
And while I gaze upon the spectacle
Of clouded splendour, on this dream-like sight
Of solemn loveliness, I think on thee,
My Brother, and on all which thou hast lost.
Nor seldom, if I rightly guess, while Thou,
Muttering the verses which I muttered first
Among the mountains, through the midnight watch
Art pacing thoughtfully the vessel's deck
In some far region, here, while o'er my head,
At every impulse of the moving breeze,
The fir-grove murmurs with a sea-like sound,
Alone I tread this path;—for aught I know,
Timing my steps to thine; and, with a store
Of undistinguishable sympathies,
Mingling most earnest wishes for the day
When we, and others whom we love, shall meet
A second time, in Grasmere's happy Vale.

NOTE.—This wish was not granted; the lamented Person not long after perished by shipwreck, in discharge of his duty as Commander of the Honourable East India Company's Vessel, the Earl of Abergavenny.

THE LEECH-GATHERER
(*Published 1807 as* Resolution and Independence)
(p. 120)

I

There was a roaring in the wind all night;
The rain came heavily and fell in floods;
But now the sun is rising calm and bright;
The birds are singing in the distant woods;
Over his own sweet voice the Stock-dove broods;
The Jay makes answer as the Magpie chatters;
And all the air is filled with pleasant noise of waters.

II

All things that love the sun are out of doors;
The sky rejoices in the morning's birth;
The grass is bright with rain-drops;—on the moors
The hare is running races in her mirth;
And with her feet she from the plashy earth
Raises a mist; that, glittering in the sun,
Runs with her all the way, wherever she doth run.

III

I was a Traveller then upon the moor;
I saw the hare that raced about with joy;
I heard the woods and distant waters roar;
Or heard them not, as happy as a boy:
The pleasant season did my heart employ:
My old remembrances went from me wholly;
And all the ways of men, so vain and melancholy.

IV

But, as it sometimes chanceth, from the might
Of joy in minds that can no further go,
As high as we have mounted in delight
In our dejection do we sink as low;
To me that morning did it happen so;
And fears and fancies thick upon me came;
Dim sadness—and blind thoughts, I knew not, nor could name.

V

I heard the sky-lark warbling in the sky;
And I bethought me of the playful hare:
Even such a happy Child of earth am I;
Even as these blissful creatures do I fare;
Far from the world I walk, and from all care;
But there may come another day to me—
Solitude, pain of heart, distress, and poverty.

VI

My whole life I have lived in pleasant thought,
As if life's business were a summer mood;
As if all needful things would come unsought
To genial faith, still rich in genial good;
But how can He expect that others should
Build for him, sow for him, and at his call
Love him, who for himself will take no heed at all?

VII

I thought of Chatterton, the marvellous Boy,
The sleepless Soul that perished in his pride;
Of Him who walked in glory and in joy
Following his plough, along the mountain-side:
By our own spirits are we deified:
We Poets in our youth begin in gladness;
But thereof come in the end despondency and madness.

VIII

Now, whether it were by peculiar grace,
A leading from above, a something given,
Yet it befell that, in this lonely place,
When I with these untoward thoughts had striven,
Beside a pool bare to the eye of heaven
I saw a Man before me unawares:
The oldest man he seemed that ever wore grey hairs.

IX

As a huge stone is sometimes seen to lie
Couched on the bald top of an eminence;
Wonder to all who do the same espy,

By what means it could thither come, and whence;
So that it seems a thing endued with sense:
Like a sea-beast crawled forth, that on a shelf
Of rock or sand reposeth, there to sun itself;

X

Such seemed this Man, not all alive nor dead,
Nor all asleep—in his extreme old age:
His body was bent double, feet and head
Coming together in life's pilgrimage;
As if some dire constraint of pain, or rage
Of sickness felt by him in times long past,
A more than human weight upon his frame had cast.

XI

Himself he propped, limbs, body, and pale face,
Upon a long grey staff of shaven wood:
And, still as I drew near with gentle pace,
Upon the margin of that moorish flood
Motionless as a cloud the old Man stood,
That heareth not the loud winds when they call;
And moveth all together, if it move at all.

XII

At length, himself unsettling, he the pond
Stirred with his staff, and fixedly did look
Upon the muddy water, which he conned,
As if he had been reading in a book:
And now a stranger's privilege I took;
And, drawing to his side, to him did say,
'This morning gives us promise of a glorious day.'

XIII

A gentle answer did the old Man make,
In courteous speech which forth he slowly drew:
And him with further words I thus bespake,
'What occupation do you there pursue?
This is a lonesome place for one like you.'
Ere he replied, a flash of mild surprise
Broke from the sable orbs of his yet-vivid eyes.

XIV

His words came feebly, from a feeble chest,
But each in solemn order followed each,
With something of a lofty utterance drest—
Choice word and measured phrase, above the reach
Of ordinary men; a stately speech;
Such as grave Livers do in Scotland use,
Religious men, who give to God and man their dues.

XV

He told, that to these waters he had come
To gather leeches, being old and poor:
Employment hazardous and wearisome!
And he had many hardships to endure:
From pond to pond he roamed, from moor to moor;
Housing, with God's good help, by choice or chance;
And in this way he gained an honest maintenance.

XVI

The old Man still stood talking by my side;
But now his voice to me was like a stream
Scarce heard; nor word from word could I divide;
And the whole body of the Man did seem
Like one whom I had met with in a dream;
Or like a man from some far region sent,
To give me human strength, by apt admonishment.

XVII

My former thoughts returned: the fear that kills;
And hope that is unwilling to be fed;
Cold, pain, and labour, and all fleshly ills;
And mighty Poets in their misery dead.
—Perplexed, and longing to be comforted,
My question eagerly did I renew,
'How is it that you live, and what is it you do?'

XVIII

He with a smile did then his words repeat;
And said that, gathering leeches, far and wide
He travelled; stirring thus about his feet

The waters of the pools where they abide.
'Once I could meet with them on every side;
But they have dwindled long by slow decay;
Yet still I persevere, and find them where I may.'

XIX

While he was talking thus, the lonely place,
The old Man's shape, and speech—all troubled me:
In my mind's eye I seemed to see him pace
About the weary moors continually,
Wandering about alone and silently.
While I these thoughts within myself pursued,
He, having made a pause, the same discourse renewed.

XX

And soon with this he other matter blended,
Cheerfully uttered, with demeanour kind,
But stately in the main; and when he ended,
I could have laughed myself to scorn to find
In that decrepit Man so firm a mind.
'God,' said I, 'be my help and stay secure;
I'll think of the Leech-gatherer on the lonely moor!'

POINT RASH-JUDGMENT[1]
(p. 44)

A narrow girdle of rough stones and crags,
A rude and natural causeway, interposed
Between the water and a winding slope
Of copse and thicket, leaves the eastern shore
Of Grasmere safe in its own privacy:
And there myself and two beloved Friends,
One calm September morning, ere the mist
Had altogether yielded to the sun,
Sauntered on this retired and difficult way.

[1] Written in 1800: W. W. says: 'The character of the eastern shore of Grasmere Lake is quite changed since these verses were written, by the public road being carried along its side. The friends spoken of were Coleridge and my Sister, and the facts occurred strictly as recorded.'

——Ill suits the road with one in haste; but we
Played with our time; and, as we strolled along,
It was our occupation to observe
Such objects as the waves had tossed ashore—
Feather, or leaf, or weed, or withered bough,
Each on the other heaped, along the line
Of the dry wreck. And, in our vacant mood,
Not seldom did we stop to watch some tuft
Of dandelion seed or thistle's beard,
That skimmed the surface of the dead calm lake,
Suddenly halting now—a lifeless stand!
And starting off again with freak as sudden;
In all its sportive wanderings, all the while,
Making report of an invisible breeze
That was its wings, its chariot, and its horse,
Its playmate, rather say, its moving soul.
——And often, trifling with a privilege
Alike indulged to all, we paused, one now,
And now the other, to point out, perchance
To pluck, some flower or water-weed, too fair
Either to be divided from the place
On which it grew, or to be left alone
To its own beauty. Many such there are,
Fair ferns and flowers, and chiefly that tall fern,
So stately, of the Queen Osmunda named;
Plant lovelier, in its own retired abode
On Grasmere's beach, then Naiad by the side
Of Grecian brook, or Lady of the Mere,
Sole-sitting by the shores of old romance.
—So fared we that bright morning: from the fields,
Meanwhile, a noise was heard, the busy mirth
Of reapers, men and women, boys and girls.
Delighted much to listen to those sounds,
And feeding thus our fancies, we advanced
Along the indented shore; when suddenly,
Through a thin veil of glittering haze was seen
Before us, on a point of jutting land,
The tall and upright figure of a Man
Attired in peasant's garb, who stood alone,
Angling beside the margin of the lake.

'Improvident and reckless,' we exclaimed,
'The Man must be, who thus can lose a day
Of the mid harvest, when the labourer's hire
Is ample, and some little might be stored
Wherewith to cheer him in the winter time.'
Thus talking of that Peasant, we approached
Close to the spot where with his rod and line
He stood alone; whereat he turned his head
To greet us—and we saw a Man worn down
By sickness, gaunt and lean, with sunken cheeks
And wasted limbs, his legs so long and lean
That for my single self I looked at them,
Forgetful of the body they sustained.—
Too weak to labour in the harvest field,
The Man was using his best skill to gain
A pittance from the dead unfeeling lake
That knew not of his wants. I will not say
What thoughts immediately were ours, nor how
The happy idleness of that sweet morn,
With all its lovely images, was changed
To serious musing and to self-reproach.
Nor did we fail to see within ourselves
What need there is to be reserved in speech,
And temper all our thoughts with charity.
—Therefore, unwilling to forget that day,
My Friend, Myself, and She[1] who then received
The same admonishment, have called the place
By a memorial name, uncouth indeed
As e'er by mariner was given to bay
Or foreland, on a new-discovered coast;
And POINT RASH-JUDGMENT is the Name it bears.

[1] i.e. D. W., W. W., Mary Hutchinson.

ALICE FELL;
OR, POVERTY
(p. 100)

The post-boy drove with fierce career,
For threatening clouds the moon had drowned;
When, as we hurried on, my ear
Was smitten with a startling sound.

As if the wind blew many ways,
I heard the sound,—and more and more;
It seemed to follow with the chaise,
And still I heard it as before.

At length I to the boy called out;
He stopped his horses at the word,
But neither cry, nor voice, nor shout,
Nor aught else like it, could be heard.

The boy then smacked his whip, and fast
The horses scampered through the rain;
But, hearing soon upon the blast
The cry, I bade him halt again.

Forthwith alighting on the ground,
'Whence comes,' said I, 'this piteous moan?'
And there a little Girl I found,
Sitting behind the chaise, alone.

'My cloak!' no other word she spake,
But loud and bitterly she wept,
As if her innocent heart would break;
And down from off her seat she leapt.

'What ails you, child?'—she sobbed, 'Look here!'
I saw it in the wheel entangled,
A weather-beaten rag as e'er
From any garden scare-crow dangled.

There, twisted between nave and spoke,
It hung, nor could at once be freed;
But our joint pains unloosed the cloak,
A miserable rag indeed!

'And whither are you going, child,
To-night along these lonesome ways?'
'To Durham,' answered she, half wild—
'Then come with me into the chaise.'

Insensible to all relief
Sat the poor girl, and forth did send
Sob after sob, as if her grief
Could never, never have an end.

'My child, in Durham do you dwell?'
She checked herself in her distress,
And said, 'My name is Alice Fell;
I'm fatherless and motherless.

'And I to Durham, Sir, belong.'
Again, as if the thought would choke
Her very heart, her grief grew strong;
And all was for her tattered cloak!

The chaise drove on; our journey's end
Was nigh; and, sitting by my side,
As if she had lost her only friend
She wept, nor would be pacified.

Up to the tavern-door we post;
Of Alice and her grief I told;
And I gave money to the host,
To buy a new cloak for the old.

'And let it be of duffil grey,
As warm a cloak as man can sell!'
Proud creature was she the next day,
The little orphan, Alice Fell!

THE SINGING BIRD
(*Published as* The Sailor's Mother)
(p. 99)

One morning (raw it was and wet—
A foggy day in winter time)
A Woman on the road I met,
Not old, though something past her prime:
Majestic in her person, tall and straight;
And like a Roman matron's was her mien and gait.

The ancient spirit is not dead;
Old times, thought I, are breathing there;
Proud was I that my country bred
Such strength, a dignity so fair:
She begged an alms, like one in poor estate;
I looked at her again, nor did my pride abate.

When from these lofty thoughts I woke,
'What is it,' said I, 'that you bear,
Beneath the covert of your Cloak,
Protected from this cold damp air?'
She answered, soon as she the question heard,
'A simple burthen, Sir, a little Singing-bird.'

And, thus continuing, she said,
'I had a Son, who many a day
Sailed on the seas, but he is dead;
In Denmark he was cast away:
And I have travelled weary miles to see
If aught which he had owned might still remain for me.

'The bird and cage they both were his:
'Twas my Son's bird; and neat and trim
He kept it: many voyages
The singing-bird had gone with him;
When last he sailed, he left the bird behind;
From bodings, as might be, that hung upon his mind.

'He to a fellow-lodger's care
Had left it, to be watched and fed,
And pipe its song in safety;—there
I found it when my Son was dead;
And now, God help me for my little wit!
I bear it with me, Sir;—he took so much delight in it.'

TO A BUTTERFLY
(p. 101)

Stay near me—do not take thy flight!
A little longer stay in sight!
Much converse do I find in thee,
Historian of my infancy!
Float near me; do not yet depart!
Dead times revive in thee:
Thou bring'st, gay creature as thou art!
A solemn image to my heart,
My father's family!

Oh! pleasant, pleasant were the days,
The time, when, in our childish plays,
My sister Emmeline and I
Together chased the butterfly!
A very hunter did I rush
Upon the prey:—with leaps and springs
I followed on from brake to bush;
But she, God love her! feared to brush
The dust from off its wings.

THE EMIGRANT MOTHER
(p. 102)

Once in a lonely hamlet I sojourned
In which a Lady driven from France did dwell;
The big and lesser griefs with which she mourned,
In friendship she to me would often tell.

This Lady, dwelling upon British ground,
Where she was childless, daily would repair
To a poor neighbouring cottage; as I found,
For sake of a young Child whose home was there.

Once having seen her clasp with fond embrace
This Child, I chanted to myself a lay,
Endeavouring, in our English tongue, to trace
Such things as she unto the Babe might say:
And thus, from what I heard and knew, or guessed,
My song the workings of her heart expressed.

I

'Dear Babe, thou daughter of another,
One moment let me be thy mother!
An infant's face and looks are thine
And sure a mother's heart is mine:
Thy own dear mother's far away,
At labour in the harvest field:
Thy little sister is at play;—
What warmth, what comfort would it yield
To my poor heart, if thou wouldst be
One little hour a child to me!

II

'Across the waters I am come,
And I have left a babe at home:
A long, long way of land and sea!
Come to me—I'm no enemy:
I am the same who at thy side
Sate yesterday, and made a nest
For thee, sweet Baby!—thou hast tried,
Thou know'st the pillow of my breast;
Good, good art thou:—alas! to me
Far more than I can be to thee.

III

'Here, little Darling, dost thou lie;
An infant thou, a mother I!
Mine wilt thou be, thou hast no fears;
Mine art thou—spite of these my tears.

Alas! before I left the spot,
My baby and its dwelling-place,
The nurse said to me, 'Tears should not
Be shed upon an infant's face,
It was unlucky'—no, no, no;
No truth is in them who say so!

IV

'My own dear Little-one will sigh,
Sweet Babe! and they will let him die.
'He pines,' they'll say, 'it is his doom,
And you may see his hour is come.'
Oh! had he but thy cheerful smiles,
Limbs stout as thine, and lips as gay,
Thy looks, thy cunning, and thy wiles,
And countenance like a summer's day,
They would have hopes of him;—and then
I should behold his face again!

V

' 'Tis gone—like dreams that we forget;
There was a smile or two—yet—yet
I can remember them, I see
The smiles, worth all the world to me.
Dear Baby! I must lay thee down;
Thou troublest me with strange alarms;
Smiles hast thou, bright ones of thy own;
I cannot keep thee in my arms;
For they confound me;—where—where is
That last, that sweetest smile of his?

VI

'Oh! how I love thee!—we will stay
Together here this one half day.
My sister's child, who bears my name,
From France to sheltering England came;
She with her mother crossed the sea;
The babe and mother near me dwell:

Yet does my yearning heart to thee
Turn rather, though I love her well:
Rest, little Stranger, rest thee here!
Never was any child more dear!

VII

'—I cannot help it; ill intent
I've none, my pretty Innocent!
I weep—I know they do thee wrong,
These tears—and my poor idle tongue.
Oh, what a kiss was that! my cheek
How cold it is! but thou art good;
Thine eyes are on me—they would speak,
I think, to help me if they could.
Blessings upon that soft, warm face,
My heart again is in its place!

VIII

'While thou art mine, my little Love,
This cannot be a sorrowful grove;
Contentment, hope, and mother's glee,
I seem to find them all in thee:
Here's grass to play with, here are flowers;
I'll call thee by my darling's name;
Thou hast, I think, a look of ours,
Thy features seem to me the same;
His little sister thou shalt be;
And, when once more my home I see,
I'll tell him many tales of Thee.'

TO THE CUCKOO
(p. 105)

O blithe New-comer! I have heard,
I hear thee and rejoice.
O Cuckoo! shall I call thee Bird,
Or but a wandering Voice?

While I am lying on the grass
Thy twofold shout I hear,
From hill to hill it seems to pass
At once far off, and near.

Though babbling only to the Vale,
Of sunshine and of flowers,
Thou bringest unto me a tale
Of visionary hours.

Thrice welcome, darling of the Spring!
Even yet thou art to me
No bird, but an invisible thing,
A voice, a mystery;

The same whom in my schoolboy days
I listened to; that Cry
Which made me look a thousand ways
In bush, and tree, and sky.

To seek thee did I often rove
Through woods and on the green;
And thou wert still a hope, a love;
Still longed for, never seen.

And I can listen to thee yet;
Can lie upon the plain
And listen, till I do beget
That golden time again.

O Blessèd Bird! the earth we pace
Again appears to be
An unsubstantial, faery place;
That is fit home for Thee!

THE RAINBOW
(*Published as* My heart leaps up when I behold)
(p. 106)

My heart leaps up when I behold
 A rainbow in the sky:
So was it when my life began;
So is it now I am a man;
So be it when I shall grow old,
 Or let me die!
The Child is father of the Man;
And I could wish my days to be
Bound each to each by natural piety.

ODE: INTIMATIONS OF IMMORTALITY FROM RECOLLECTIONS OF EARLY CHILDHOOD

The Child is father of the Man;
And I could wish my days to be
Bound each to each by natural piety.

(p. 106)

I

There was a time when meadow, grove, and stream,
The earth, and every common sight,
 To me did seem
 Apparelled in celestial light,
The glory and the freshness of a dream.
It is not now as it hath been of yore;—
 Turn wheresoe'er I may,
 By night or day,
The things which I have seen I now can see no more.

II

The Rainbow comes and goes,
And lovely is the Rose,
The Moon doth with delight
Look round her when the heavens are bare;
Waters on a starry night
Are beautiful and fair;
The sunshine is a glorious birth;
But yet I know, where'er I go,
That there hath past away a glory from the earth.

III

Now, while the birds thus sing a joyous song,
And while the young lambs bound
As to the tabor's sound,
To me alone there came a thought of grief:
A timely utterance gave that thought relief,
And I again am strong:
The cataracts blow their trumpets from the steep;
No more shall grief of mine the season wrong;
I hear the Echoes through the mountains throng,
The Winds come to me from the fields of sleep,
And all the earth is gay;
Land and sea
Give themselves up to jollity,
And with the heart of May
Doth every Beast keep holiday;—
Thou Child of Joy,
Shout round me, let me hear thy shouts, thou happy Shepherd-boy!

IV

Ye blessèd Creatures, I have heard the call
Ye to each other make; I see
The heavens laugh with you in your jubilee;
My heart is at your festival,
My head hath its coronal,
The fulness of your bliss, I feel—I feel it all.
Oh evil day! if I were sullen
While Earth herself is adorning,
This sweet May-morning,

And the Children are culling
    On every side,
  In a thousand valleys far and wide,
    Fresh flowers; while the sun shines warm,
And the Babe leaps up on his Mother's arm:—
    I hear, I hear, with joy I hear!
    —But there's a Tree, of many, one,
A single Field which I have looked upon,
Both of them speak of something that is gone:
    The Pansy at my feet
    Doth the same tale repeat:
Whither is fled the visionary gleam?
Where is it now, the glory and the dream?

V

Our birth is but a sleep and a forgetting:
The Soul that rises with us, our life's Star,
    Hath had elsewhere its setting,·
    And cometh from afar:
    Not in entire forgetfulness,
    And not in utter nakedness,
But trailing clouds of glory do we come
    From God, who is our home:
Heaven lies about us in our infancy!
Shades of the prison-house begin to close
    Upon the growing Boy,
      But He
Beholds the light, and whence it flows,
    He sees it in his joy;
The Youth, who daily farther from the east
    Must travel, still is Nature's Priest,
    And by the vision splendid
    Is on his way attended;
At length the Man perceives it die away,
And fade into the light of common day.

VI

Earth fills her lap with pleasures of her own;
Yearnings she hath in her own natural kind,

And, even with something of a Mother's mind,
    And no unworthy aim,
    The homely Nurse doth all she can
To make her Foster-child, her Inmate Man,
    Forget the glories he hath known,
And that imperial palace whence he came.

VII

Behold the Child among his new-born blisses,
A six years' Darling of a pigmy size!
See, where 'mid work of his own hand he lies,
Fretted by sallies of his mother's kisses,
With light upon him from his father's eyes!
See, at his feet, some little plan or chart,
Some fragment from his dream of human life,
Shaped by himself with newly-learned art;
    A wedding or a festival,
    A mourning or a funeral;
      And this hath now his heart,
    And unto this he frames his song:
      Then will he fit his tongue
To dialogues of business, love, or strife;
    But it will not be long,
    Ere this be thrown aside,
    And with new joy and pride
The little Actor cons another part;
Filling from time to time his 'humorous stage'
With all the Persons, down to palsied Age,
That Life brings with her in her equipage;
    As if his whole vocation
    Were endless imitation.

VIII

Thou, whose exterior semblance doth belie
    Thy Soul's immensity;
Thou best Philosopher, who yet dost keep
Thy heritage, thou Eye among the blind,
That, deaf and silent, read'st the eternal deep,

Haunted for ever by the eternal mind,—
    Mighty Prophet! Seer blest!
    On whom those truths do rest,
Which we are toiling all our lives to find,
In darkness lost, the darkness of the grave;
Thou, over whom thy Immortality
Broods like the Day, a Master o'er a Slave,
A Presence which is not to be put by;
Thou little Child, yet glorious in the might
Of heaven-born freedom on thy being's height,
Why with such earnest pains dost thou provoke
The years to bring the inevitable yoke,
Thus blindly with thy blessedness at strife?
Full soon thy Soul shall have her earthly freight,
And custom lie upon thee with a weight,
Heavy as frost, and deep almost as life!

IX

    O joy! that in our embers
    Is something that doth live,
    That nature yet remembers
    What was so fugitive!
The thought of our past years in me doth breed
Perpetual benediction: not indeed
For that which is most worthy to be blest;
Delight and liberty, the simple creed
Of Childhood, whether busy or at rest,
With new-fledged hope still fluttering in his breast:—
    Not for these I raise
    The song of thanks and praise;
    But for those obstinate questionings
    Of sense and outward things,
    Fallings from us, vanishings;
    Blank misgivings of a Creature
Moving about in worlds not realised,
High instincts before our mortal Nature
Did tremble like a guilty Thing surprised:
    But for those first affections,
    Those shadowy recollections,
Which, be they what they may.

Are yet the fountain light of all our day,
Are yet a master light of all our seeing;
    Uphold us, cherish, and have power to make
Our noisy years seem moments in the being
Of the eternal Silence: truths that wake,
       To perish never;
Which neither listlessness, nor mad endeavour,
       Nor Man nor Boy,
       Nor all that is at enmity with joy,
       Can utterly abolish or destroy!
       Hence in a season of calm weather
       Though inland far we be,
Our Souls have sight of that immortal sea
       Which brought us hither,
     Can in a moment travel thither,
And see the Children sport upon the shore,
And hear the mighty waters rolling evermore.

          x

Then sing, ye Birds, sing, sing a joyous song!
       And let the young Lambs bound
       As to the tabor's sound!
We in thought will join your throng,
       Ye that pipe and ye that play,
       Ye that through your hearts to-day
       Feel the gladness of the May!
What though the radiance which was once so bright
Be now for ever taken from my sight,
       Though nothing can bring back the hour
Of splendour in the grass, of glory in the flower;
       We will grieve not, rather find
       Strength in what remains behind;
       In the primal sympathy
       Which having been must ever be;
       In the soothing thoughts that spring
       Out of human suffering;
       In the faith that looks through death,
In years that bring the philosophic mind.

XI

And O, ye Fountains, Meadows, Hills, and Groves,
Forebode not any severing of our loves!
Yet in my heart of hearts I feel your might;
I only have relinquished one delight
To live beneath your more habitual sway.
I love the Brooks which down their channels fret,
Even more than when I tripped lightly as they;
The innocent brightness of a new-born Day
　　　　Is lovely yet;
The Clouds that gather round the setting sun
Do take a sober colouring from an eye
That hath kept watch o'er man's mortality;
Another race hath been, and other palms are won.
Thanks to the human heart by which we live,
Thanks to its tenderness, its joys, and fears,
To me the meanest flower that blows can give
Thoughts that do often lie too deep for tears.

TO THE SMALL CELANDINE
(p. 118)

Pansies, lilies, kingcups, daisies,
Let them live upon their praises;
Long as there's a sun that sets,
Primroses will have their glory;
Long as there are violets,
They will have a place in story:
There's a flower that shall be mine,
'Tis the little Celandine.

Eyes of some men travel far
For the finding of a star;
Up and down the heavens they go,
Men that keep a mighty rout!
I'm as great as they, I trow,
Since the day I found thee out,
Little Flower—I'll make a stir,
Like a sage astronomer.

Modest, yet withal an Elf
Bold, and lavish of thyself;
Since we needs must first have met
I have seen thee, high and low,
Thirty years or more, and yet
'Twas a face I did not know;
Thou hast now, go where I may,
Fifty greetings in a day.

Ere a leaf is on a bush,
In the time before the thrush
Has a thought about her nest,
Thou wilt come with half a call,
Spreading out thy glossy breast
Like a careless Prodigal;
Telling tales about the sun,
When we've little warmth, or none.

Poets, vain men in their mood!
Travel with the multitude:
Never heed them; I aver
That they all are wanton wooers;
But the thrifty cottager,
Who stirs little out of doors,
Joys to spy thee near her home;
Spring is coming, Thou art come!

Comfort have thou of thy merit,
Kindly, unassuming Spirit!
Careless of thy neighbourhood,
Thou dost show thy pleasant face
On the moor, and in the wood,
In the lane;—there's not a place,
Howsoever mean it be,
But 'tis good enough for thee.

Ill befall the yellow flowers,
Children of the flaring hours!
Buttercups, that will be seen,
Whether we will see or no;

Others, too, of lofty mien;
They have done as worldlings do,
Taken praise that should be thine,
Little, humble Celandine

Prophet of delight and mirth,
Ill-requited upon earth;
Herald of a mighty band,
Of a joyous train ensuing,
Serving at my heart's command,
Tasks that are no tasks renewing,
I will sing, as doth behove,
Hymns in praise of what I love!

I WANDERED LONELY AS A CLOUD
(p. 109)

I wandered lonely as a cloud
That floats on high o'er vales and hills,
When all at once I saw a crowd,
A host, of golden daffodils;
Beside the lake, beneath the trees,
Fluttering and dancing in the breeze.

[Continuous as the stars that shine]
And twinkle on the milky way,
They stretched in never-ending line
Along the margin of a bay:
Ten thousand saw I at a glance,
Tossing their heads in sprightly dance.

The waves beside them danced; but they
Out-did the sparkling waves in glee:
A poet could not but be gay,
In such a jocund company:
I gazed—and gazed—but little thought
What wealth the show to me had brought:

For oft, when on my couch I lie
In vacant or in pensive mood,
They flash upon that inward eye
Which is the bliss of solitude;
And then my heart with pleasure fills,
And dances with the daffodils.

THE GLOW-WORM

(*Published 1807 as* Among all lovely things my Love had been)
(p. 111)

Among all lovely things my Love had been;
Had noted well the stars, all flowers that grew
About her home; but she had never seen
A Glow-worm, never one, and this I knew.

While riding near her home one stormy night
A single Glow-worm did I chance to espy;
I gave a fervent welcome to the sight,
And from my Horse I leapt; great joy had I.

Upon a leaf the Glow-worm did I lay,
To bear it with me through the stormy night:
And, as before, it shone without dismay;
Albeit putting forth a fainter light.

When to the Dwelling of my Love I came,
I went into the Orchard quietly;
And left the Glow-worm, blessing it by name,
Laid safely by itself, beneath a Tree.

The whole next day, I hoped, and hoped with fear;
At night the Glow-worm shone beneath the Tree:
I led my Lucy to the spot, 'Look here!'
Oh! joy it was for her, and joy for me!

THE COCK IS CROWING
(*Published as* Written in March, while resting on the bridge
at the foot of Brother's Water)
(p. 111)

The cock is crowing,
The stream is flowing,
The small birds twitter,
The lake doth glitter,
The green field sleeps in the sun;
The oldest and youngest
Are at work with the strongest;
The cattle are grazing,
Their heads never raising;
There are forty feeding like one!

Like an army defeated
The snow hath retreated,
And now doth fare ill
On the top of the bare hill;
The Ploughboy is whooping—anon—anon:
There's joy in the mountains;
There's life in the fountains;
Small clouds are sailing,
Blue sky prevailing;
The rain is over and gone!

THE REDBREAST AND THE BUTTERFLY
(p. 112)

Art thou the bird whom Man loves best,
The pious bird with the scarlet breast,
Our little English Robin;
The bird that comes about our doors
When Autumn-winds are sobbing?
Art thou the Peter of Norway Boors?
Their Thomas in Finland,
And Russia far inland?

The bird, that by some name or other
All men who know thee call their brother,
The darling of children and men?
Could Father Adam open his eyes
And see this sight beneath the skies,
He'd wish to close them again.
—If the Butterfly knew but his friend,
Hither his flight he would bend;
And find his way to me,
Under the branches of the tree:
In and out, he darts about;
Can this be the bird, to man so good,
That, after their bewildering,
Covered with leaves the little children,
    So painfully in the wood?

What ailed thee, Robin, that thou couldst pursue
    A beautiful creature,
That is gentle by nature?
Beneath the summer sky
From flower to flower let him fly;
'Tis all that he wishes to do.
The cheerer Thou of our in-door sadness,
He is the friend of our summer gladness:
What hinders, then, that ye should be
Playmates in the sunny weather,
And fly about in the air together!
His beautiful wings in crimson are drest,
A crimson as bright as thine own:
Would'st thou be happy in thy nest,
O pious Bird! whom man loves best,
Love him, or leave him alone!

I'VE WATCHED YOU NOW A FULL HALF-HOUR
(*Published as* To a Butterfly)
(p. 113)

I've watched you now a full half-hour,
Self-poised upon that yellow flower;
And, little Butterfly! indeed
I know not if you sleep or feed.
How motionless!—not frozen seas
More motionless! and then
What joy awaits you, when the breeze
Hath found you out among the trees,
And calls you forth again!

This plot of orchard-ground is ours;
My trees they are, my Sister's flowers;
Here rest your wings when they are weary;
Here lodge as in a sanctuary!
Come often to us, fear no wrong;
Sit near us on the bough!
We'll talk of sunshine and of song,
And summer days, when we were young;
Sweet childish days, that were as long
As twenty days are now.

I HAVE THOUGHTS THAT ARE FED BY THE SUN[1]
(p. 114)

I have thoughts that are fed by the sun.
    The things which I see
    Are welcome to me,
    Welcome every one:
I do not wish to lie
    Dead, dead,

[1] See *P.W.*, vol. IV, p. 365. These lines are headed in the MS. 'Half an hour afterwards', and are preceded by two verses in similar style celebrating the silence and peace of his bedroom.

Dead without any company;
    Here alone on my bed,
With thoughts that are fed by the Sun,
And hopes that are welcome every one,
    Happy am I.

O Life, there is about thee
A deep delicious peace,
I would not be without thee,
    Stay, oh stay!
Yet be thou ever as now,
Sweetness and breath with the quiet of death,
Be but thou ever as now,
    Peace, peace, peace.

THE TINKER
(p. 116)

Who leads a happy life
If it's not the merry Tinker,
Not too old to have a Wife;
Not too much a thinker?
Through the meadows, over stiles,
Where there are no measured miles,
Day by day he finds his way
Among the lonely houses:
Right before the Farmer's door
Down he sits; his brows he knits;
Then his hammer he rouzes;
Batter! batter! batter!
He begins to clatter;
And while the work is going on
Right good ale he bouzes;
And, when it is done, away he is gone;
    And, in his scarlet coat,
    With a merry note,
    He sings the sun to bed;
    And, without making a pother,
Finds some place or other
For his own careless head.

When in the woods the little fowls
Begin their merry-making,
Again the jolly Tinker bowls
Forth with small leave-taking:
Through the valley, up the hill;
He can't go wrong, go where he will:
    Tricks he has twenty,
    And pastimes in plenty;
He's the terror of boys in the midst of their noise;

When the market Maiden,
Bringing home her lading,
Hath pass'd him in a nook,
With his outlandish look,
And visage grim and sooty,
Bumming, bumming, bumming,
What is that that's coming?
Silly maid as ever was!
She thinks that she and all she has
Will be the Tinker's booty:
At the pretty Maiden's dread
The Tinker shakes his head,
Laughing, laughing, laughing,
As if he would laugh himself dead.
And thus, with work or none,
The Tinker lives in fun,
With a light soul to cover him;
And sorrow and care blow over him,
Whether he's up or a-bed.

CHILDREN GATHERING FLOWERS
(*Published as* Foresight)
(p. 117)

That is work of waste and ruin—
Do as Charles and I are doing!
Strawberry blossoms, one and all,
We must spare them—here are many:
Look at it—the flower is small,
Small and low, though fair as any:
Do not touch it! summers two
I am older, Anne, than you.

Pull the primrose, sister Anne!
Pull as many as you can.
—Here are daisies, take your fill;
Pansies, and the cuckoo-flower:
Of the lofty daffodil
Make your bed, or make your bower;
Fill your lap and fill your bosom;
Only spare the strawberry-blossom!

Primroses, the Spring may love them—
Summer knows but little of them:
Violets, a barren kind,
Withered on the ground must lie;
Daisies leave no fruit behind
When the pretty flowerets die;
Pluck them, and another year
As many will be blowing here.

God has given a kindlier power
To the favoured strawberry-flower.
Hither soon as spring is fled
You and Charles and I will walk;
Lurking berries, ripe and red,
Then will hang on every stalk,
Each within its leafy bower;
And for that promise spare the flower!

THIS IS THE SPOT[1]
(p. 121)

This is the spot:—how mildly does the sun
Shine in between the fading leaves! the air
In the habitual silence of this wood
Is more than silent; and this bed of heath—
Where shall we find so sweet a resting-place?
Come, let me see thee sink into a dream
Of quiet thoughts, protracted till thine eye
Be calm as water when the winds are gone
And no one can tell whither. My sweet Friend,
We two have had such happy hours together
That my heart melts in me to think of it.

STANZAS IN THE MANNER OF
THOMSON'S 'CASTLE OF INDOLENCE'
(*Published as* Stanzas written in my Pocket-copy of
Thomson's 'Castle of Indolence')
(p. 123)

Within our happy Castle there dwelt One
Whom without blame I may not overlook;
For never sun on living creature shone
Who more devout enjoyment with us took:
Here on his hours he hung as on a book,
On his own time here would he float away,
As doth a fly upon a summer brook;
But go to-morrow, or belike to-day,
Seek for him,—he is fled; and whither none can say.

Thus often would he leave our peaceful home,
And find elsewhere his business or delight;
Out of our Valley's limits did he roam:
Full many a time, upon a stormy night,

---

[1] These lines, called in the MS. (MS. M, copied 1803–4) 'Travelling', have a very early origin and belong to the Alfoxden period. The last six lines are found in the second part of 'Ode to Lycoris' (i.e. D. W.), written in 1817. See *P.W.*, vol. IV, p. 97.

His voice came to us from the neighbouring height:
Oft could we see him driving full in view
At mid-day when the sun was shining bright;
What ill was on him, what he had to do,
A mighty wonder bred among our quiet crew.

Ah! piteous sight it was to see this Man
When he came back to us, a withered flower,—
Or like a sinful creature, pale and wan.
Down would he sit; and without strength or power
Look at the common grass from hour to hour:
And oftentimes, how long I fear to say,
Where apple-trees in blossom made a bower,
Retired in that sunshiny shade he lay;
And, like a naked Indian, slept himself away.

Great wonder to our gentle tribe it was
Whenever from our Valley he withdrew;
For happier soul no living creature has
Than he had, being here the long day through.
Some thought he was a lover, and did woo:
Some thought far worse of him, and judged him wrong;
But verse was what he had been wedded to;
And his own mind did like a tempest strong
Come to him thus, and drove the weary Wight along.

With him there often walked in friendly guise,
Or lay upon the moss by brook or tree,
A noticeable Man with large grey eyes,
And a pale face that seemed undoubtedly
As if a blooming face it ought to be;
Heavy his low-hung lip did oft appear,
Deprest by weight of musing Phantasy;
Profound his forehead was, though not severe;
Yet some did think that he had little business here:

Sweet heaven forefend! his was a lawful right;
Noisy he was, and gamesome as a boy;
His limbs would toss about him with delight,
Like branches when strong winds the trees annoy.

Nor lacked his calmer hours device or toy
To banish listlessness and irksome care;
He would have taught you how you might employ
Yourself; and many did to him repair,—
And certes not in vain; he had inventions rare.

Expedients, too, of simplest sort he tried:
Long blades of grass, plucked round him as he lay,
Made, to his ear attentively applied,
A pipe on which the wind would deftly play;
Glasses he had, that little things display,
The beetle panoplied in gems and gold,
A mailèd angel on a battle-day;
The mysteries that cups of flowers enfold,
And all the gorgeous sights which fairies do behold.

He would entice that other Man to hear
His music, and to view his imagery:
And, sooth, these two were each to the other dear:
No livelier love in such a place could be:
There did they dwell—from earthly labour free,
As happy spirits as were ever seen;
If but a bird, to keep them company,
Or butterfly sate down, they were, I ween,
As pleased as if the same had been a Maiden-queen.

I GRIEVED FOR BUONAPARTÉ
(*Published as* 1801)
(p. 127)

I grieved for Buonaparté, with a vain
And an unthinking grief! The tenderest mood
Of that Man's mind—what can it be? what food
Fed his first hopes? what knowledge could *he* gain?
'Tis not in battles that from youth we train
The Governor who must be wise and good,
And temper with the sternness of the brain
Thoughts motherly, and meek as womanhood.
Wisdom doth live with children round her knees:

Books, leisure, perfect freedom, and the talk
Man holds with week-day man in the hourly walk
Of the mind's business: these are the degrees
By which true Sway doth mount; this is the stalk
True Power doth grow on; and her rights are these.

OUR DEPARTURE
(*Published as* A Farewell)
(p. 129)

Farewell, thou little Nook of mountain-ground,
Thou rocky corner in the lowest stair
Of that magnificent temple which doth bound
One side of our whole vale with grandeur rare;
Sweet garden-orchard, eminently fair,
The loveliest spot that man hath ever found,
Farewell!—we leave thee to Heaven's peaceful care,
Thee, and the Cottage which thou dost surround.

Our boat is safely anchored by the shore,
And there will safely ride when we are gone;
The flowering shrubs that deck our humble door
Will prosper, though untended and alone:
Fields, goods, and far-off chattels we have none:
These narrow bounds contain our private store
Of things earth makes, and sun doth shine upon;
Here are they in our sight—we have no more.

Sunshine and shower be with you, bud and bell!
For two months now in vain we shall be sought;
We leave you here in solitude to dwell
With these our latest gifts of tender thought;
Thou, like the morning, in thy saffron coat,
Bright gowan, and marsh-marigold, farewell!
Whom from the borders of the Lake we brought,
And placed together near our rocky Well.

We go for One to whom ye will be dear;
And she will prize this Bower, this Indian shed,
Our own contrivance, Building without peer!
—A gentle Maid, whose heart is lowly bred,
Whose pleasures are in wild fields gatherèd,
With joyousness, and with a thoughtful cheer,
Will come to you; to you herself will wed;
And love the blessed life that we lead here.

Dear Spot! which we have watched with tender heed,
Bringing thee chosen plants and blossoms blown
Among the distant mountains, flower and weed,
Which thou hast taken to thee as thy own,
Making all kindness registered and known;
Thou for our sakes, though Nature's child indeed,
Fair in thyself and beautiful alone,
Hast taken gifts which thou dost little need.

And O most constant, yet most fickle Place,
That hast thy wayward moods, as thou dost show
To them who look not daily on thy face;
Who, being loved, in love no bounds dost know,
And say'st, when we forsake thee, 'Let them go!'
Thou easy-hearted Thing, with thy wild race
Of weeds and flowers, till we return be slow,
And travel with the year at a soft pace.

Help us to tell Her tales of years gone by,
And this sweet spring, the best beloved and best;
Joy will be flown in its mortality;
Something must stay to tell us of the rest.
Here, thronged with primroses, the steep rock's breast
Glittered at evening like a starry sky;
And in this bush our sparrow built her nest,
Of which I sang one song that will not die.

O happy Garden! whose seclusion deep
Hath been so friendly to industrious hours;
And to soft slumbers, that did gently steep
Our spirits, carrying with them dreams of flowers,

And wild notes warbled among leafy bowers;
Two burning months let summer overleap,
And, coming back with Her who will be ours,
Into thy bosom we again shall creep.

THE SUN HAS LONG BEEN SET
(*Published as* Evening Voluntaries, VIII)
(p. 134)

The sun has long been set,
   The stars are out by twos and threes,
The little birds are piping yet
   Among the bushes and trees;
There's a cuckoo, and one or two thrushes,
And a far-off wind that rushes,
And a sound of water that gushes,
And the cuckoo's sovereign cry
Fills all the hollow of the sky.
   Who would go 'parading'
In London, and 'masquerading,'
On such a night of June
With that beautiful soft half-moon,
And all these innocent blisses?
On such a night as this is!

SONNET COMPOSED UPON WESTMINSTER BRIDGE, SEPTEMBER 3, 1802
(p. 151)

Earth has not anything to show more fair:
Dull would he be of soul who could pass by
A sight so touching in its majesty:
This City now doth, like a garment, wear
The beauty of the morning; silent, bare,
Ships, towers, domes, theatres, and temples lie
Open unto the fields, and to the sky;
All bright and glittering in the smokeless air.

Never did sun more beautifully steep
In his first splendour, valley, rock, or hill;
Ne'er saw I, never felt, a calm so deep!
The river glideth at his own sweet will:
Dear God! the very houses seem asleep;
And all that mighty heart is lying still!

FAIR STAR OF EVENING
(*Published as* Sonnet composed by the sea-side, near Calais,
August, 1802)
(p. 152)

Fair Star of evening, Splendour of the west,
Star of my Country!—on the horizon's brink
Thou hangest, stooping, as might seem, to sink
On England's bosom; yet well pleased to rest,
Meanwhile, and be to her a glorious crest
Conspicuous to the Nations. Thou, I think,
Shouldst be my Country's emblem; and shouldst wink,
Bright Star! with laughter on her banners, drest
In thy fresh beauty. There! that dusky spot
Beneath thee, that is England; there she lies.
Blessings be on you both! one hope, one lot,
One life, one glory!—I, with many a fear
For my dear Country, many heartfelt sighs,
Among men who do not love her, linger here.

IT IS A BEAUTEOUS EVENING, CALM
AND FREE[1]
(p. 153)

It is a beauteous evening, calm and free,
The holy time is quiet as a Nun
Breathless with adoration; the broad sun
Is sinking down in its tranquillity;
The gentleness of heaven broods o'er the Sea:

[1] Composed at Calais, August 1802.

Listen! the mighty Being is awake,
And doth with his eternal motion make
A sound like thunder—everlastingly.
Dear Child! dear Girl! that walkest with me here,
If thou appear untouched by solemn thought,
Thy nature is not therefore less divine:
Thou liest in Abraham's bosom all the year;
And worshipp'st at the Temple's inner shrine,
God being with thee when we know it not.

DARK AND MORE DARK THE SHADES OF EVENING FELL

(*Published as* Sonnet composed after a journey across the
Hambleton Hills, Yorkshire)
(p. 156)

Dark and more dark the shades of evening fell;
The wished-for point was reached—but at an hour
When little could be gained from that rich dower
Of prospect, whereof many thousands tell.
Yet did the glowing west with marvellous power
Salute us; there stood Indian citadel,
Temple of Greece, and minster with its tower
Substantially expressed—a place for bell
Or clock to toll from! Many a tempting isle,
With groves that never were imagined, lay
'Mid seas how steadfast! objects all for the eye
Of silent rapture; but we felt the while
We should forget them; they are of the sky,
And from our earthly memory fade away.

APPENDIX II

Two poems by
Dorothy Wordsworth

ADDRESS TO A CHILD, DURING A BOISTEROUS WINTER EVENING[1]

What way does the Wind come? What way does he go?
He rides over the water, and over the snow,
Through wood, and through vale; and o'er rocky height,
Which the goat cannot climb, takes his sounding flight;
He tosses about in every bare tree,
As, if you look up, you plainly may see;
But how he will come, and whither he goes,
There's never a scholar in England knows.

He will suddenly stop in a cunning nook,
And ring a sharp 'larum;—but, if you should look,
There's nothing to see but a cushion of snow
Round as a pillow, and whiter than milk,
And softer than if it were covered with silk.
Sometimes he'll hide in the cave of a rock,
Then whistle as shrill as the buzzard cock;
—Yet seek him,—and what shall you find in the place?
Nothing but silence and empty space;
Save, in a corner, a heap of dry leaves,
That he's left, for a bed, to beggars or thieves!

As soon as 'tis daylight to-morrow, with me
You shall go to the orchard, and then you will see
That he has been there, and made a great rout,
And cracked the branches, and strewn them about;

[1] Probably written by D. W. in 1806, and addressed to W. W.'s children John and Dora. W. W. published it in his *Poems* (1815); in the edition of 1845 he identified it as 'By my Sister'.

Heaven grant that he spare but that one upright twig
That looked up at the sky so proud and big
All last summer, as well you know,
Studded with apples, a beautiful show!

Hark! over the roof he makes a pause,
And growls as if he would fix his claws
Right in the slates, and with a huge rattle
Drive them down, like men in a battle:
—But let him range round; he does us no harm,
We build up the fire, we're snug and warm;
Untouched by his breath see the candle shines bright,
And burns with a clear and steady light;
Books have we to read,—but that half-stifled knell,
Alas! 'tis the sound of the eight o'clock bell.
—Come now we'll to bed! and when we are there
He may work his own will, and what shall we care?
He may knock at the door,—we'll not let him in;
May drive at the windows,—we'll laugh at his din;
Let him seek his own home wherever it be;
Here's a *cozie* warm house for Edward and me.

A WINTER'S RAMBLE IN GRASMERE VALE[1]

A Stranger, Grasmere, in thy vale,
All faces then to me unknown,
I left my sole companion-friend
To wander out alone.

Lured by a little winding path,
Quickly I left the publick road,
A smooth and tempting path it was
By sheep and shepherds trod.

[1] An unpublished poem, written by D. W. in 1834, when she was an invalid, and preserved among the Dove Cottage Papers. It commemorates her first walk alone after she and W. W. arrived in their 'chosen vale', four days before Christmas 1799.

Eastward, towards the lofty hills
That pathway led me on
Until I reach'd a stately rock
With velvet moss o'ergrown.

With russet oak, and tufts of fern
Its life was richly garlanded;
Its sides adorned with eglantine
Bedropped with hips of glossy red.

Beneath that Rock my course I stayed,
And, looking to its summit high,
'Thou wear'st', said I, 'a splendid garb,
Here winter keeps his revelry.

What need of flowers? the splendid moss
Is gayer than an April mead,
More rich its hues of varied green,
Orange and gold and glowing red.'

—Beside that gay and lovely Rock
There came with merry voice
A foaming Streamlet glancing by:
It seemed to say 'Rejoice!'

My youthful wishes all fulfill'd—
Wishes matured by thoughtful choice,
I stood an *Inmate* of this Vale,
How *could* I but rejoice?

INDEX

OXFORD

MORE OXFORD PAPERBACKS

A complete list, including The World's Classics, Twentieth-Century Classics, OPUS, Past Masters, Oxford Authors, Oxford Shakespeare, and Oxford Paperback Reference, is available in the UK from the General Publicity Department, Oxford University Press, Walton Street, Oxford OX2 6DP.

In the USA, complete lists are available from the Paperbacks Marketing Manager, Oxford University Press, 200 Madison Avenue, New York, NY 10016.

LETTERS OF DOROTHY WORDSWORTH

A Selection

Edited by Alan G. Hill

In this selection of Dorothy Wordsworth's letters, a companion
to Dorothy's *Journals*, Alan G. Hill presents seventy complete
letters drawn from the new and enlarged edition of *The Letters of
William and Dorothy Wordsworth* (of which he is General Editor).
They have been chosen to provide a portrait of the writer and her
milieu, and can be read as a continuous narrative, following the
course of her life from youth until the onset of her last tragic
illness.